Reading, Thinking, and Concept Development

READING, *Thinking,* AND CONCEPT DEVELOPMENT

STRATEGIES
FOR THE
CLASSROOM

**Theodore L. Harris and
Eric J. Cooper** Editors

College Entrance Examination Board
New York, 1985

Acknowledgments

This volume would not have been possible without the support of several individuals. Foremost, we wish to thank Stephen Ivens for his vision, guidance, and direction throughout the various stages of this project. We also wish to thank Sandra MacGowan for her enthusiastic support during the editing of the document; and thanks to all the authors for their excellent contributions and patience over the two years it took to bring this volume to publication.

Authors are encouraged to express freely their professional judgment. Therefore, points of view or opinions stated in this book do not necessarily represent official College Board position or policy.

Editorial inquires concerning this book should be addressed to: Editorial Office, The College Board, 45 Columbus Avenue, New York, New York 10023-6917.

Copies of this book may be ordered from College Board Publications, Box 886, New York, New York 10101. The price is $19.95.

ISBN: 0-87447-219-9

Printed in the United States of America.

9 8 7 6 5 4 3 2

Contents

Foreword

In 1977 the College Board joined a research effort, begun by the Board of Regents of the State University of New York, the New York State Education Department, and Touchstone Applied Science Associates, to develop a new technology for the assessment of comprehension. Funded by the Carnegie Corporation, the project resulted in the Degrees of Reading Power (DRP) program. Its goal, as designed by New York State and the collaborating institutions, is aimed at improving reading comprehension instruction—a goal that we believe can best be achieved through the integration of comprehension assessment and instruction. To support this integration, the College Board created a staff development component for the Degrees of Reading Power program to complement its efforts in comprehension assessment. This new component drew on the expertise of many of the leading authorities in the field of reading research to determine how comprehension instruction can best be achieved in the classroom.

The staff development component started as a series of workshops for administrators and teachers in school systems that had adopted the Degrees of Reading Power tests. These workshops were designed to help schools develop a coherent curriculum and provide sound comprehension instruction. While we are pleased that the workshops have been well received, our success has created a demand that simply cannot be met. Leading authorities in reading are, by definition, limited in number, as are school resources to cover the costs of a series of staff development workshops. Therefore, we are pleased that the consultants who have played such a major role in helping us were willing to contribute articles to this volume. The expertise the authors bring to the task is unquestioned: their concern for students genuine; their faith in schools and teachers unwavering.

The articles that follow focus on comprehension and concept development, which we believe should be the central core of an effective educational program. Comprehension *can* be taught and it *can* be assessed. If this collection assists educators in their thinking about comprehension instruction, and provides the classroom teacher with practical strategies for students faced with comprehending text at a particular level of difficulty, then our objectives for publishing it will have been realized.

Stephen H. Ivens
The College Board

Preface

The intent of this volume is to equip teachers with a repertoire of skills and strategies for improving text comprehension, and thus help them better understand the teaching-learning processes involved. Information about the how and why of comprehension presently is scattered and not readily available in a comprehensive, practical way. The authors of these articles seek to fill this void by endeavoring to explain not only *how* comprehension processes may be fostered, but *why* the procedures work in terms of current comprehension theory.

The proposed instructional strategies are meant to be used selectively to complement, not to replace, the broad array of comprehension skills and abilities that the experienced teacher already possesses. These strategies are prescriptive, outlining specific ways of processing text to achieve certain comprehension and cognitive goals. They represent alternatives that the teacher may tap to help students gain confidence and proficiency in comprehending the printed page, be the text narrative or expository. They may serve as adjuncts to the many other aspects of comprehension, such as the intricacies involved in the interpretation of literature or the precise understanding of an abstract scientific concept. The fact that examples of the strategies are given at several grade levels, elementary and secondary, further enhances their applicability in the classroom.

There is justified concern and discontent over the failure of American schools to effectively teach text comprehension. It is only very recently that scholars from many fields of language study have collaborated to find out why this is so and to suggest what can be done about it in the classroom. As a result, we have learned more about the nature of comprehension and have generated more positive ways of improving comprehension in the last two decades than in the many previous decades. Yet it is not so much that through the newer cognitive psychology we are discovering new concepts related to comprehension; rather, we are learning to more fully appreciate the staggering intricacies of comprehension and cognitive processes, which need to be slowed down, analyzed, and resynthesized for effective learning. For the most part, the emerging terminology—*schema, prediction, macrostructure,* and the like—represent long-established concepts; but now we are giving such concepts a new instructional priority.

The crux of the newer point of view in teaching comprehension has to do with the relation of process to content: the dynamics of the teaching-learning situation, which must be recognized and implemented to achieve the desired comprehension outcome. In reexploring old notions of teaching comprehension, we have learned that frequently we have short-circuited or omitted critical phases of comprehension-learning processes. In assessing comprehension, we often have accepted a token response for understanding. Likewise we have been guilty of teaching isolated intellectual skills rather than functional ones that can be incorporated into effective comprehension strategies.

This volume attempts to demonstrate how such practices may be avoided. It speaks to teachers—not only to classroom teachers but to supervisors of teachers and to teachers of teachers at professional training levels—to view comprehension with enlightened eyes and to take vigorous steps to help students unlock the doors to the mysterious realm of comprehension and thinking. It speaks to adoption committees, local and state, to insist upon more adequate attention to the provision of effective guidance materials used to teach comprehension. It also speaks to publishers to recognize the validity of this knowledge and to cooperate with the teaching profession in producing improved materials for teaching comprehension.

The scope of the articles in this volume is wide, ranging from highly specific, narrowly-focused teaching-learning approaches to broad ones; from strategies that emphasize group interaction to those primarily content-centered. The topic of readability—"matching reading materials to readers"—is discussed in detail, with specific aids for the teacher in selecting materials to enhance the attainment of comprehension. The volume opens and closes with consideration of the vital role played by teacher's manuals in determining how comprehension is actually taught in the classroom. The present inadequate provisions of the typical teacher's manual for guiding comprehension are discussed by Durkin in the Introduction, and some hopeful signs of change in modifying adoption procedures to improve instructional procedures are described by Osborn and Stein in the concluding article. To those who have always conceived of the effective teacher as one who knows when and how to deviate from a teacher's manual, this volume offers timely assistance to all who seek to help students bring to reading the joy of understanding.

Theodore L. Harris
Professor Emeritus, School of Education
University of Puget Sound

Eric J. Cooper
The College Board

Introduction

The Center for the Study of Reading (CSR), now a well-known source of comprehension research, was established at the University of Illinois in 1976 with support from the National Institute of Education (NIE). Its assigned mission was to conduct research that, combined with studies from other sources, would eventually yield data capable of attaining one of NIE's goals: to improve comprehension instruction in our elementary schools.

While the goal was both laudable and welcome, the implicit assumption that students already were receiving comprehension instruction was puzzling—at least to me. Having done classroom-observation research for almost twenty years without ever seeing any, I naturally wondered whether NIE's assumption was incorrect or whether I had overlooked comprehension instruction, as it had never been the pre-established focus of a study. But, then, neither had comprehension assessment, which was observed repeatedly at all grade levels.

IDENTIFYING CSR'S RESPONSIBILITY

Because it was important to know whether the Center's responsibility was to initiate what did not exist or to improve what did, a classroom-observation study was planned for grades 3 through 6. Those levels were chosen with the assumption that if instruction in how to understand connected text *was* being offered, more would be found in grades 3 through 6 than in grades 1 and 2. The request to observe the best teachers in a school was made with the assumption that they were more likely to provide comprehension instruction than less effective teachers. Because a pilot study, in which the reading period in 23 classrooms was observed, once reinforced the belief that comprehension instruction was rare (Durkin, 1977), one further decision was to include social studies classes in the research, again as a way of maximizing the likelihood that comprehension instruction would be found if not during reading then in social studies, where the difficulty of textbooks always has been an obvious source of comprehension problems.

Durkin, D. "Comprehension Instruction—Where Are You?" Reading Education Report No. 1. Urbana: University of Illinois, Center for the Study of Reading, 1977.

In the pilot study, 39 teachers in 14 school systems each were observed on three successive days. Everything that was seen during the 17,997 minutes of observing was timed and then described according to categories identified with the help of the pilot study. The categories covered teacher behavior (e.g., waits, teaches, assesses, assigns) as well as the various components of reading (e.g., decoding, vocabulary knowledge, comprehension). Since data from the study are available elsewhere (Durkin, 1978-79), only a few of the findings will be cited.

CONCEPTION OF COMPREHENSION INSTRUCTION

Before the pilot study was begun, the literature was searched for a conception of comprehension instruction that would define the focus for the larger study. None was found, however. For the more encompassing research, therefore, *comprehension instruction* was defined as what a teacher does to help students understand, or work out, the meaning of connected text. Help was expected to come in a form that would include various combinations of imparting information, offering explanations, providing examples and nonexamples, modeling, posing questions, and so on. Subject matter for such instruction was expected to include topics such as the functions of various kinds of punctuation, anaphoric devices, similes, and cohesive ties. The instruction might be a preplanned lesson (objective, instruction, practice, application) or onthe-spot teaching prompted by one or more students' problems in understanding a particular type of structure or, for instance, an unusual use of language in a given piece of text.

While the major contributions that factors such as world knowledge and purposes for reading make to comprehension were clearly recognized, attention to them was not viewed as being comprehension instruction. Nor were questions, posed by teachers, that have to do with the products of comprehension. Distinctions thus were made between what this writer views to be *facilitating* comprehension (e.g., establishing purposes for reading); *teaching* comprehension (e.g., explaining appositives and their functions); and *assessing* comprehension (e.g., having children retell a story they read).

Durkin, D. "What Classroom Observations Reveal about Reading Comprehension Instruction." *Reading Research Quarterly* 14 (1978-79), 481-533.

Classroom Observation Study

In spite of the steps taken to maximize the likelihood that comprehension instruction would be found, little was seen. None was offered during social studies; and of the 11,587 minutes spent observing reading, only 45 minutes of the teachers' time went to helping students understand, or work out, the meaning of connected text. Since the 45 minutes included 12 separate instances of instruction, the average length of the episodes was only 3.7 minutes. One example of comprehension instruction, which lasted 4 minutes, is described below:

> Following a basal manual's suggestion, a teacher said to a group of students that *and* and *but* are words that sometimes connect other words to make a long sentence. Still adhering to the manual's recommendation, the teacher wrote on the board *Pollywog sat in Mrs. Weaver's class and looked out the window and prayed for rain.* After the group read the sentence aloud, the teacher continued using the manual and asked whether or not someone could say what one short sentence in the long one was. A child responded, "Pollywog sat in Mrs. Weaver's class." When another child said, "Looked out the window," in response to the teacher's request for the second short sentence, he was told to start with "Pollywog." The same reminder was necessary when another child said the third sentence was "Prayed for rain."

The above episode is referred to for two reasons. First, it demonstrates that excessively demanding standards were not used to define comprehension instruction and thus do not account for its scarcity. The episode also exemplifies characteristics of the little comprehension instruction that was found. To be more specific, the "teaching" was not only brief but also lacked any attempt to relate in some explicit way what was being done to how to read—in this case, to how to understand, or work out, the meaning of complex sentences. The episode is also typical in that the teacher followed a manual, did no more nor less than what it recommended, then shifted (as did the manual) to a written assignment. It was these latter characteristics that required frequent use of the term *mentioning* in reporting findings from the research. Mentioning was defined as, "Saying just enough about a topic to allow for an assignment related to it."

Workbook and ditto-sheet assignments turned out to be so common everywhere that it was tempting to conclude that a substantial amount of what was observed was a means for getting to written exercises, many of which dealt with topics that were related neither to each other nor to what the students were reading in their textbooks. That such a conclusion may be at least partially accurate was suggested in the very first classroom that was visited. Working with a group of poor readers, the teacher appeared to rush through preparations for reading a selection, even though prereading activities are especially necessary for such students. Why the teacher went so quickly was clarified later when she said to the group, "I want you to get two workbook pages done by 10 o'clock." This was just one of the many times when "covering material" was a more accurate description of what was seen than was "teaching reading." Because of the frequency of written assignments, it was not unexpected to find that 14.4 percent of the time spent observing the teachers was assigned to the category "gives assignment." Nor is it surprising to learn in reports of other classroom studies (Anderson, 1984) that students may spend as much as 70 percent of their time doing assignments.

The fact that a considerable amount of the teachers' time (17.7 percent) went to assessing comprehension was not surprising either, since observing in classrooms over a long period of time consistently revealed much assessment via questions. Especially noticeable in this more recent research was the teachers' concern for whether answers were right or wrong, not for what responses might suggest for future instruction or immediate help. The typical procedure, then, was for a teacher to ask a question and to continue calling on students until one gave the expected answer. Another question then was posed, and the same routine was followed.

It is also important to note that at no time did any of the observed teachers have students return to the text for such reasons as to cite evidence for their answers. Nor was a text ever examined for constructions that might cause problems, for unusual uses of words, or, for example, for words that signal opinions or cause-effect relationships. Failure to return to the text for a specific purpose minimized the likelihood of "on-the-spot" comprehension instruction, which may at times be more effective than preplanned lessons since it deals with an existing problem.

Basal Manual Study

It was not only what the teachers did (and did not do) but also the remarkable similarity of their behavior that prompted the question, "Why did 39 teachers from 14 school systems look the same in how

Anderson, L. "The Environment of Instruction: The Function of Seatwork in a Commercially Developed Curriculum." In *Comprehension Instruction*. G. G. Duffy, L. R. Roehler, and J. Mason (eds.), New York: Longman, 1984, 93-103.

they used their time?" Since all were using one or more basal series, the logical next step was to examine basal manuals to see what they suggest for teaching comprehension. Because data from this second study also have been reported elsewhere (Durkin, 1981), only a brief summary of the findings will be given here.

Manuals covering kindergarten through grade 6 from five basal reader programs were read word for word, primarily to learn about the kind and number of procedures that were suggested for comprehension instruction. (The definition of comprehension instruction remained the same for this second study.) The close examination of the manuals was required not only because exactly correct data were the target but also because the manuals' recommendations are not always labeled correctly. In one first-grade manual, for instance, a procedure for teaching the word *yellow* was called "study skills." Of special relevance to the research was the large number of manual segments in all five programs that described ways to assess comprehension, yet referred to them as "instruction." To cite an example, teachers were directed to read aloud a paragraph about a boy making a cake for his father's birthday that included words that help in following a sequence (e.g., *first, later*). Subsequent to the oral reading, teachers were directed to ask questions listed beneath the paragraph that had to do with what the boy did first, what he did next, and so on. Nowhere on the page was any reference made to the signal words or to what might be done to get students to take advantage of those words in reconstructing the sequence in which the described events occurred. Nonetheless, the recommended procedure was labeled "instruction with signal words for sequence." (It should be noted that nothing had been done with such words in the earlier manuals in this series.)

When labels were ignored, what had been seen in the 39 classrooms characterized the manuals: *much* comprehension assessment and relatively little comprehension instruction. Not unexpectedly, references to practice exercises originating in workbooks and ditto sheets were exceedingly numerous. Like those in the classrooms, assignments dealt with brief pieces of text, covered many different topics, and often bore no relationship to selections in the readers.

Because comprehension instruction was the central concern of this study, a few additional comments about how the manuals handled it are in order.

Durkin, D. "Reading Comprehension Instruction in Five Basal Reader Series." *Reading Research Quarterly* 16 (1981), 515-544.

How Basal Manuals Deal with Teaching Comprehension

One very pronounced characteristic of all the manuals was the tendency to teach by implication rather than with direct, explicit instruction. This was illustrated in the 4-minute episode referred to earlier when the classroom-observation research was described. The same pervasive characteristic can be illustrated further with what was done with the fact that authors reveal the traits of their characters both directly and indirectly. Only one series suggested making that fact explicit with the help of brief paragraphs in which the traits of a girl were described directly with adjectives and indirectly with references to her behavior. In contrast, all the other series dealt with the same topic by listing questions about the traits of characters, omitting any recommendation to help students see that the traits were communicated by different means, some requiring inferences. Since all five series did include direct, explicit comprehension instruction for various topics at various but unpredictable times, why none provided it consistently has no apparent explanation.

Another characteristic of the manuals was to equate definitions with instruction and, by so doing, to stop short of being instructive for comprehending. The tendency of all the manuals not to go beyond definitions can be illustrated with the way they dealt with first-person and third-person narration. While the two types were defined repeatedly, no manual ever suggested procedures for helping students see the relevance of knowing about the two kinds of perspectives for reading. This was the case even when selections in the basal reader included both types of stories.

What the five series did with facts and opinions makes the same point. While *fact* and *opinion* were both defined and illustrated with what seemed like excessive repetition, nothing was ever suggested to clarify for students how knowing about facts and opinions should enter into the reading of an advertisement or an expository selection about a topic that is either controversial or incompletely understood. The generous amount of attention that definitions received was only one of the many times when manuals treated means as ends in themselves.

At certain places, the sequence of instruction in the manuals also had to be questioned. In one case, for example, how to skim a page to find answers to questions was described very briefly. Next came the recommendation to have students return to a certain page in the selection that they had just read and discussed so that they could skim it to find answers to two suggested questions. The problem, of course, is that the students already would know the answers, having just finished—if the teacher followed manual recommendations—a very detailed question-answer review of the story.

Unquestionably, the topic receiving the most frequent and persistent attention in all five programs was "main idea." A brief description of what is done with that topic will allow for a summary of the treatment of comprehension instruction in general.

To begin, even though *main idea* is not the easiest concept to grasp, it received attention as early as first grade, in one case with the unhelpful advice to teachers, "Introduce the word *idea*." (Other nonspecific suggestions began, "Lead the children to generalize that. . . ." and "Guide the pupils to conclude that. . . .") The initial treatment of main ideas inevitably used narrative material (paragraphs referred to as "stories"), even though expository text is the natural home for main ideas. "Instruction" took the form of calling attention to main ideas communicated in topic sentences, which were obviously displayed in the publishers' paragraphs. When the focus shifted to practice exercises, as it often did, not all the paragraphs contained main ideas. However, that problem was resolved with the use of multiple-choice formats in which the expected response often could be identified by eliminating obviously incorrect answers. Even though much space in manuals, workbooks, and ditto sheets dwelled on main ideas, only one of the five series—and this occurred once—ever suggested to teachers that they explain to students that attending to the main ideas of paragraphs helps in remembering an author's key points.

To summarize, comprehension instruction in the five basal programs was flawed not only by its paucity and indirect, nonspecific nature but also by the omission of attention to the value of why something was being taught. In spite of the scarcity, too much was done with some topics whereas others were treated briefly or not at all. In contrast to the small amount of comprehension instruction, the space allotted in the manuals to comprehension assessment and to comprehension practice in the form of brief exercises was clearly excessive.

OTHER RESEARCH

Concurrent with and subsequent to the studies that have been described in this introduction, a considerable amount of research was done by others with the hope of learning more about the comprehension process and about the implications of what was learned for instructional programs. Without question, what has emerged from this "veritable explosion of studies" (Guthrie, 1980) has produced valuable, insightful information. Equally visible, however, are a number of problems, three of which will be discussed briefly.

The first problem, which will make communication between researchers, authors of instructional materials, and teachers unnecessarily difficult, is disagreement over the meaning of comprehension *instruction*. According to Duffy and Roehler (1982), one of the most common and also incorrect referents for "instruction" in research reports is repeated exposure, otherwise known as *practice*. My own conclusion, based on research reports, articles, and reading methodology textbooks, is that the most common referent is activating and adding to children's knowledge of whatever it is that is relevant for reading a particular selection. If this conclusion is correct, it verifies the accuracy of a prediction that Carl Bereiter (1978) made when he said that it would eventually be concluded that "the way to improve comprehension is to stuff children's heads with 'subject matter' so that, whatever they're asked to read, they will stand a chance of already knowing quite a bit about it" (p. 7). The move by basal publishers to include much more expository material in their texts may be further evidence of the correctness of Bereiter's prediction. (Another reason may be the very large number of studies concerned with expository rather than narrative text.) In any case, the many different procedures now being called "instruction" are serving to obscure rather than illuminate its meaning.

A second problem that surfaces when the existing literature is reviewed is the tendency of many researchers and writers to lump together "comprehension" and "retention," much as if the two were the same. While it is certainly true that it is of little value to comprehend a piece of text only to forget what it said, comprehending and remembering what was comprehended are hardly identical, a fact overlooked—or at least not made explicit—in studies concerned with topics such as summarizing. Even though the excellent work that has been done on how to teach students to summarize ultimately should have a positive impact on what students are able to retain from their reading, it still must be recognized that it is impossible to summarize what was not

Guthrie, T. "Research Views." *Reading Teacher* 33 (1980), 880-882.

Duffy, G. G. and L. R. Roehler, "The Illusion of Instruction." *Reading Research Quarterly* 17 (1982), 438-445.

Bereiter, C. "Discourse Type, Schema, and Strategy—A Viewpoint from the Standpoint of Instructional Design." Paper presented at AERA Annual Meeting, Toronto, Canada, March 28, 1978.

understood in the first place. How to help students achieve that understanding—other than to "stuff their heads" with information—is in my opinion a neglected concern among most researchers doing comprehension studies, since relatively few seem to be concerned at present with the bottom-up side of the reading process. Instead, what is becoming an almost monotonous amount of attention is going to schema theory and its implications for reading. As a result, the profession has gone from one lop-sided position in which the text was all that counted to another in which world knowledge is winning everyone's attention.

A third problem is that the haste to learn about comprehension has discouraged both researchers and consumers of their reports from taking the time to realize in a very conscious way that *much* remains to be investigated before recommendations for improving students' comprehension abilities are warranted. After all, until there has been the time (and interest) to carry out studies that extend over a period of time and that include subjects at various grade levels, nobody is in a position to tell teachers exactly what they should and should not do. Highly premature, for instance, is a statement such as the following, which appears in the Preface of a reading methodology textbook: "No longer do teachers need lament the lack of appropriate knowledge and methods for teaching comprehension" (McNeil, 1984). "Haste makes waste" may be just the right slogan to keep in mind as we find ourselves passing through an era marked by unprecedented interest in reading comprehension.

RESPONSES TO THE RESEARCH

The collection of articles that follow illustrates one development that has occurred since reports of the studies just described were published. Numerous attempts now are being made to specify what is essential for comprehending connected text, to clarify differences between teaching and testing comprehension, and to describe examples of comprehension instruction that are suitable for both elementary and secondary students, and that stay clear of the flaws found in the instruction provided by basal manuals. While such efforts merit loud applause, they are not sufficient to effect much improvement in what is done with comprehension in classrooms. This is the case because the only source of help that stands a chance of having a widespread impact on teachers is manuals; consequently, only when teacher's guides reflect what is now known about comprehension and how to teach it can we expect to see major changes in what is done to teach students how to comprehend.

McNeil, D. *Reading Comprehension*. Glenview, Ill.: Scott, Foresman and Company, 1984.

Based on two conferences held with representatives of publishers, it is clear that needed changes will be made in basal manuals only when the marketplace demands them. Or, as one after another publisher stated or inferred, "We give our customers what they want." To get groups such as textbook selection committees to want the right thing, teachers and administrators need much education about what exists and what is needed in manuals and practice materials. Meanwhile, teachers who always have done a good job will continue to do even better with the help of books such as this one.

Dolores Durkin
Professor, Elementary and Early Childhood Education
University of Illinois, Urbana-Champaign

Reading, Thinking, and Concept Development

Part I
Explicit Comprehension Skills Teaching

In recent years, there has been a lively debate between those who advocate teaching comprehension by direct-skills techniques and those who advocate primary attention to the cultivation of cognitive strategies. A frequent implication of proponents of the latter position is that comprehension does not depend upon learned skills but on carefully nurtured cognitive strategies.

It seems reasonable to recognize that comprehension in fact depends upon a number of learned abilities, from the specific skill learning described in this section to the more general strategies described in later sections. Cognitive strategies require the possession of both an array of specific skills and the concepts essential for their implementation. Part of the difficulty that has clouded this debate and has obstructed clear-cut signals for the improvement of comprehension is the varying interpretations given to the terms *skill* and *strategy*. While the term *strategy* properly refers to "a systematic plan for achieving a specific goal or result," the term *skill* has acquired a very elastic set of meanings. These meanings may range from the highly specific, such as eye-movement skills, to the very complex, such as certain thinking and study skills, which may be thought of as virtually synonymous with *strategy*. The reader would be well-advised to note the apparent meanings attributed to these terms at various points in this volume.

A perennial problem in the teaching of skills is the successful transfer of initiative from the teacher-demonstrator to the student-learner. In teaching basic comprehension skills, is there a general model of explicit skills instruction that can effectively aid this transfer? Following a discussion of research in comprehension instruction, Pearson and Leys suggest how one might teach the comprehension skill of main idea explicitly in a procedure that gradually moves the responsibility for learning from teacher to students. The authors' suggestion of the impact that prior knowledge has on the teaching of main idea and other concepts has important implications for instruction and will be discussed throughout this volume.

"Teaching" Comprehension

P. David Pearson

Margie Leys

In the last five years, much has been written about the lack of instruction provided by teachers (Durkin, 1978–1979; Duffy and McIntyre, 1980) and teacher's manuals (Durkin, 1981; Beck, McKeown, McCaslin, and Burkes, 1979) to help children learn the dazzling array of comprehension skills we require them to perform as they prove to us—by completing workbook pages, passing end-of-unit or end-of-level mastery tests, or living through the administration of a standardized test—that they can or cannot understand what they read. Implicit in such criticism are the assumptions that teachers ought to teach children *how* to comprehend and that basal manuals ought to give teachers guidance concerning *how* to teach children *how* to comprehend.

We do not necessarily disagree with these assumptions. In fact, our basic goal in this essay is to illustrate what *explicit* instruction in comprehension skills might look like if we ever ran across it. But we want to make clear at the outset that the evidence in favor of teaching comprehension skills directly and explicitly is not as overwhelming as one might suppose and that there are alternative points of view on the issue.

WHAT FOSTERS COMPREHENSION?

Consider, for example, the possibility (implicit, if not explicit, in the view of Goodman and Goodman, 1979, or Harste, Burke, and Woodward, 1982) that the entire skills orientation (Harste and Burke, 1977) misses the point about comprehension in particular and reading in general. What may really matter is putting children in a supportive environment, giving them material to read that is written naturally (using the same kind of language that they are used to hearing being spoken), and providing them with the opportunity to develop very real and personal reasons for reading a selection (I want to know more about X; I want to write a story about Y; I want to read story Z to my friends). It might be true that when children are placed in such a situation, the issue of success or failure in comprehension does not even arise because children will, almost by definition, comprehend what they read to the degree they need to in order to satisfy their goals. In such a functionally oriented environment, comprehension, like decoding, becomes a means to an end rather than an end in itself: Comprehension is something you do because it helps you reach that larger and personally more relevant goal. Within such a perspective, the whole issue of comprehension skills and comprehension instruction becomes irrelevant. What matters are relevance and functionality. The teacher's role is not to impart wisdom from his or her *fount of knowledge* but to arrange conditions to help learning occur, to provide information when asked to do so by a student (this might even mean telling a student what you got out of reading a story or a paragraph), and to help children realize the range of goals and functions that reading can serve.

Consider another possibility. We know that the knowledge students accumulate over time has a powerful influence on their ability to recall information from a text, to answer either open-ended or multiple-choice questions about a passage, or to perform virtually any other comprehension task we may put in their way. Perhaps the whole notion of a skill or a strategy (by either we mean a context-free and content-free procedure for completing some kind of task; in other words, a procedure that is not dependent on the selection you are reading or the situation you are in) is ill-conceived because what really determines your ability to perform any of the so-called skills (finding the main idea, determining sequence, distinguishing statements of fact from opinion, for example) is *how much you already know* about the topic under discussion in the text. If this were true, then the best course of action to improve reading comprehension, however one defined it, might be to help students learn more about everything!

We suspect that this dilemma of prior knowledge applies to some of our traditional skills but not to others. How does one construct a main idea for a paragraph when none is explicitly stated? How can you know what those four sentences are all about *unless you know what they are all about?* How can you distinguish between literal comparison statements (a lime is like a lemon) and figurative comparisons (billboards are like warts) unless you know that limes really are like lemons and billboards are only metaphorically like warts? But notice that you can tell that some statements are likely to be statements of opinions because they contain a judgmental word (good, bad, best, etc.) or a linguistic hedge (might, ought, should, must). Or you might be able to tell that A caused B because of the force of the linguistic connective *because* in the sentence. (The rocket crashed *because* it ran out of liquid oxygen.)

These are difficult issues. And we do not think final answers exist for any of them. But we are willing to risk the attempt to illustrate what we think *explicit* instruction in comprehension tasks might look like. We undertake this risky venture because we believe that even if teachers cannot really *teach* comprehension skills, they can provide some *help and guidance* along a student's path to becoming an independent comprehender and learner. They can share with students the secrets of their own successes as language users.

MODEL FOR TEACHER-STUDENT RESPONSIBILITY IN INSTRUCTION

A convenient way to conceptualize the range of teacher behaviors in providing help and guidance has been developed by Pearson and Gallagher (1983, after Campione, 1981) and is represented in the figure on page 6. According to their model, instruction varies as a function of the relative degree of responsibility accepted by teachers and/or students for completion of any given task. At the leftmost edge of the figure, the teacher accepts all the responsibility and the student none. At the rightmost edge, the student accepts all the responsibility and the teacher none. In between these two extremes, responsibility is shared by teacher and student. The 100 percent teacher condition is what we mean by modeling; the 100 percent student condition is what we mean by independent practice or application. In between are varying instances of guided practice. The trick, of course, in any instructional program (we doubt that anyone would deny such a goal) is to bring students to accept 100 percent of the responsibility. Only partially in jest, we like to call it a model of "planned obsolescence" in teaching.

A MODEL OF EXPLICIT INSTRUCTION

PROPORTION OF RESPONSIBILITY FOR TASK COMPLETION

ALL TEACHER   JOINT RESPONSIBILITY   ALL STUDENT

MODELING   GUIDED PRACTICE   PRACTICE OR APPLICATION

Gradual Release of Responsibility

To illustrate the application of this model, contrast Durkin's comments in this volume and her findings about what was going on in classrooms (1978–79), what was being suggested in basal manuals, and the oft-quoted admonition that "children learn to read by reading" (1981) with the methodology pursued by either Palincsar and Brown (1983) or Gordon and Pearson (1983). Durkin found that the dominant teacher practices used to promote reading comprehension were asking students questions about selections they had just read and having students complete workbook pages and worksheets on their own. In both cases, teachers begin and end their instructional cycles in the rightmost region of the model. Students begin by practicing and, if they fail to demonstrate mastery of a particular skill, they continue to practice the behavior. It is what traditionally has been labeled a "teaching by testing" approach to comprehension, or what we might call a practice-only approach to comprehension. The assumption seems to be that students will learn the appropriate behavior if they are exposed to enough instances of the criterion task. Notice, however, that precisely the same assumption underlies the "children learn to read by reading" philosophy; what differs between the two is the nature of the materials they are exposed to—compartmentalized skill activities versus real text. The role of the teacher in either situation is to find the appropriate practice materials for the students (and, we suppose, to provide some feedback on how they are doing at key points along the way). By contrast, the work of Palincsar and Brown (1983) and Gordon and Pearson (1983) assumes that instruction begins on the leftmost edge of the graph and works its way along that diagonal to eventually end up in a practice-only situation; however, before that practice-only phase, the teacher has been heavily involved in the instructional situation, first by modeling the criterion behavior and then by sharing responsibility for that behavior with the students.

While several studies have illustrated the efficacy of the gradual release of responsibility philosophy implied in the model (Palincsar and Brown, 1983; Gordon and Pearson, 1983; Raphael and Pearson, 1982; Raphael, Wonnacott, and Pearson, 1983; Paris, Lipson, Cross, Jacobs, DeBritto, and Oka, 1982), one should not conclude that all children should be taught using such a philosophy for all tasks they need to learn in order to become expert readers. There are likely to be both children and tasks for whom and which the philosophy is neither necessary nor appropriate. Indeed, a major research endeavor facing the reading field is to discover the set of student and task characteristics that define the range of effectiveness for competing instructional strategies.

THREE EXAMPLES OF TEACHER GUIDANCE

In the remainder of this essay, we provide three examples of what we think the kind of teacher guidance and help implied by the model might look like. We have purposely chosen two examples of the mundane and much maligned skill called "finding the main idea." We have chosen it because of its ubiquity (it is taught in virtually every grade and every reading series) and because it represents a challenge to our whole notion of explicit instruction (recall that earlier we suggested that it might rest more on prior knowledge than on any content-free procedure). In the first of our examples we offer a lesson plan (one that might even appear in a teacher's manual) to help grade 2 students select explicitly stated main-idea statements; in the second, we provide a scenario of a discussion in which the teacher is trying to help grade 8 students select appropriate main-idea statements that are not part of the target paragraphs. Our third example provides a sample lesson for teaching high school students how to write a summary.

Example: Grade 2, Small-Group Reading Class—A Lesson Plan for Introducing Explicitly Stated Main Ideas

Anchor point: Children have had experience with explicitly stated main ideas located at the beginning of paragraphs.

Step One: Teacher Models and Explains

Review with children what they already know about main ideas. Tell them that today they will learn something new about finding main ideas and you will show them what you mean. (Put a paragraph on the overhead projector and read it to the children.)

Example: 1. Jeff could hear toads and bullfrogs. 2. He also could hear an owl. 3. Then he heard something moving in the bushes. 4. Jeff heard many noises the night he slept in the woods.

For each sentence, explain to the children why it is or is not the main idea of the paragraph. For example, "Sentence 2 can't be the main idea of this paragraph because it only tells about one noise that Jeff heard. It is a detail sentence. Only sentence 4 tells us what the whole paragraph is about—that Jeff heard many noises. The other sentences tell about the different noises that Jeff heard."

A diagram may make the relationship between the main idea sentence and the detail sentences clearer for the children.

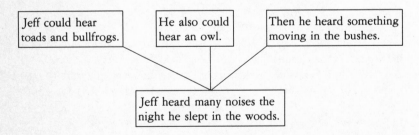

Remind students that in their earlier work they found the main idea sentences at the beginning of a paragraph. Tell them that sometimes writers place them at the end of a paragraph instead of at the beginning.

When looking for the main idea sentence they need to look in both places.

Step Two: Guided Practice

Put another paragraph on the chalkboard and read it to the class. This time tell them you will work together to determine which sentence tells what the whole paragraph is about.

Example: 1. Jessica invited all the kids. 2. Brock got the balloons. 3. Anne brought a cake. 4. And Katie brought the ice cream. 5. Everyone did something for the surprise birthday party.

Take the first sentence and explain why it is or is not the main idea sentence of the paragraph. Then ask for a volunteer to work through each of the sentences in the paragraph. The paragraph could be diagrammed as in the previous example.

Step Three: Teacher Reviews the Concept Being Taught

Elicit from the students what it is that makes a sentence a main idea sentence.

Step Four: Independent Practice

The children now have worked with main idea sentences at the beginning and at the end of paragraphs. For independent practice, give them a worksheet that contains both types of paragraphs. This variation will give you information about whether or not a child is just selecting the last sentence or working through each sentence in the manner that you have just modeled.

Here are two sample paragraphs that could appear on the same worksheet:

Example: 1. She cleaned out her locker and her desk. 2. Later that day, her friends had a party for her. 3. She cried as she said goodbye to everyone. 4. Alison was very sad on her last day at school.

Example: 1. Kids in our class have many different pets. 2. Amelia has a raccoon. 3. Clair has a snake. 4. Elizabeth just got a horse. 5. And Megan has five goats!

The difficulty of the task can be altered by the type of response used. The easiest form is to have the children select an answer from a set of choices. The task would be more difficult if you asked the children to find the main idea sentence in the paragraph.

Step Five: Application

Discuss with the children why it is a useful skill to be able to identify main ideas and how this skill can help them understand what they read. Have children look for main ideas in appropriate stories and expository text. Be sure that the material you use actually contains explicitly stated main ideas.

Example: Grade 8, Whole Social Studies Class—Implicit Main Ideas

Anchor point: beginning of the year.

Mrs. Hargrave: One comprehension exercise that you've all done many times is finding the main idea of a paragraph. You've probably done this mostly in reading class, but this is a useful skill for reading and understanding any kind of material. By now, you know quite a bit about main ideas. Let's review what you know. What can you tell us about main ideas? (Teacher writes the students' points on the chalkboard.)

Clyde: Not all paragraphs have a main idea.

Sally: It's the first sentence that gives you the main idea.

Sam: Not always! Sometimes it's the last one.

Jeff: Lots of times I can't find it.

Mrs. Hargrave: What do you mean?

Jeff: Sometimes we're told to figure out the main idea and I can't always find it.

Mrs. Hargrave: Yes, sometimes I have that problem too. When the main idea isn't directly stated, you, as a reader, have to figure out what the author is trying to tell you in that paragraph. Here's what you've told us so far about main ideas.

1. Not all paragraphs have a main idea—they are just a list of details.
2. Sometimes the first sentence is the main idea.
3. Sometimes the last sentence is the main idea.
4. Sometimes the main idea isn't given—you have to figure it out.

Today we're going to work on point four, that is, how to figure out the main idea of a paragraph when it isn't stated. (Teacher puts a paragraph on the overhead projector.) Let's read this paragraph and I'll show you what I mean.

> Many individual householders in the villages of India can no longer afford to own camels. One of these animals now costs about $400 to buy and about $3 a day to feed. Furthermore, the buying power of most Indian families has declined in recent years. Poor returns for the produce they grow, larger families, and India's general inflation have reduced the standard of living for most villagers. Many people who once earned a living as camel drivers have been forced to find other kinds of work to support their families.[1]

Here are four sentences. (Teacher puts these on the overhead projector.)

1. The camel was once the principal means of transportation in India.
2. Only the very poor can afford to own a camel in India.
3. Several factors have made owning a camel too costly for Indian villagers.
4. It costs $400 to buy a camel.

One sentence is a statement of the main idea of this paragraph. It's sentence 3. It can't be sentence one, since the paragraph doesn't tell us this information. It can't be sentence 2, since it is the opposite of what the paragraph tells us. And it can't be sentence 4 because it is too specific; other information is included in the paragraph that is not covered by this statement. Only sentence 3 covers all the information, the details, given in the whole paragraph.

Mrs. Hargrave: Let's try another paragraph. This time I won't do all the work; you can do part of it. (Teacher puts the paragraph on the overhead projector and reads it to the students.)

> In India, camels once served as the principal means of transportation. These animals also were used in agriculture for work such as plowing. Traditionally, the status of a family in the community was judged by the number of camels it owned. Camels were also part of an Indian bride's dowry. Before India became an independent country in 1947, states like Rajasthan were ruled by feudal kings. For centuries these kings kept large numbers of camels for both pageantry and military purposes. The tradition of maintaining camels in the military continues in a limited way; even today the Indian government keeps a camel corps to patrol the Pakistan border. And camels still appear in ceremonial pageants.

---

1. All passages in this section are reprinted with permission from the *Ginn Reading Program,* Level 15 (Clymer, Venezky, and Indrisano, 1982).

Here are four sentences. Let's see if any of these is a statement of the main idea of the whole paragraph. (Teacher puts sentences on the overhead projector and reads the first one.)

1. Camels were once a measure of Indian social status.

Who can tell us about the first sentence?

Richard: I don't think it's the main idea because it's too specific; there's more in the paragraph than stuff about social status.

Mrs. Hargrave: Good point. What about sentence 2?

2. Through tradition and culture, Indian life has been linked to the camel.

Nicholas: I think so; that sentence seems to cover everything.

Mrs. Hargrave: Well, let's look at the other two statements, then we can come back to sentence 2 and see if you still think it's the main idea. What about sentence 3?

3. Though camels are slow and clumsy, many people still prefer them to cars.

Laura: No, that isn't given in the paragraph.

Mrs. Hargrave: Yes, Laura, you're correct. What about sentence 4?

4. Camels are useful for many things.

Clay: No, that's too general; it doesn't really tell us anything important.

Mrs. Hargrave: That's good, Clay. Nicholas, what do you think now about sentence 2?

Nicholas: It covers everything, and besides, none of the others were the main idea!

Mrs. Hargrave: We've worked through this example and have learned something else about main ideas. I'll add this to our list on the board: A main idea tells us what the whole paragraph is about. Now I have an exercise for you to try. I've taken some paragraphs from your social studies book and I want you to determine which of the four sentences that follows each paragraph is a statement of the main idea of that paragraph. Any questions? In our everyday reading we don't have someone listing four choices of what the main idea of a paragraph could be. We have to create for ourselves a statement of the main idea. On

Monday, we'll try to create a statement of the main idea for paragraphs without stated main ideas. Here is the exercise.

> Today, paved roads connect Indian towns that were once separated by spans of desert sand. Vehicles such as buses, trucks, jeeps, bicycles, and pushcarts carry people, produce, and products in all directions. Because of the dramatic rise in the prices of gasoline and oil, some transporters are using camels to pull very heavy loads on wagons equipped with old airplane tires. This kind of camel-carrying power is especially useful for carrying great loads of grain for short distances.

1. Rising fuel costs have made camels practical for pulling heavy loads.
2. Paved roads and motor vehicles have made camels obsolete.
3. According to the census of 1972, there are a million camels in India.
4. Camels are useful for carrying great loads of grain.

Example: Grades 10–11, Whole Class–Content Area—A Lesson Plan for Teaching Summarization

Anchor point: Day one of a series of lessons. Students have had some instruction and practice writing summaries in their reading classes.

Necessary Materials

You will need the handout "How to Write a Summary" (see the Appendix at the end of this article). It consists of three sections:

1. General steps
2. Specific rules for creating summaries
3. A final suggestion for how to polish a summary

Also, you will need a sample passage that you can use to demonstrate to the students how to create a summary by applying the general steps and rules in the handout. You will want to make a copy of your polished summary to give to the students. Finally, you will need two passages for the students to summarize.

Step One: Teacher Models and Explains

Tell students that over the next few days you will be teaching them how to write summaries and explain how this can be useful to them.

Review with students what they already know about summaries.

Elicit a definition of a summary. Here is a working definition (after Day, 1980):

> A summary is a shortened version of a text. It is a concentrate of the original. It says basically the same thing as the original passage does, but it says it in fewer words. That is why it is called a summary. It is short.
>
> A summary does not contain your opinions. You may think that the author of a text is crazy and that the text is full of lies. But you don't say so in your summary. A summary is only a short version of the text. It is a reduction of the original text, nothing more.

Pass out the Appendix and explain to students that if they follow these rules and general steps they will be able to write better summaries. Read the rules to the students in this order: general steps 1 and 2, the four summarization rules, general steps 3 and 4, and the final suggestion. Then tell the students that you will show them how to follow the suggestions in the handout.

Put the following passage on the overhead projector:

Phylum Pyrrophyta

Since ancient times, sailors have been mystified by seeing the ocean's waters glow at night. We know today that a group of protists is responsible for this. The ability of a living organism to produce light is described as *bioluminescence* (bi o lu m nes' ns). The light is produced by *dinoflagellates* (din o flaj' lats). They contain chlorophyll and use it in photosynthesis. They also contain other pigments, and many of them appear reddish in color. Almost all dinoflagellates live in salt water.

Dinoflagellates have two flagella, which lie in grooves on the cell wall. One of the flagella circles about the middle of the organism, while the other trails out behind. The trailing flagellum propels the organism, while the circular one seems to be used for steering.

The cell wall of dinoflagellates is made of cellulose, like that of true plants. In some dinoflagellates the wall is smooth and in one piece. In other dinoflagellates the cell wall is made of many separate pieces that are cemented together. This type of wall looks like armor plating.

At certain times dinoflagellates suddenly start to reproduce in tremendous numbers. This gives rise to the condition known as *red tide*. Biologists are not sure why this happens, but it happens every year somewhere along the Atlantic or Pacific coast. The dinoflagellates can reach concentrations of 60 million per liter of water. The reddish color of the organisms gives the name to the tide.

Some dinoflagellates release poisons into the water. The large number of these organisms present during a red tide produce enough poison to kill many fish. Mussels and clams can accumulate the poison without being killed. But people who eat contaminated shellfish during a red tide can become quite ill. A red tide on the coast of New England in the summer of 1972 caused many people to be hospitalized.[2]

Now demonstrate general steps 1 and 2 (state the general theme and determine the main points). Next, apply the summarization rules, marking the text as you demonstrate each rule:

1. Circle all lists and suggest appropriate superordinate terms for each list.
2. Underline all topic sentences; write topic sentences for paragraphs that lack them.
3. Cross out all redundant information.
4. Show how certain paragraphs can be condensed, that is, joined together.

Now demonstrate general steps 3 and 4 (rethink, and check and double check). Read your summary as it exists. Finally, use the final suggestion to complete the summary. Hand out a "polished" version of the summary to the students.

Example of a Summary

Unicellular algae in the phylum Pyrrophyta are responsible for casting a mysterious glow over the evening ocean. These algae, otherwise known as *dinoflagellates,* are made of celluloid walls that are either smooth or bricklike in appearance. They travel by the aid of two flagella.

Because of their peculiar reproduction habits and reddish-colored pigment, dinoflagellates are also responsible for the toxic tide referred to as the *red tide.* Since some dinoflagellates release poisons, people who eat shellfish during red tide can become ill.

Step Two: Review the Concept Being Taught

Review with the students the definition of a summary and the general steps and rules used to write a summary.

It will take about 25 to 35 minutes to complete Steps One and Two. If you have enough time, continue with Steps Three and Four. If not, begin instruction for Day Two with a review, Step Two, and then continue with Steps Three and Four.

Step Three: Guided Practice

Give the students a short passage (three to four paragraphs) and as a group do general steps 1 and 2 and apply the summarization rules and

---

2. This passage is reprinted with permission from Silver Burdett (Smallwood and Alexander, 1981).

the final suggestion. (Note: you will need a new passage.) Try to let the students do as much of the work as they can, but be sure to offer feedback and suggestions for revision if students are off course. This phase is characterized by lots of negotiation among members of the group, successive refinement, and group consensus.

Step Four: Independent Practice

Give the students another short passage and have them create a summary for that passage, using the general steps and summarization rules handout. Collect these summaries and give the students individualized written feedback on their work. The feedback to the students should refer to their use and/or misuse of the rules and/or the general steps on the handout.

Step Five: Application

Your goal in teaching this skill is to get the students to use summary writing as one of their learning and studying strategies. As soon as possible, have students start applying this skill in their content area texts. Some text is easier to summarize than others; check to ensure that the material you assign is appropriate for the task. Gradually move students into more difficult material. Explain to the students that this skill is a very useful way to check their understanding of what they have read. Also, if their text contains chapter summaries, discuss how these can be useful for preview and review of the material.

CONCLUSION

As we indicated at the outset of this article, we do not think that final answers exist for the question of just how explicit instruction on reading comprehension tasks should be. Two issues should prevent you from accepting our advice uncritically. First, the influence of prior knowledge on comprehension tasks may prevent context-free instruction on some tasks. Second, "skills" as we presently define them might not even be necessary if we adopted a more functionally oriented view of literacy education. Nonetheless, we hope that we have given you some useful prototypes that you can put to work in your own situation. But these prototypes are nothing more than exemplary guidelines; they are not above revision and alteration for your classroom and students. We would prefer that teachers *adapt* rather than *adopt* our suggestions.

APPENDIX. HOW TO WRITE A SUMMARY

General Steps

1. *Make sure you understand the text.* Ask yourself, "What was this text about? What did the writer say?" Try to say the general theme to yourself.
2. *Look back.* Reread the text to make sure you got the theme right. Also read to make sure that you really understand what the important parts of the text are. Star the important parts. *Now use the four specific rules for writing a summary.*
3. *Rethink.* Reread a paragraph of the text. Try to say the theme of that paragraph to yourself. Is the theme a topic sentence? If it is missing, have you written it in the margin?
4. *Check and double check.* Did you leave in any lists? Make sure you don't list things in your summary. Did you repeat yourself? Make sure you didn't. Did you skip anything? Is all the important information in the summary?

Rules

1. *Collapse lists.* If you see a list of things, try to think of a word or phrase name for the whole list. For example, if you saw a list like eyes, ears, neck, arms, and legs, you could say body parts. Or if you saw a list like ice skating, skiing, or sledding, you could say winter sports.
2. *Use topic sentences.* Often authors write a sentence that summarizes a whole paragraph. It is called a topic sentence. If the author gives you one, you can use it in your summary. Unfortunately, not all paragraphs contain topic sentences. That means you may have to make up one for yourself. If you don't see a topic sentence, make up one of your own.
3. *Get rid of unnecessary detail.* Some text information can be repeated in a passage. In other words, the same thing can be said in a number of different ways, all in one passage. Other text information can be unimportant, or trivial. Since summaries are meant to be short, get rid of repetitive or trivial information.
4. *Collapse paragraphs.* Paragraphs are often related to one another. Some paragraphs explain one or more paragraphs. Some just expand on the information presented in other paragraphs. Some paragraphs are more necessary than other paragraphs. Decide which paragraphs should be kept or gotten rid of, and which might be joined together.

A Final Suggestion

Polish the summary. When a lot of information is reduced from an original passage, the resulting concentrated information often sounds very unnatural. Fix this problem and create a more natural-sounding summary. Adjustments may include but are not limited to: paraphrasing, the insertion of connecting words like "and" or "because," and the insertion of introductory or closing statements. Paraphrasing is especially useful here for two reasons: one, because it improves your ability to remember the material and two, it avoids using the author's words, otherwise known as plagiarism.

About the Authors

P. David Pearson is Chairman of the Department of Elementary and Early Childhood Education, University of Illinois, Urbana-Champaign.

Margie Leys is a doctoral student, Department of Elementary and Early Childhood, at the University of Illinois, Urbana-Champaign.

References

Beck, I. L., M. G. McKeown, E. S. McCaslin, and A. M. Burkes. *Instructional Dimensions That May Affect Reading Comprehension: Examples from Two Commercial Reading Programs.* Pittsburgh: University of Pittsburgh, Learning Research and Development Center, 1979.

Campione, J. *Learning, Academic Achievement, and Instruction.* New Orleans: Paper delivered at the Second Annual Conference on Reading Research and the Study of Reading, April 1981.

Clymer, T., R. L. Venezky, and R. Indrisano. *Chains of Light, Level 15.* Ginn Reading Program. Lexington, MA: Ginn and Co., 1982.

Day, J. D. "Teaching Summarization Skills: A Comparison of Training Methods." University of Illinois at Urbana-Champaign: Unpublished doctoral dissertation, 1980.

Duffy, G. and L. McIntyre. *A Qualitative Analysis of How Various Primary Grade Teachers Employ the Structured Learning Component of the Direct Instruction Model When Teaching Reading.* Research Series No. 80. Michigan: Institute for Research on Teaching, Michigan State University, 1980.

Durkin, D. "What Classroom Observations Reveal about Reading Comprehension Instruction." *Reading Research Quarterly* (1978-79) 14, 481–533.

Durkin, D. "Reading Comprehension Instruction in Five Basal Reader Series." Reading Research Quarterly 16 (1981).

Durkin, D. "Do Basal Manuals Teach Reading Comprehension?" In R. C. Anderson, J. Osborn, and R. J. Tierney (Eds.), *Learning to Read in American Schools.* Hillsdale, N.J.: Erlbaum, 1984.

Goodman, K. S. and Y. M. Goodman. *Theory and Practice of Early Reading* (Vol. 1). Hillsdale, N.J.: Erlbaum, 1979.

Gordon, C. and P. D. Pearson. *The Effects of Instruction in Metacomprehension and Inferencing on Children's Comprehension Abilities* (Tech. Rep. No. 277). Urbana: University of Illinois, Center for the Study of Reading, 1983.

Hare, V. C. and K. M. Borchardt. "Direct Instruction of Summarization Skills." *Reading Research Quarterly,* in press.

Harste, J. C. and C. L. Burke. "A New Hypothesis for Reading

Teacher Research: Both Teaching and Learning of Reading Are Theoretically Based." In P. D. Pearson and J. Hansen (Eds.), *Reading: Theory, Research and Practice.* Twenty-sixth yearbook of the National Reading Conference. Clemson, S.C.: National Reading Conference, 1977.

Harste, J. C., C. L. Burke, and V. A. Woodward. "Children's Language and World: Initial Encounters with Print." In J. A. Langer and M. T. Smith-Burke (Eds.), *Reader Meets Author/Bridging the Gap: A Psycholinguistic and Sociolinguistic Perspective.* Newark, Del.: IRA, 1982.

Palincsar, A. and A. Brown. *Reciprocal Teaching of Comprehension-Monitoring Activities* (Tech. Rep. No. 269). Urbana: University of Illinois, Center for the Study of Reading, 1983.

Paris, S. G., M. Y. Lipson, D. R. Cross, J. E. Jacobs, A. M. DeBritto, and E. R. Oka. *Metacognition and Reading Comprehension.* Chicago: Research colloquium presented at the annual meeting of the International Reading Association, April 1982.

Pearson, P. D. and M. C. Gallagher. "The Instruction of Reading Comprehension." *Contemporary Educational Psychology* (1983) 8, 317–344.

Raphael, T. E. and P. D. Pearson. *The Effects of Metacognitive Strategy Awareness Training on Students' Question-Answering Behavior* (Tech. Rep. No. 238). Urbana: University of Illinois, Center for the Study of Reading, 1982.

Raphael, T. E., C. A. Wonnacott, and P. D. Pearson. *Metacognitive Training in Question-Answering Strategies: Implementation in a Fourth Grade Developmental Reading Program* (Tech. Rep. No. 284). Urbana: University of Illinois, Center for the Study of Reading, 1983.

Smallwood, W. L. and P. Alexander. *Biology.* Morristown, N.J.: Silver Burdett, 1981.

As previously indicated by Pearson and Leys, learning to identify or to infer the main idea of passages has long been one of the most prevalently taught aspects of comprehension instruction. In fact many educators consider it to be the most important skill of reading comprehension but at the same time one of the most difficult to teach. Will inductive, direct instruction in the skills of categorizing and classifying help students improve their ability to identify main ideas? Williams proposes a model, with demonstrated success, for teaching the concept of main idea.

How to Teach Readers to Find the Main Idea

Joanna P. Williams

Teaching children to "find the main idea" has long been part of reading instruction, and lessons on this topic appear over a wide range of grade levels. As widespread as this instructional focus is, however, children often cannot find the main idea even in rather simple texts (Baumann, 1983).

Recently we have completed the development and evaluation of an instructional program that focuses on teaching specific strategies for identifying the main idea in short expository paragraphs (Williams, Taylor, Jarin, and Milligan, 1983). Our project was an attempt to design a program that was based on certain fundamental and classic principles of instruction, and on implications for instruction drawn from recent advances in theories of text processing. The text materials used in the instructional sequence came from a series of our experiments (Williams, Taylor, and Ganger, 1981; Taylor and Williams, 1983; Williams, Taylor, and de Cani, in press; Williams, in press), which also provided some of the base for the instructional design.

We make no claims that the ability to identify main ideas is, in any real sense, different from any other comprehension—comprehension that involves making inferences, for example. It is clear from the

21

demonstrations of schema theorists (Anderson, 1984; Rumelhart, 1980) that a reader always brings prior knowledge to the task of understanding text and that such background information interacts with the text information in cognitive processing. When does one comprehension task end and another begin? A consideration of such matters is beyond the scope of this paper. The focus here is strictly on attempts to improve children's ability in the traditional and ubiquitous task called "finding the main idea."

Our program was based on the idea that comprehension of the main idea rests strongly on basic categorization and classification skills (Williams, in press), and this paper presents a description of an inductive concept-identification model of text processing, proposed as the basis of an instructional model. Also three sample lessons are outlined, two of which are derived from our instructional program. The third lesson, suitable for more advanced students, is based on the same instructional model.

Successful instruction usually reflects the application of certain fundamental, classic principles. Teachers should start a lesson by modeling the criterion performance, and instruction should move gradually to the point at which the student can perform the task independently. Both the instructional tasks and the response-demands should be arranged into easy-to-difficult sequences. Feedback should be provided, and there should be sufficient repetition and practice at each step of the sequence, which should occur in a variety of formats in order to promote transfer. Our program incorporated these basic principles in its design.

CATEGORIZATION AND TEXT PROCESSING

When children begin to read, they are already highly proficient in their ability to categorize the world (Mervis, 1980). Indeed, even toddlers can sort familiar objects into categories. Preschoolers also can easily provide an appropriate general category label for a group of familiar objects, i.e., "toys." In fact, probably no laboratory task has yet demonstrated the extent to which young children have these abilities. We believe that an effective instructional technique consists of showing children that this same classification model underlies certain aspects of text processing, i.e., finding the main idea. That is, we demonstrate that what one does when one reads a paragraph in order to get the main idea is similar to what one does when referring to a group of objects by means of a summary (category) label. The instruction consists of juxtaposing known categories and relevant text examples, and it provides the child with the familiar model of classification as a framework (schema) for the new concept of main idea.

Of course, we also *tell* the child what a main idea is, and this certainly can help. But a definition is not necessarily as potent as a couple of well-chosen examples. Moreover, the most valuable examples most likely derive from an already understood concept.

These notions are consonant with recent theoretical work on text comprehension. Kintsch and van Dijk (1978), for example, talk about the development of *macrostructure*. As people read text, they convert sentences to propositions, and at the same time they delete, generalize, and integrate those propositions. These latter macroprocesses yield a macrostructure, which can be defined as those propositions in the text that represent the information that would appropriately summarize that text. These macroprocesses are, of course, basic cognitive processes that underlie all human abilities, not just language comprehension, let alone just written language comprehension.

The following paragraph illustrates the similarity between text processing and simple classification:

> Cowboys had many jobs to do. Cowboys had to protect the herd from cattle robbers. They had to brand cattle to show who owned them. They had to ride around the ranch to keep cattle from straying too far.

In this paragraph, each of the last three sentences entails (i.e., semantically implies) the topical macroproposition expressed in the first sentence (van Dijk, 1980, p. 46). The first sentence, then, is an explicit expression of the macrostructure, a sentence that summarizes the entire text.

Expressions of macrostructure do not have to appear explicitly in the text, of course. If the topic sentence were to be removed from the above paragraph, readers would be able to generate the macroproposition underlying the paragraph by reading the detail sentences; and if they were asked to write a summary sentence for the paragraph, they would most likely come up with a sentence similar to the topic sentence presented above (Williams, Taylor, and Ganger, 1981).

Obviously, natural text is much more complex and varied than a simple classification model, strictly applied, can handle. The ability to deal with such complexities—and, at more advanced levels, to make the adjustments in the basic model that are necessary in order to process sophisticated text—derives from gradual refinements in macroprocessing ability as the child develops and as he or she gains further experience.

Example Lesson 1

In this introductory lesson, the child is provided with the already familiar classification model as a framework for the unfamiliar concept of main idea. The lesson as written is suitable for a learning-disabled child who attains the third- or fourth-grade level on a standardized reading test but who nonetheless often fails to "get the point." With suitable modifications it would also be appropriate early in comprehension instruction for nondisabled students, i.e., toward the end of the first grade or at the beginning of the second grade. The explicit presentation of the classification model provides a familiar schema and serves to orient the pupil to the task.

Excerpts from the teacher's script (Williams et al., 1983), which can serve as a *framework* for an actual lesson, are presented here. (More or fewer examples will be appropriate, for example.)

Begin by laying out a variety of pens, pencils, and crayons. "What do we call these things all together?" (Things we use for writing.) "Good. Now, what kinds of things do we use for writing?" (We use *pens.* Make a separate pile of pens. We use *pencils.* Make another separate pile. We use *crayons.* Make another separate pile.) "Let's review." (Place writing implements in one pile.) "What are all these?" (Things used for writing.) "What kinds of things do we use to write?" (Pens, pencils, and crayons.) "So, we have many different things to write with. Can you think of something else that we write with that I don't have here?" (Chalk.) "Good. Those are all things used for writing."

Next, place a variety of buttons on the table. "What are these called?" (Buttons.) "What kinds of buttons do you see?" (Plastic buttons, wooden buttons, metal buttons.) Separate the buttons into three piles as in the above example, and then move them back into one pile. "All of these are buttons. But we found out something about buttons —they're made out of different materials. So, we can look at different *kinds* of buttons."

Next, write a list of words on the board: *dollar, money, dime, penny.* "Which word in this list tells about all the other words?" *(Money.)* "Good. Why?" *(Money* tells what all the others are about.) Erase *money* from the list; rewrite it above the others so it's the topmost word and underline it.

Write another list on the board and read it aloud. *"Dusting the furniture, scrubbing the floors, making the beds, washing the dishes.* What are all these phrases about?" *(Cleaning the house.)* Write the phrase above the others, and underline it. "*That* phrase tells the most important idea of all these phrases."

Mount a list of sentences, each written on a separate strip of paper, on a felt board and read aloud. *"There are many ways to use paper; paper is used to write letters; paper is used to write book reports; it is used for drawing pictures.* Which sentence tells what the others are about?" *(There are many ways to use paper.)* Underline the sentence. "This sentence tells the most important idea of all the sentences. These other sentences (point to them) are all about different ways to use paper."

Now write a paragraph with no topic sentence about the materials from which buttons are made. Generate an appropriate topic sentence, and remind the students of their earlier classification of real buttons.

DEFINITION OF MAIN IDEA

One difficulty with much current instruction is that the definition of *main idea* has not been spelled out clearly. The lack of an explicit, consistent definition makes it difficult to select or construct good instructional texts. Often, the lack of clarity in the materials used leads to fuzzy, debatable "main ideas" that do not allow clear illustration of the concept and thereby do not provide good feedback to students.

This problem can be avoided by defining *main idea* more rigorously. We have done this by using the terms provided in van Dijk's (1980) analysis. Let us return to our sample paragraph. We can define both a *general topic* for this paragraph, i.e., *cowboys*, and a *specific topic*, i.e., *cowboys have many jobs*. The point is that there are various levels of macrostructure, some more general and inclusive than others.

The point is that text materials for teaching should be designed, at least in the initial stages of instruction, so that there is a clear main idea, one that fits into some definite structure. We think that the van Dijk formulation is a good foundation: it does not cover all paragraphs, but it is general and inclusive and clear enough to serve as the structure for initial materials. Later in instruction, more varied and flexible paragraph structures are warranted.

Example Lesson 2

This lesson focuses on finding the specific topic of a paragraph. It assumes proficiency in finding the general topic, which is the focus of a great deal of the existing instructional material on main idea. Indeed, we believe that rather too much emphasis is placed on general topic and not enough on more challenging tasks for which children actually need more help. We present here the teaching script for a single paragraph; the actual lesson would contain similar work on several paragraphs. (It should be noted that the lesson on specific topic does not directly follow Lesson 1 in our instructional program.)

This lesson also is suitable for learning-disabled children who score at the third- or fourth-grade level on standardized reading tests *and* who can identify the general topic of a single paragraph. With modification, such a lesson also could be used with beginning readers. For example, a teacher might decide not to teach the terminology *general topic* and *specific topic* or might prefer not to use handouts.

Distribute a handout on which is printed each of the paragraphs to be used in the lesson. Put the first paragraph on the chalkboard, and ask a child to read it aloud.

> Squirrels live in different parts of the United States. The gray squirrel is often seen in parts in the eastern United States. The red squirrel lives in forests in the Rocky Mountains. The round-tailed ground squirrel is common in the desert.

"When I ask you what this paragraph is about, what is the first thing that comes to mind?" (Squirrels.) Children circle each instance of the word *squirrels* on their handout; circle instances on the chalkboard example. "Good. Squirrels is called the *general topic* of this paragraph." Write the term on the board. "What does the paragraph tell *about* squirrels?" (Where squirrels live.) Children underline the instances— the different places—that are mentioned in the paragraph; underline them on the chalkboard example. "Does the paragraph tell us *everything* we know about squirrels?" (No.) "Good. For example, it does not tell what squirrels like to eat, or how they care for their young. *This* paragraph tells only about the different places where squirrels live. We call this information about the squirrels the *specific topic* of this paragraph." Write the term on the board; under it, write *where squirrels live* with a list of the different places. "The specific topic tells us more information about the general topic. Once we figure out the general topic of a paragraph, we have to look further and figure out the specific topic."

CATEGORIZATION AND LEARNING FROM TEXT

So far, we have been assuming that readers understand what cowboys are, what jobs are, and that branding cattle, protecting the herd, and so forth are examplars of the category of jobs. Thus we have been talking about simple comprehension and not the more complex situation that occurs when readers are learning from text, as when they have an understanding of the category "jobs," but have never known before reading a paragraph that branding cattle is one of a cowboy's jobs.

We also have been talking about a model of concept identification rather than of concept formation. The reader who is reading a series of detail sentences of the type shown above presumably has an understanding that the activities specified in those sentences are jobs. (Of course, this may not always be true. It may be that a reader has never learned before that an individual might get paid for performing a particular activity. But we have not dealt so far with the formation— or expansion—of categories.)

The model, however, can be extended to cover such situations. When people read, they usually assume that the text will contain only relevant information (cf. Grice's [1975] cooperative principle). Thus, in terms of our simple paragraphs, the reader under ordinary conditions will expect that all the detail sentences serve as positive exemplars of the main idea. Consider a reader who has read enough of the paragraph above (with or without a topic sentence) to have formed, however hazily, the mental representation, "This is about cowboys' jobs," and who then comes upon a sentence whose underlying proposition he or she cannot identify as an exemplar of the general category "jobs." The reader may change his or her identification of that proposition to include it in his or her set of exemplars, i.e., relabel it "a job." In this case, the reader would be learning from the text.

On the other hand, he or she might reject the proposition as an exemplar and enlarge the representation of what the paragraph is about; this is in fact what proficient readers do with simple paragraphs (Williams, Taylor, and de Cani, in press). For example, if a sentence such as "Cowboys sing and dance every evening" were encountered in the sample paragraph, a young reader might infer that singing and dancing are jobs that cowboys do; or a reader who is more proficient might offer as a topic sentence, "Cowboys do many different things at work and play." It should be noted that in both cases readers are assuming that the text is well organized and that the information it presents is relevant. Only in extreme cases will readers reject anomalous portions of text instead of trying to make sense of them and incorporate them into their representations (Markman, 1981).

Example Lesson 3

This lesson deals with content-area instruction for normally-achieving junior high school students (seventh grade).[1] Long before this point

---

1. The author is grateful to David Fairfield for suggesting Lesson 3 and to Mr. Linn Marks for valuable comments on an earlier version of this paper.

in a student's education, of course, he or she already has internalized
the basic categorization model inherent in text processing, even if that
model has never been made explicit in the student's early instruction.
This internalized model makes it possible for text structures to be used
to expand conceptual knowledge. In other words, the student reads to
learn.

A text several paragraphs long is presented. After reading the passage, students are given three statements and are asked to select the one
that best represents the main idea of the passage. The statements are
written such that one is totally irrelevant, the second is related to the
text but comprised of minor details, and the third is the best representation of the main idea. Students can eliminate the first statement quickly
and thus narrow the choice to two items. "If they select statement 2,
it is easy to show why it is incorrect: details vs. main idea" (Putnam,
1974, p. 42).

Later items can be constructed to "fine tune" the skill. For example,
the extraneous statement can be eliminated and replaced by one that
contains relevant, althouh very minor, information. A second statement
can contain the main idea, stated very poorly, and the third statement
can be the main idea expressed well. Once again, the choice can be
quickly narrowed to two, and if the student chooses the main idea
poorly expressed, "It is easy to teach the reasons why: one is more
encompassing or it includes only the main point" (Putnam, 1974, p.
42). Such exercises can be used and elaborated on in order to help
develop the ability to learn from text.

Following is a sample text (Buggey, Danzer, Mitsakos, and Risinger,
1980) and two exercise items based on the text:

Abolitionists, regardless of their approach, ran into many problems.

Southerners looked upon abolitionists as troublemakers. Lunsford Lane
was tarred and feathered when he returned to North Carolina to purchase
his family's freedom.

State legislators in the South appealed to each northern legislature to stop
abolitionists' activities in their states. Although they received little support
in the state legislatures, they were able to gather the votes to pass a "gag"
rule in the United States House of Representatives. This law set aside all
petitions relating to abolition. Adopted in 1836, the measure was not with-
drawn until 1844.

But prejudice was not limited to the slaveholding South. Abolitionist
speakers in both North and South often were pelted with rotten eggs.
William Lloyd Garrison was more than once run out of town on the end of
a rope.

Townspeople in Canterbury, Connecticut, broke into Prudence Crandall's school for black girls, destroyed furniture, broke windows, threw filth into the water well, and eventually succeeded in forcing the school to move out of town.

Even among the abolitionists, prejudice could be seen. One antislavery society became quite alarmed when it was suggested that blacks be invited into membership. Many members felt it was acceptable to invite blacks to attend, but not be put on "equality with ourselves." In this society, those members who favored equality for all, black and white, finally won out.

It may be said that the abolitionists were both successful and unsuccessful in their reform movement. They were unsuccessful in convincing southern slaveholders to abolish slavery. They were successful in getting many people in the North ready for the struggle ahead.

Exercise 1: Choose the statement that best expresses the main idea of the passage.

1. State legislators worked differently in the North and South.
2. Abolitionists met a lot of resistance to their antislavery views.
3. All abolitionists were against slavery, but some of them opposed equality.

The student is encouraged to consider only the information that is relevant to the text and eliminate immediately that which is irrelevant or absurd. In this exercise, statement 1 can be eliminated outright. The passage mentions state legislators in the larger context of abolitionists' activities, but the entire passage hardly could be said to be reflected in this statement. In the second elimination, one must decide which statement is more important, more relevant, more central to the text. Statement 3 is true and can be found in the text, but it is not central to the complete passage. Statement 2 summarizes the main idea of the passage, and for this reason it is preferable to the last statement.

By varying the choices, the exercise becomes somewhat more challenging.

Exercise 2: Choose the statement that best represents the main idea of the passage:

1. There was resistance in the North to education for blacks.
2. Abolitionists were subject to frequent harassment.
3. Abolitionists had to deal with both internal and external problems.

Since all the statements are consonant with the text, the task becomes considerably more difficult. Statement 1 is definitely true, as illustrated in the fifth paragraph. However, once applied to the entire text, it easily can be demonstrated that the main idea of that paragraph, i.e., the resistance to education for blacks, is only one aspect in the broader context of problems encountered by blacks and the abolitionist advocates. Once this statement is eliminated, the student must determine which of the remaining statements, both expressions of the main idea, is the better of the two. While statement 2 expresses the central theme of the text, statement 3 is more encompassing and therefore is the better choice.

SUMMARY

In summary, a concept-identification model of text processing has been proposed as the basis for an instructional model. Several lessons have been outlined to illustrate how the model can be used.

About the Author

Joanna P. Williams is Professor, Department of Educational Psychology, at Teachers College, Columbia University.

References

Anderson, R. C. "Role of the Reader's Schema in Comprehension, Learning, and Memory." In R. C. Anderson, J. Osborn, and R. J. Tierney, (Eds.), *Learning to Read in American Schools.* Hillsdale, N.J.: Lawrence Erlbaum Associates, 1984.

Baumann, J. F. "Children's Ability to Comprehend Main Ideas in Content Textbooks." *Reading World* (1983) 22, 322–331.

Buggey, Danzer, Mitsakos, Risinger. *America! America!* Glenview, Ill.: Scott Foresman and Company, 1980.

Grice, H.P. "Logic and Conversation." In P. Cole and J. L. Morgan (Eds.), *Syntax and Semantics, Vol. 3: Speech Acts.* New York: Seminar Press, 1975.

Kintsch, W. and T. A. van Dijk. "Toward a Model of Text Comprehension and Production." *Psychological Review* (1978) 85, 363–394.

Markman, E. M. "Comprehension Monitoring." In W. P. Dickson (Ed.), *Children's Oral Communication Skills.* New York: Academic Press, 1981.

Mervis, C. B. "Category Structure and the Development of Categorization." In R. J. Spiro, B. C. Bruce, and W. F. Brewer (Eds.), *Theoretical Issues in Reading Comprehension.* Hillsdale, N.J.: Lawrence Erlbaum Associates, 1980.

Putnam, L. R. "Don't Tell Them to Do It . . . Show Them How." *Journal of Reading* (1974) 17.

Rumelhart, D. E. "Schemata: The Building Blocks of Cognition." In R. J. Spiro, B. C. Bruce, and W. F. Brewer (Eds.), *Theoretical Issues in Reading Comprehension.* Hillsdale, N.J.: Lawrence Erlbaum Associates, 1980.

Taylor, M. B. and J. P. Williams. "Comprehension of Learning-Disabled Readers: Task and Text Variations." *Journal of Educational Psychology* (1983) 75, 743–751.

van Dijk, T. A. *Macrostructures.* Hillsdale, N.J.: Lawrence Erlbaum Associates, 1980.

Williams, J. P. "Categorization, Macrostructure, and Finding the Main Idea." *Journal of Educational Psychology,* in press.

Williams, J. P., M. B. Taylor, and J. S. de Cani. "Constructing Macrostructure for Expository Text." *Journal of Educational Psychology*, in press.

Williams, J. P., M. B. Taylor, and S. Ganger. "The Effect of Text Variation at the Level of the Individual Sentence on the Comprehension of Simple Expository Paragraphs." *Journal of Educational Psychology* (1981) 73, 851–865.

Williams, J. P., M. B. Taylor, D. C. Jarin, and E. S. Milligan. *Determining the Main Idea of Expository Paragraphs: An Instructional Program for the Learning-Disabled and Its Evaluation* (Technical Report No. 25). New York: Teachers College, Columbia University, Research Institute for the Study of Learning Disabilities, 1983.

Anaphoric reference is among the elements of text cohesion that have received considerable attention in relation to reading comprehension. For example, it has been suggested that the distance between a pronoun and its referent can affect comprehension. Will specific attention in the classroom to how words are frequently used to refer to other words lead to improved text comprehension? Johnson presents a number of exercises designed to develop an understanding of such anaphoric relationships as a comprehension aid.

Developing Comprehension of Anaphoric Relationships

Dale D. Johnson

Readers must deal with anaphoric relationships in everything they read. In this article, the term *anaphoric relationship* is used in an inclusive sense to denote the direction indicated by a reference term, either backward or forward. Technically, the term *anaphora* means "backward reference"—the use of a word or group of words to substitute for a preceding word or group of words; *cataphora* means "forward reference"—the use of a word or group of words to substitute for a following word or group of words. Anaphoric references are far more common than cataphoric references. In the sentence, "Eric yanked the door open and he stormed into the room," *he* is the anaphoric term for the antecedent, *Eric.* In "The puma gracefully leaped from the tree. The sleek cat was a natural predator," *sleek cat* is the backward reference replacement for *puma.* In "We ducked when they shouted 'Fore!' This can, at times, be a dangerous game," *This* is the anaphoric term for the unstated antecedent, *golf.* In "They were really wild today. My class was just about out of control," the forward reference term *They* is encountered before the word *class* to which it refers. While there are many types of anaphora, the most familiar are the pronouns.

What differentiates a unified text from lists of sentences in paragraph form is the author's use of reference terms and other cohesive ties of text structure, such as substitution, ellipsis, conjunction, and lexical cohesion as described by Halliday and Hasan (1976). Chapman recently observed, "For a text to be recognized as a text rather than as a haphazard collection of sentences, it must have an orderly and cohesive construction. . . . This concept is attractive not only for the way in which it establishes the basic notion of tying parts of a text together but also for its great potential as a tangible teaching technique. . . . It gives teachers, and through them, their pupils, a notion that they can readily understand the concept of tying things together by means of suitable knots."[1] Everything we read contains features of cohesion, and the reader who is unable to process such connections is unquestionably going to suffer comprehension loss. Anaphoric elements of text structure must be dealt with for comprehension to occur.

Solid instruction is needed to help students deal with anaphoric relationships. Good writers make plentiful use of these features of text structure and good comprehenders must process them accurately. This article describes several teaching strategies designed to help students comprehend the anaphoric relationships found in all levels and types of written material. The comprehension instructional activities presented here are based upon the abbreviated listing of anaphoric relations summarized by Pearson and Johnson (1978, pp. 124–25).

ANAPHORIC RELATIONS

Relation	*Example*	*Possible Comprehension Questions*
Pronouns: I, me, us, you, he, him, she, her, we, they, them.	Mary has a friend named John. She picks him up on the way to school. They walk home together too.	Who gets picked up? Who picks him up? Name the person who gets picked up.
Locative (location) pronouns: here, there.	The team climbed to the top of Mt. Everest. Only a few people have been there.	Where have only a few people been? Name the place where only a few people have been.

---

1. Chapman, John, *Reading Development and Cohesion*. (London: Heinemann Educational Books, 1983), pp. 46, 48.

Deleted nouns: usually an adjective serves as the anaphora.	The students scheduled a meeting but only a few attended. Apparently several went to the beach. Others attended a dance in the gym. Only the most serious actually came to the meeting. (Notice that each adjective phrase or adjective refers to students.)	Who went to the beach? Who attended the dance in the gym? What does the word *others* refer to?
Arithmetic anaphora.	Mary and John entered the building. The former is tall and lovely. The latter is short and squatty. The two make an interesting couple.	Who is tall and lovely? Who makes an interesting couple? What does the word *two* refer to?
Class inclusive anaphora: a superordinate word substitutes for another word.	1. The dog barked a lot. The animal must have seen a prowler.	1. What animal must have seen a prowler?
	2. The lion entered the clearing. The big cat looked graceful as it surveyed its domain.	2. What cat looked graceful? What does the word *cat* refer to?
	3. John was awakened by a siren. He thought the noise would never stop.	3. What noise did John think would never stop?

Inclusive anaphora: that, this, the idea, the problem, these reasons. Can refer back to an entire phrase, clause, or passage.	1. (After twenty pages discussing the causes of Civil War.) For these reasons, the South seceded from the Union.	1. Why did the South secede from the Union?
	2. Someone was pounding on the door. This (or it) surprised Mary.	2. What surprised Mary?
	3. Crime is getting serious in Culver. The police have to do a better job to solve this problem.	3. What do the police have to do a better job about?
	4. "Do unto others as you would have them do unto you." Such an idea has been the basis of Christian theology for 2,000 years.	4. What has been the basis of Christian theology for 2000 years?
Deleted predicate adjective: so is, is not, is too (also), as is.	1. John is dependable. So is Henry.	1. Is Henry dependable?
	2. John is dependable. Susan is not.	2. Is Susan dependable?
	3. The lion was large but graceful. The tiger was too.	3. Describe the tiger.

4. The lion, as is the tiger, is large but graceful.

4. Describe the tiger.

Proverbs: so does can, will have, and so on (or), can, does, will too (or), can does, will not, as did, can, will.

1. John went to school. So did Susan.

1. What did Susan do?

2. John went to school. Susan did too.

2. What did Susan do too?

3. Henry will get an A. So will Theresa.

3. What will Theresa do?

4. Amy can do a cartwheel. Matthew cannot.

4. Can Matthew do a cartwheel? What can't Matthew do?

5. Mom likes bologna. Dad does not.

5. Does Dad like bologna?

6. John likes, as does Henry, potato chips.

6. What does Henry like? Does Henry like potato chips?

The "possible comprehension" questions in the chart are types of questions teachers can ask during the discussion of a passage to focus students' attention on anaphoric relationships. In addition to good solid teacher-led discussion that uses such focus questions, there are a number of paper-and-pencil activities that can provide students with practice in dealing with these cohesive features of text. Some are at the sentence level and others use longer units of discourse.

The remainder of this article presents examples of different types of paper-and-pencil anaphoric practice. First, three kinds of activities are shown; then, examples for intermediate, middle, and high school students are presented.

THREE TYPES OF INSTRUCTIONAL ACTIVITIES

Stevenson and Baumann (1981) have recommended three categories of paper-and-pencil activities designed to provide learners with practice in anaphoric resolution: "Find the Antecedent," "Anaphoric Substitutes," and "Question and Answer."

"Find the Antecedent"

This activity requires students to locate and identify antecedents for anaphoric terms. For young children, this should involve simple sentences and sentence pairs; for older students, paragraphs or passage-length selections may be used.

Directions: Circle the word or words that mean the same as the italicized word or words.
a. Sam went fishing all morning. *He* caught two bass and a perch.
b. My bike is very old. For my birthday I'm going to get a new *one.*
c. Mary scored two goals in last night's soccer game. Mary's teammate, Susan, *did too.*
d. Terry and Tom went swimming. *Both* had a great time.
e. The Brownies went to visit the Fire Station, but *several* couldn't go because they had the flu.

Directions: The following story has several italicized words. Try to figure out what other word or words mean the same as the italicized parts. Write your answers on the spaces below.

$$\begin{matrix} & 1 & & 2 \end{matrix}$$

My name is Tom. *I* have a best friend whose name is Jim. *We* have a lot in
$$\begin{matrix} 3 \end{matrix}$$
common. *I* like to ride bikes and so does Jim. Jim likes to play soccer, and
$$\begin{matrix} 5 & 6 & 7 & & 8 \end{matrix}$$
so do I. As *I* said, *my friend* and I enjoy doing the *same things.*

1. _____   5. _____

2. _____   6. _____

3. _____   7. _____

4. _____   8. _____

Note: This activity can be made less difficult by providing students with a list of answer choices.

"Anaphora Substitution"

This activity requires students to substitute an anaphoric term for a clearly identified antecedent. The following activities are similar to the "Find the Antecedent" exercises, except that students need to select an abbreviated, more efficient way of stating repeated information.

Directions: Each of the following sentences has one or more italicized words. From the list at the bottom of the page, select the word that means the same as the italicized part and write that word on the blank.

a. *John* went on a trip to New York.

a. _____

b. Mary built a *doghouse.* She made the doghouse for her pet poodle.

b. _____

c. Nancy went to Bear Lake Camp last summer. She had never been to *Bear Lake Camp* before.

c. _____

d. Mark hit a home run, and Tom *hit a home run.*

d. _____

e. Martha got some new building blocks for her birthday, but her brother broke the *new building blocks.*

e. _____

them   did too   he   his   there   it

"Question and Answer"

Requiring students to answer questions about anaphoric relationships will help them make these associations and ultimately improve reading comprehension. The following activity is designed for this purpose, but it is also suitable to evaluate students' ability to comprehend anaphora.

Directions: Read the following sentences and short paragraphs, and answer the questions that follow.

a. John had a birthday. Because of this, Sally gave him a new watch.
Who received the gift?_____ Why was the gift given?_____

b. Martin and Monica made an attractive couple. The woman wore a long black coat, and the man wore a white coat with tails.
Whose coat was white?_____ Whose coat was black?_____

c. John is thrifty, but Mary isn't. The boy always saves his allowance, but the girl always spends her money on gum and candy.
Is Mary thrifty?_____ Who would have more money?_____
Who do you think would be better at blowing bubbles?_____

d. Ronald owns an antique bicycle. He got it from his grandfather who used it when he was a child. At that time, the bicycle was considered to be very "fancy."
From whom did Ronald get the bicycle?_____
Who first owned the bicycle?_____
When was the bicycle considered to be "fancy"?_____

e. The Boy Scouts scheduled an activity day last Saturday. The scouts could

choose what they wanted to do. Some learned how to tie knots. Most of the scouts went to the movie on bear hunting. Only a few decided to learn sign language. At the end of the day, everyone got together for cookies and hot chocolate.
How many scouts ate cookies and hot chocolate?_____
Did many scouts choose to learn how to tie knots?_____
What was the most popular activity?_____
What was least popular?_____

INSTRUCTIONAL ACTIVITIES FOR INTERMEDIATE, MIDDLE, AND HIGH SCHOOL STUDENTS

Intermediate Grades

Four instructional examples follow. The first two use the anaphoric substitution format (in these examples, pronoun substitutes). The remaining two are examples of question-and-answer activities using short-story-length passages.

Directions: Read each sentence and notice the italicized word or words. Write a pronoun that could replace the italicized words.
1. *The captain* is in charge of the ship._____
2. *Mares* are female horses._____
3. *Ike and I* found facts about the Milky Way._____
4. *The Rainbow and the Sea Witch* were clipper ships._____
5. *Frank* reported on Mount Everest._____
6. *A husky* is an Eskimo dog._____
7. *Ericka* showed a model of a fruit fly._____
8. *John F. Kennedy and Lyndon B. Johnson* were presidents._____
9. *Victoria and I* went on a tour of O'Hare Airport._____
10. Luis talked about *space travel.* _____
11. Bill showed how to make *pies.* _____
12. Mike told *Harry* about pole vaulting._____
13. The class buried *the time capsule.* _____
14. We use *microscopes* in science class._____
15. A report on England was given by *Zelda.* _____
16. Ms. Low helped *Sally and me.* _____
17. This picture was painted by *Ms. Lopez.* _____

Directions: Rewrite each of these sentences, substituting a pronoun for the italicized word or words.
1. *Sherlock Holmes* is a storybook detective.

2. *Bees* collect nectar from flowers.

_____

3. *An aquarium* should be cleaned weekly.

_____

4. *Billie Jean King* has won many tennis titles.

_____

5. *Ben and I* are learning to make a pizza.

_____

6. Masons build with *stone.*

_____

7. Many people wear *hats.*

_____

8. The worker bees take care of *the queen.*

_____

9. The sandwiches were eaten by *Fran and me.*

_____

10. The computer was run by *Mr. Boyd.*

_____

Directions: Some words refer to other words in the sentence in this story. Read the story and answer the questions that follow.

Three Pigs in Custody
by Brothers Grimm, April 1, 1853

[1]"We were sick and tired of having our homes blown down," said Curly Pig as he and his brothers were taken into custody by local police for the murder of C. Lupus Wolf.

[2]The three Pig brothers moved to town about two months ago in order to open a bakery. [3]Curly built a home of straw. [4]Oinky built a home of twigs. [5]Pinky built a home of bricks.

[6]It seems that every time the moon was full, C. Lupus Wolf went down to Maple Street and blew Curly's and Oinky's homes over, which forced them to take refuge with Pinky. [7]C. Lupus scrambled all over the roof trying to slide down the chimney.

[8]This month's fiasco was one time too many. [9]When C. Lupus slid down the chimney, a pot of boiling water was waiting for him. [10]C. Lupus was

singed. [11]Maybe the Pig brothers should have gotten official help before taking such drastic steps.

[12]As they were led away, the brothers said that they hoped people would understand how irritating it was to have to rebuild their homes every month.
1. In sentence 1, who does *We* refer to?_____
2. In sentence 6, who does *them* refer to?_____
3. In sentence 8, what does *one time too many* refer to?_____
4. In sentence 9, who does *him* refer to?_____
5. In sentence 11, what does *such drastic steps* refer to?

_____

6. In sentence 12, who does *they* refer to?_____

Directions: Some words refer to other words in the sentences in this story. Read the story and answer the questions that follow.

Woodland Woman to Wed
by Charles Willis, April 1, 1697

[1]A very happy Ms. Snow White announced her engagement yesterday. [2]She made the announcement from the forest home of dwarf friends. [3]Ms. White also told of the hardships she has endured lately.

[4]Ms. White is the daughter of Baron White. [5]Three years ago, when Baron White remarried, problems started. [6]The new wife found out that her magic mirror thought Ms. White the fairest in the land. [7]Ordered to do away with Ms. White, a kind huntsman turned her loose in the woods. [8]She wandered for a few days. [9]Then she was taken in by seven dwarfs.

[10]When Ms. White ate a poisoned apple sent by the evil wife, the dwarfs prepared a glass coffin. [11]Prince Charming saw the entombed woman. [12]He wanted to save her. [13]He attempted to move the coffin. [14]It dropped. [15]The poisoned apple was dislodged. [16]After a short friendship, Ms. White came to love the Prince.

[17]Ms. White smiled happily as she said, "It was all worth it. [18]I'm sure that I will be happy at the palace. [19]I intend to have a hand in the policymaking in this kingdom."
1. In sentence 1, who does *her* refer to?_____
2. In sentence 2, who does *she* refer to?_____
3. In sentence 6, who does *her* refer to?_____
4. In sentence 7, who does *her* refer to?_____
5. In sentence 11, who does the *entombed woman* refer to?_____
6. In sentence 12, who does *he* refer to?_____
7. In sentence 14, what does *it* refer to?_____
8. In sentence 17, what does *it* refer to?_____

Middle School

The activities for middle school students use expository text and an exchange of business letters. The first activity follows the question-answer format and the remaining activities require the students to find the antecedents.

Directions: Anaphoric words take the place of other words in sentences and may refer to people, places, a number of things, or whole ideas. Read the passage and then answer the questions that follow.

[1]Extraordinary animals and beasts have always intrigued humans. Tales about *them* abound in legends, myths, folklore, and literature. One of these legendary beasts is the Abominable Snowman.

[2]As the story is told, the *creature* dwells in the Great Himalaya Mountains of South Central Asia. Descriptions about the manlike ape or apelike man often are exaggerated, but the consensus from *there* is that it is approximately 8 feet (2½ meters) in height and has a mass of hair covering its body. Reports state that the Snowman walks upright, and its large size is confirmed by the huge tracks it leaves in the snow. Several photographs of these tracks have been taken, and *this* possibly has led to a continuation of the belief in the monster.

[3]The Snowman is called "yeti" by the inhabitants of Tibet; this word literally means "dweller among the rocks." Not only have the people of Tibet claimed to have seen "yeti," but *so have* explorers, guides, military personnel, and merchants.

[4]In 1960, Sir Edmund Hillary, the noted New Zealand explorer, searched for the Abominable Snowman in the hills of the Himalayas. One year later, *he* concluded that "yeti" was nonexistent. Today many doubt Hillary's *position* and their interest is piqued when yet another sighting is reported.

1. To what does *them* refer in the first paragraph?_____
2. To what does *creature* refer in the second paragraph?_____
3. For what word(s) does *there* substitute in the second paragraph?

_____

4. To what idea does *this* refer in the second paragraph?

_____

5. For what word(s) does *so have* substitute in the third paragraph?

_____

6. To whom does *he* refer in the last paragraph?_____
7. To what idea does *position* refer in the last paragraph?

_____

Directions: Read the following three letters. The italicized pronouns refer to nouns mentioned earlier in each letter. In the spaces provided below each letter, write the noun each pronoun replaced. Then answer the questions that follow.

14 Lookout Drive
Melon City, Ohio 28994
October 14, 19___

Yaeger's Discount Center
Main Street
Melon City, Ohio 28995

Dear Mr. Yaeger:

I am not the type of person who writes complaint letters to presidents of department stores. Usually, if a store has treated me unfairly, I just don't give ¹*it* any more of my business. However, I have had a number of problems with your store, and I have no choice except to make sure ²*they* are worked out.

To begin with, I went into your store about six months ago to buy a clock radio. ³*It* was to have been a birthday present for my husband. ⁴*He* already had ⁵*one,* but I had broken it. In any case, I walked into your store intending to buy a clock radio and walked out having bought a $700 bedroom set. In truth, I had no need for a bedroom set. I'm still not sure why I bought ⁶*one.* But having bought it, I expected to receive it in good condition. This letter is to inform you that its condition was anything but good—on the contrary, ⁷*it* was terrible. The wood not only was scratched in many places, but ⁸*it* also was broken! I look to you for a solution to this problem.

Yours truly,
Kate Levin

1. _____   5. _____

2. _____   6. _____

3. _____   7. _____

4. _____   8. _____

9. To what problem is Kate Levin referring in the last sentence of her letter?

_____

Dear Ms. Levin:

I was shocked to read of the shabby condition in which our merchandise reached you. Believe me, "Yaeger's" does not believe in unhappy customers. We strive to please ¹*them.* When we learn of a situation such as yours, we do everything we can to correct [2]*it.* To that end, I offer you a choice. You may choose to have all four pieces replaced by a set in perfect condition. Or—to prove our sincere regrets—you may return [3]*them* for a complete refund.

I have passed your letter on to the agent in charge of complaints. I think you will find her eager to settle your complaint. In fact, Mrs. Partridge is probably the best person to settle [4]*it,* since it was she who sold you the furniture in the first place.

> Yours truly,
> Harold Yaeger

1. _____   3. _____

2. _____   4. _____

5. In the first paragraph, to what idea does *To that end* refer?

_____

Dear Mr. Yaeger:

A lot has happened in the two weeks since I first wrote to you. I am getting used to the scratches on the furniture. [1]*They* lend a certain "antique mood" to the bedroom set. I have already replaced the four broken dowels, so [2]*they* don't annoy me as much as they used to. True, the finish was darker. But since [3]*it* wasn't applied very well to begin with, I don't believe anyone will notice the difference.

Please tell Mrs. Partridge not to get in touch with me. Make sure that [4]*she* understands not to contact me by phone, by mail, or in person. I think it is always best to be perfectly clear about things. Confusion spreads so easily these days. [5]*It* should be fought at all costs, I always say. That is why I now repeat that Mrs. Partridge has no reason to get in touch with me. I have no complaints. I don't even mind that the clock radio stopped working. After all, we did get eight days of use out of [6]*it.*

> Yours truly,
> Kate Levin

1. _____   4. _____

2. _____   5. _____

3. _____   6. _____

High School

The first example contains several anaphora beyond simple pronouns. Students must locate the appropriate antecedents. They need to answer questions about the paragraphs in the second example. Antecedent location is required in the two letters presented in the last example.

Directions: Authors often use anaphoric words to replace other words in their writing. For example in the sentence, "Tawney was a pretty cat, but the animal scratched all the furniture," *the animal* is used to replace cat. Read this selection and note the italicized words. Write the word or words they replace in the spaces below.

The woodwind instruments commonly used today belong to three families: flutes, clarinets, and oboe.

Of *these,* [1] the flutes have the highest pitch. The two principal kinds are the concert flute and the piccolo. The *latter* [2] is a lighter instrument, often used by marching bands. The light, bright tone of the concert flute often is employed by composers to carry the melody of a piece of music.

Instruments of the clarinet family have a tone lower than flutes but higher than oboes. There are several types of these *midrange instruments.* [3] Each has a particular range; *those of higher tone* [4] are used in marching bands to play music scores for violin.

So are certain light instruments of the oboe family. *This group* [5] includes the concert oboe and the bassoon. The *second of these* [6] has the lowest tone of all the woodwinds. It often is used for comical effect.

All these uses [7] make the woodwinds particular favorites of composers and arrangers. *Most* [8] can be found in even the smallest concert orchestras and marching bands.

1. these _____
2. latter _____
3. mid-range instruments _____
4. those of higher tone _____
5. this group _____
6. second of these _____
7. all these uses _____
8. most _____

Directions: Replacement words are used to take the place of other words in a passage. Read the two passages and answer the questions that follow each passage.

Geraldine paused outside her apartment building. She bent over and pulled up her knee socks. The rubber bands she was using to hold *them* up made her legs itch. She debated whether or not she should take the bands off. Then she noticed some boxes and pieces of furniture sitting in front of the building. Much to her dismay, *several* looked familiar. Geraldine rushed up to her apartment. There, she found her sister Anita, crying. Geraldine and her mother had been evicted.

1. To what does *them* refer? _____
2. To what does the underlined *several* refer? _____
3. Where did Geraldine find her sister? _____

After eating a lunch that she barely tasted, Geraldine went back to school. But her mind was not on school work. She worried about her mother's illness, where *they* were going to live, and what they would do about the furniture. But she could not solve *any of those things*. She went to biology class, listened to her teacher talk about nutrition, and then wondered how her body knew what she would need tomorrow. *That* seemed impossible, since she did not know where she would even be tomorrow. She went to math class and asked herself what squares and triangles had to do with real problems. The *ones* that she had seemed more important than those in the book.

4. To whom does *they* refer? _____
5. What are *any of those things* that Geraldine cannot solve?

_____

6. What is *that* which seems impossible to Geraldine?

_____

7. To what does *ones* refer? _____

Directions: Read the following two letters. Each of the italicized pronouns was used in place of another word or phrase. On the blanks following the letters, write the word or phrase that each pronoun replaced.

Dear Face Up Cream Company:

In your ads you promise that customers can get their money back if [1]*they* are not completely satisfied with Face Up Cream. I want my $4.27 back because your Face Up Cream did not satisfy me. In fact, [2]*it* was worse than unsatisfactory, it was a disaster! My skin did not clear up in two days, as you claimed it would, but [3]*it* got worse. You claimed that I would soon become "a number one member of the in crowd," but my closest friends are now avoiding me because they are afraid my condition is contagious. It does not help to tell [4]*them* that [5]*it* is not something they can catch. They are not around long enough for me to tell them anything. So please give me back my money!

Yours truly,
Suzie Pittel

Dear Ms. Pittel:

We regret that you have doubts about Face Up Cream's ability to clear up your skin problem and to boost your standing among the smart set. Clearly, there is a problem. We ask, however, whether ⁶*it* lies with Face Up Cream or with the way in which you used our product. After all, no skin cream can produce miracles. Nevertheless, ⁷*it* can hide blemishes and as a result boost an individual's confidence. Did you believe that all of your blemishes would disappear in two days? Unfortunately, blemishes are just not eliminated that easily. ⁸*They* require months of dedicated Face Up Cream application. This kind of treatment will definitely show amazing results not only on your face but also in your social life. We promise that ⁹*it* will bring your fair-weather friends running back to you. Please understand that we appreciate the pain you have suffered already, and to show our sincere concern, we will send you a six-month supply of Face Up Cream for only $12.54. ¹⁰*That* is one-third off the regular price! After six months, if you are still not completely satisfied, we will, of course, be happy to refund your money.

                                        Yours truly,
                                        Face Up Cream Company

1. _____   6. _____

2. _____   7. _____

3. _____   8. _____

4. _____   9. _____

5. _____   10. _____

SUMMARY

Readers encounter anaphoric relations in everything they read. It is difficult to read more than two sentences without having to deal with one. The sentence you just read contains two anaphoric relations—*it* and *one*. This article has shown the role of anaphora in text structure cohesion and has presented an abbreviated list of anaphora types, examples, and possible comprehension questions for use in discussion of a passage. The kinds of instructional activities that comprise the bulk of the article can be easily constructed by teachers interested in providing comprehensive instruction in anaphora resolution. Writers will not and should not decrease their use of these cohesive ties; therefore, it is up to teachers to prepare their students to cope with such relationships and to guard against unnecessary comprehension loss.

About the Author

Dale D. Johnson is Professor, Department of Curriculum and Instruction, at the University of Wisconsin at Madison.

References

Chapman, L.J. *Reading Development and Cohesion.* London: Heinemann Education Books, 1983.

Halliday, M. and R. Hasan. *Cohesion in English.* London: Longman, 1976.

Pearson, P. and D. Johnson. *Teaching Reading Comprehension.* New York: Holt, Rinehart, and Winston, 1978.

Stevenson, A. and F. Baumann. "Comprehension of Anaphora: Teaching Children to Comprehend Pronoun Referents." Paper presented at Wisconsin State Reading Association Spring Conference, Oconomowoc, Wisconsin, May 19–21, 1981.

Part II
Precomprehension and Postcomprehension Strategies

An outstanding teacher of English literature to college freshmen made a revealing remark in the early 1940s: "I used to spend five minutes making a reading assignment for the next day. I now find that I spend from 30 to 40 minutes preparing the students to read the assignment." This teacher rightly anticipated one of the major effects, though somewhat belated, of the newer cognitive psychology upon comprehension instruction: the need to thoroughly prepare students for reading by activating their background knowledge and experience in relation to what is about to be read.

The first three articles in this section demonstrate different ways to involve students in meaningful and motivating prereading activities. The final article discusses postinstructional assessment strategies to avoid an improper assessment of a student's comprehension. Since the question is the most common means of assessing comprehension, it is reasonable to suppose that unless a student understands what a question calls for, either explicitly or implicitly, the desired response will not be forthcoming *even if available.* Response instruction, designed to clarify what type, level, and structure of response is expected to a given question, is a logical complement to process-oriented comprehension instruction.

A large body of research indicates that prior knowledge is a critical factor in comprehension. How may students and teachers become more aware of what students already know about a topic and use this information advantageously before reading a given selection? Langer and Purcell-Gates describe a three-phase, problem-oriented prereading plan (PReP) that features much classroom discussion with "communication prompts and probes" to help students use prior knowledge in developing effective comprehension strategies.

Knowledge and Comprehension: Helping Students Use What They Know

Judith A. Langer
Victoria Purcell-Gates

This article addresses a problem common to teachers of all subjects. Whether in science, social studies, literature, or mathematics, textbooks are often difficult for students to understand. Although teachers use a variety of prereading activities to prepare students, we continue to seek new ways to help them comprehend the textbook material we ask them to read.

A series of results from our research studies (Langer 1980, 1981, 1982, 1984a,b) have led us to rethink the notion of prereading discussions. Many such discussions lead us to incorrectly estimate what students know about a particular topic—to believe that students know more (or less) about a particular topic than they actually do. If students offer the response we expect, it is easy to assume they understand, and if they give a response *we* do not understand or did not expect, it is too easy to assume *they* don't understand. To really understand what students know and mean requires discussion, and in

particular, discussion in which students and teachers listen to one another.

Our work suggests that students have a rich background of life's
experiences that can help them understand even highly technical academic prose. However, too often this potentially useful knowledge is
expressed in personal (home talk) language as opposed to academic
(school talk) language. The words and ideas that come to the students'
minds may not be the responses teachers expect when asking prophead-
ing questions. Early in their school lives, students learn that their home-
talk associations are not likely to be what the teacher is looking for, and
begin to withhold their ideas—ideas they might otherwise use to make
sense of the technical material they read in school.

In this article, we will present a prereading activity designed to help
both students and teachers become aware of what students already
know about a specific topic. This activity, called the Pre-Reading Plan
(PReP), can be used with students in grades 3 through 12, in all subject
areas. Before presenting the activity, let us first explore a bit more
deeply why some frequently used teaching practices may fail to prepare
students to read their textbooks.

VOCABULARY REVIEW

Picture, if you will, a fourth-grade classroom in which a group of
students have been assembled for a prereading activity to prepare them
to read a social studies chapter on "Forms of Government." Following
the suggestions in the teacher's guide, the teacher has placed 10 vocabulary words from the chapter on the chalkboard and is attempting to
find out if any of the students can "say what the words mean."

Teacher: Who can tell us what *democracy* means? (A few students tenta-
tively raise their hands while the rest of the students gaze somewhat
anxiously at their desks.)

Teacher: Joseph?

Joseph: My daddy belong to the democracy party!

Teacher: You mean the Democratic party. That's nice. Anyone else?
Joan?

Joan: Democracy is . . . I don't know.

Teacher: Anyone else? James?

James: Democracy is the form of government of our government!

Teacher: Good! That's right. Democracy is a form of government. Now, who can give us a new sentence, using your own words, to include the word *democracy?*

Let us examine this fairly typical scenario. First, what was the purpose of this activity? Why did the teacher ask the vocabulary definition question? What knowledge did the teacher expect to tap or teach? In this case, the teacher wished to prepare the students for reading the chapter, to introduce them to the technical words they did not already know or remind them of the meanings they only partially knew before reading those words in the text.

This justification presupposes that teachers can prepare someone for a thinking activity simply by adding new knowledge, and that students who are told the meaning of a word will be able to comprehend that word upon seeing it in a text.

OUTSIDE-IN AND INSIDE-OUT INSTRUCTION

The first assumption implies a passive stance on the part of the student, as if a teacher can help students learn by assigning them to find definitions and then use the new words in sentences. In this sort of teacher-directed (outside-in) activity, students are expected to accept new words much as children accept having rainboots put on, by adding new parts to the outside frame. This view of the learner as a passive recipient of information has been rejected by decades of cognitive research (Piaget, 1954; Neisser, 1976; Anderson, 1977; Rumelhart, 1977). We know that learning is in large part directed from the inside out. The student comprehends new ideas by relating the new ones to ideas, experiences, and language that already make sense to the student, and by stretching these already-held meanings in an attempt to understand the new. Meanings are not constructed outside the student's background of knowledge by guessing definitions and putting words into sentences. Any activity that presupposes a passive stance on the part of the learner is doomed from the start.

The second assumption, that the meaning of a word lies in its top-level, surface definition, also has been rejected by recent research (Goodman and Goodman, 1978; Harste, Burke, and Woodward, 1982; Anderson, 1977). We now know that knowledge is always, to a certain extent, idiosyncratic; it is built from the inside out. Knowledge is based on individual experiences and shaped as learners fit these experiences into their own individual frameworks for understanding the world. People continually make sense of the world using their existing knowledge to interpret new information. Being able to make sense of the world involves not merely using terse language to frame a definition, but describing and elaborating concepts by linking them to other understandings. If a student has had no experience with a particular concept, a definition will make no real sense unless it can be linked to what is already known. These links help learners make sense from the inside out, from their home-talk world of personal language and experience to the school-talk world of academic thought and technical language.

Comprehension research consistently has confirmed these basic tenets. Readers must be active constructors of meaning if they are to understand what the author is saying. The students themselves must make the connections; no one else can make them for the students because no one else shares the personal knowledge used to makes sense of the world. Thus, hard as we try, no one but the students can fashion the links that will be meaningful.

WORDS VS. CONCEPTS

In the vocabulary-review scenario presented above, none of the students considered what they already knew about the concept *democracy*. Instead, they tried to guess what their teacher expected, if they tried to respond at all. Unfortunately, such activities fall short of preparing students to read their texts with greater comprehension. First, vocabulary words are chosen because they are "new"; that is, they are not in the students' reading or speaking vocabularies. The rationale for choosing the words to be taught is simply that they are unknown and, if taught, they will then be known. No credence is given to the fact that the words represent whole networks of concepts that may be necessary for understanding the text. Surely, simply knowing that democracy is a form of government, or even knowing that it is a form of government by the people exercised either directly or by representation, will not get a student very far in a history text unless the principles underlying societies, governments, and forms of rules and laws also are understood.

Another problem with vocabulary-review activities is that they often present a large number of words. This may seem reasonable if words selected for review are seen as members of a word bank, but not if they are simply labels for underlying complicated concepts. While ten new labels may not be too many, ten new concepts are likely to be overwhelming.

IMITATION DISCUSSION AND INSTRUCTIONAL DIALOGUE

Beyond the issue of what and how much is presented in a prereading activity lies the problem of communication between teacher and students. Outside the classroom, when we want to discover what someone knows about a given topic, we generally would say, "What do you know about sky diving?" or "Do you know anything about wind surfing?" This reveals that the questioner would like to know more about the topic and expects a meaningful response, either indicating lack of knowledge or a report of known information. The person questioned is likely to respond with the requested information, and the person who initiated the question is likely to continue the conversation with a request for elaboration or further information (e.g., "You mean you use your body weight to turn the thing?").

Unlike real-life discussion in which the participants work together to make sense, classroom discussion is often more limited; the participants do not seem to use conversation in a cooperative learning enterprise. Instead, the discussion becomes an "imitation" of real conversation. If a teacher asks, "Can you tell me what *democracy* means?" the student usually will assume that the teacher has a particular response in mind, and that some sort of judgment about the student's knowledge will be made based on the response. This expectation calls for a different type of thinking, a different type of conversation, and a different type of response than is found in our real-life example. No longer do the persons questioned search their memories for what they may know about the topic. Instead they try to fashion an "appropriate" response —a recitation of what they have learned—for which they will be evaluated favorably.

Early in their school careers, students learn that only certain types of responses are likely to bring favorable evaluations; these responses generally contain school-type, academic language. James's response, "a form of government," is typical of the "academese" students learn to adopt in school. Because they have been trained to focus on the content being taught (if not learned), teachers unconsciously listen for academic language and react positively to it when they hear it. School language often makes it seem as though students know the concept when in fact all they demonstrate is that they can use academese effectively. Too often teachers stop here instead of probing further to understand what students know and how deeply they know it.

THE PReP

The Pre-Reading Plan was developed to foster an instructional dialogue that differs in intent and communicative result from the activities we have been describing. PReP is directed by a real desire to *hear* what the students know. This intent shapes the language used by the teacher and by the students.

The PReP is a diagnostic/instructional activity that is the product of extensive research (Langer, 1980, 1981, 1982, 1984b; Langer and Nicolich, 1981). It is based on three theoretical notions:

1. Knowledge about a topic influences how well a text is understood. What a person knows, how well that knowledge is organized in memory, and how it is used during reading are all somewhat idiosyncratic, based on personal knowledge and experiences.
2. The instructional environment influences the background knowledge and strategies readers use when they read a text. When teachers and students focus on what they understand rather than on right answers, real communication is more likely to take place.
3. Better comprehenders monitor their comprehension by
   - being aware of what they do and do not know
   - understanding the task demands
   - judging whether or not a bit of information is text related
   - taking steps to increase the likelihood of understanding the text.

The PReP is a three-step activity that is useful for both instruction and assessment. Presented before students begin reading their texts, the plan helps the teacher determine how much background knowledge a student has about a particular topic and how that knowledge is organized; the language a student uses to express the knowledge; and how much concept teaching (if any) may be necessary before the student is likely to comprehend the text. Instructionally, the activity helps students become aware of what they already know about the topic; build on this knowledge in the context of the group's elaboration of related language and concepts; and refine predictions of what the content of the text will contain, which will facilitate learning from the text.

Preparing for PReP

Before beginning the discussion, the teacher needs to review the text to be assigned and choose three to five key concepts which can be represented by a word, phrase, or picture. For example, if the text deals with the branches of government, "congress" might be one of the concepts selected. A picture of the Supreme Court in action might also be presented.

Three Phases of PReP

Phase 1

The first phase is basically a free-association task. In this phase, initial associations with a particular concept are elicited.

Teacher: Before we read about the United States' form of government, tell me anything, anything at all, that comes to your mind when you hear this word (see this picture, etc.).

As the students respond, the teacher writes their associations on the chalkboard, overhead projector overlay, or chart paper. It is important that all responses be accepted in a nonjudgmental manner. Also, the students should be encouraged to think of as many ideas as they can about the concept.

Phase 2

When all students have had an opportunity to respond, the teacher begins the second phase of the activity, which involves reflecting on the initial associations.

Teacher: What made you think of . . . ?

This phase helps students become aware of what they know and judge whether or not it is likely to relate to the text they will soon read. They also reflect and build upon what they already know through listening to and interacting with the teacher and the other members of the group.

Phase 3

During the third phase of the activity, the students are given an opportunity to reformulate their ideas.

Teacher: Based on our discussion, have you any new ideas about the word (the picture, etc.)?

The students now can shape, through language, associations that have been elaborated or altered as a result of the discussion. Because they have had an opportunity to probe their own memories, listen to others, and reflect upon this process, the responses elicited during this phase often are more refined than those elicited during the first phase.

From the beginning, students are aware that they are doing the PReP because they are preparing to read about a particular topic. The entire activity takes place in the context of the to-be-read material. However, this does not mean that, as the third phase is concluded, they are asked to predict what the text will say. Rather, they are pointed in the direction of the text, and the ownership of the knowledge remains theirs.

In summary, the three phases of PReP involve: (1) initial associations with the concept; (2) reflections on these initial associations; and (3) reformulation of knowledge. Table 1 portrays these three phases.

TABLE 1. THREE PHASES OF PReP

Phase	*Teacher*	*Students*
1	"Tell me anything you think of when you hear. . . . "	free associate/access prior knowledge
2	"What made you think of. . . . "	reflect on thought processes, organization of knowledge
3	"Do you want to add to or change your first response?"	reformulate and refine responses

---

Assessing Student Knowledge

Student responses generally will fall into three categories, which can be used by the teacher to assess the complexity of the students' knowledge. Previous studies have shown these categories to be good predictors of students' recall of a particular passage and to be independent of IQ and overall reading ability (Langer, 1980; Langer, 1984b; Langer and Nicolich, 1981).

1. *Much prior knowledge.* Much knowledge about a concept is displayed if students respond during phase one with superordinate concepts, definitions, analogies, or linkages with other concepts

indicative of high-level integration of ideas. They will show an encompassing knowledge of the topic.

2. *Some prior knowledge. Some* knowledge about the topic is reflected in responses that take the form of examples, attributes, or defining characteristics. Students will know bits of information about the topic.

3. *Little prior knowledge. Little* knowledge is indicated by responses that focus on low-level associations, morphemes, "sound alikes," or somewhat irrelevant first-hand experiences. This sort of knowledge is peripheral and diffuse. (See Table 2 for examples of responses at each of the three levels.)

TABLE 2. THE ORGANIZATION OF TOPIC-SPECIFIC KNOWLEDGE

Much Knowledge

superordinate concept—higher class category
    e.g., *fascism*: "One of the various forms of political rule."

definitions—precise meaning
    e.g., *dictator*: "A ruler with absolute authority over the government of a people."

analogies—substitution of comparison for a literal concept or literal expression
    e.g., *court*: "Court is the scale that weighs your destiny."

linking—connecting one concept with another
    e.g., congress: "Congress is like parliament in that both. . ."

Some Knowledge

examples—appropriate class, but more specific
    e.g., *government*: "Dictatorship."

attributes—subordinate to larger concept
    e.g., *court*: "Trust in the judgment of others."

defining characteristics—defines a major aspect of the concept
    e.g., *government*: "Makes laws"

Little Knowledge

associations—tangential cognitive links
    e.g., *congress*: "Important people."

morphemes—smallest units of meaning such as prefixes, suffixes, and
  root words
    e.g., *binary*: "Bicycle."

sound alikes—similar phonemic units
    e.g., *gerrymander*: "Salamander."

first-hand experiences—tangential responses based on current exposure
    e.g., *Iran*: "News on television."

no apparent knowledge

Generally, students with *much* prior knowledge are able to comprehend the text without assistance; those with *some* prior knowledge may
need the watchful eye of the teacher to help them along the way; and
those with *little* prior knowledge are in need of direct concept instruction before they can be expected to comprehend the text. Of course,
some texts use such convoluted sentence structures or such abstract
language that they create processing problems even for students who
know a good deal about the topic.

EXAMPLES OF PReP IN USE

The remainder of this article will be devoted to examples of the PReP
being used with several different types of reading material at different
grade levels.

Example: Grade 5, Social Studies Class

A fifth-grade class was about to read a section of their social studies
text that dealt with the U.S. form of government. Their teacher was
concerned about the heavy concept load of the chapter and wished to
find out what the students already knew about the topic. The teacher
previewed the chapter and chose three basic concepts. A portion of the
PReP activity that followed for the key word *congress* is presented
below. The categorizations of the students' responses are listed along
the right margin.

Phase 1

Teacher: Before we read the next section of our social studies book
about the U.S. government, I want each of you to tell anything, any-

thing at all, that comes to your mind when you hear the word *congress.*

As the students responded, the teacher wrote their responses on the chalkboard. Each response was accepted in a nonjudgmental and interested way by the teacher.

Bill: A part of our government where they make the laws.	Much: definition
Megan: It's in Washington, D.C.	Some: attribute
Gabe: A law-making body of government.	Much: superordinate/ definition
Alan: On T.V.	Little: association
Jennifer: Makes laws.	Some: defining characteristic
John: Congo.	Little: morphemic association

Phase 2

Teacher: Now I'd like you each to tell me what made you think of what you said. Megan, you said, "It's in Washington, D.C." What made you think of that?

Each of the students was asked in turn what made them think of their individual responses.

Megan: My dad went to Washington, D.C., on a business trip a couple of months ago. He brought pictures back and he told us about how he went to see the White House where the President is and he went to see the congress.

Through this discussion, Megan was able to connect what she had learned from her father, complete with his personal impressions, with the concept of *congress* about to be met in print.

Gabe: I was thinking about all the parts of our government. I picture congress as the part that makes the laws.

Alan also was able to explore and expand his thinking as he told how he hears and sees news about congress on television.

Phase 3

Teacher: Now that we have talked about this and before we read the text, do any of you want to add to or change what you have said about the term *congress?*

Megan: A group of elected people   Much: definition
who meet in Washington, D.C., to
debate and make laws for the
country.

Megan thus was able to give a more precise definition of the concept. Her memory of what she had heard from her father, which she had connected to what had been said in the discussion by other members in the group, helped her to do this.

Alan: Important people argue about   Some: attribute
what the . . .

Alan was able to expand on his memory of hearing about congress on television by recalling some of the issues surrounding the television announcements.

Through this activity, the teacher was able to assess what each student knew about the social studies material they would read. The teacher decided that Gabe and Bill were well-prepared to read the assigned chapter. Megan probably could read the material successfully, but Jennifer would need extra help to link what she knew to the content of the chapter. Alan and John would need some additional instruction on the concept itself before they could be expected to comprehend the social studies text (see Pearson and Johnson, 1978, for suggestions for concept instruction).

Example: Grade 8, Science Class

In a science classroom, at the eighth-grade level, students were preparing to read about *photosynthesis* in their texts. The teacher preceded their reading with a PReP activity to help them recall and organize what they already knew about this concept and to determine which students were ready to read the material. The portion of the activity below focused on the concept of *photosynthesis.* Other key words selected were *cycle* and *oxygen.*

Phase 1

Teacher: We're going to be reading about a process called *photosynthesis* in our texts. I'd like you to tell me anything that comes to mind when you hear the word *photosynthesis*. I'll write what you say on the board. Anyone?

During this phase it became apparent that none of the students had *much* knowledge of the concept. The following is typical of the responses.

Joan: Sun shining on a plant.	Some: defining characteristic
Jack: Photograph.	Little: morphemic association
Marian: Pictures.	Little: morphemic association
Zachary: Something to do with science.	Little: association

Phase 2

Teacher: Now I'd like each of you to think about what you said and to try to tell us what made you think of that response.

Jack: Photosynthesis sounded like *photograph*. The first part of it, anyway.

Marian: Yeah. I thought at first you said *photograph* and that made me think of *pictures*.

Joan: I remembered reading in a book about photosynthesis. There was this picture that showed rays coming out of the sun and going down to a plant. I just remembered the picture when I heard that word.

Zachary: I just remembered hearing the word in another science class.

During this activity, the teacher helped the group see that they did know something about the concept. A discussion grew out of the meaning of the *photo* morpheme and how it would be related to the sun and plants. This helped all of the students refine their responses in the third phase and helped some of them raise the level of their responses.

Phase 3

Teacher: Now that we've been thinking about this for a while, do any of you want to change or add to your previous responses, before we read about *photosynthesis?*

Joan: It is when the sun shines on   Much: definition
plants and that helps the plants give
oxygen.

Zachary: Sun and plants.   Some: defining
                                              characteristics

Jack and Marian still had only *little* prior knowledge, but they refined
their previous responses by adding *light,* which they may have connected to their earlier *photograph* responses.

The teacher concluded that although Joan could successfully read the
text, the others needed help building the concept from what they knew
before reading about it. Jack and Marian were helped to see that they
already knew about the morpheme *photo* and the role of light in the
process of photography. They then could extend this knowledge to the
role of light in the process of photosynthesis. Of course, further concept
teaching took place but always beginning with the students' own knowledge as displayed through their own language.

Example: Grade 11, Literature Class

Our final example of the PReP comes from an eleventh-grade literature class. The class was about to read a series of selections that deal
with the concept of *justice.* Their literature selections included excerpts
from *The Book of Job* and Dante's *Inferno.* In addition to selecting the
concept of *justice* for the PReP activity, the teacher also had chosen the
key words of *fairness* and *retribution.*

Phase 1

Teacher: Tell me anything you think of when you hear the word *justice.*

As the students responded, the teacher recorded their comments uncritically on an overhead projector overlay. The students all seemed to
possess at least *some* knowledge of the concept.

Alice: Being fair.   Some: defining
                                              characteristic

Carol: It's when a murderer is caught,   Some: example
tried, and executed.

Jason: When my mother believes me   Some: example
when I tell the truth, even though it
looks like I might be lying.

Robert: Fair handling—due reward.   Much: definition

Melanie: A basic concept underlying   Much: linking
our system of law. No matter how
rich or poor you are, you are treated
equally in the eyes of the law.

Phase 2

Teacher: I'd like each of you to tell me how you thought of your associations to the word *justice.* What were you thinking of when you chose your responses?

Robert: I was thinking about how my parents try to reward us when we deserve it and punish us when we deserve it. That seems just. Also, other authority groups should do the same—schools, employers, governments, courts.

Note that this part of the activity gave the teacher a chance to probe Robert's initial bookish definition to see if he did, in fact, understand the concept of *justice.* From his response to this probing, it became apparent that Robert had given a great deal of thought to the concept of justice.

Carol: Whenever I hear the word *justice,* I always think of crime shows and people being punished by the courts.

Phase 3

Teacher: Now that you have had a chance to reflect on your thinking about this term, do any of you wish to add to or change your original response?

Jason: Means getting what you   Much: superordinate
deserve.

Carol: Getting punished if you are   Much: superordinate
guilty and not getting punished if you
are innocent.

Before allowing the students to begin reading, the teacher helped them to see that they possessed quite definite ideas about the concept of justice based on experiences in their own lives. When they thought of these experiences and ideas and reflected upon how the ideas were formed in their minds, they were ready to learn and assess how the Bible treats the subject and how Dante treats it.

These three instances of the classroom use of PReP demonstrate its application at different levels with different topics. The principles behind it make it quite useful in all subject areas. It provides a way for students to become aware of what they know about a given topic and to reflect and build upon that knowledge. It also gives the teacher a way to assess the degree of knowledge students already have about a particular topic. It does this in such a way that students are not led to give "canned" responses with little meaning behind them.

As teachers, we all can recall instances, such as the science example above, when the content and language of the text was far from the experience of our students. Our dilemma is to bridge the gap in a substantive way. This involves helping students become aware of what they already know and then helping them build on that knowledge so that they can use it to gain new knowledge.

We also can recall situations such as the example from the literature class in which we knew our students had a great deal of experience to bring to the text. The task here is to help students recall those experiences and reflect upon them so that they are consciously assimilating the written material through the filter of their own relevant knowledge.

How we, as teachers, approach what our students already know leads in turn to how they will approach their texts. To help students use what they already know, classroom discussions need to give students room to tell what they know, in their own language. PReP is one way to accomplish this.

About the Authors

Judith A. Langer is Associate Professor, School of Education, at Stanford University.

Victoria Purcell-Gates is a doctoral student, Department of Language and Literacy, at the University of California at Berkeley.

References

Anderson, R. C. "The Notion of Schemata and the Educational Enterprise." In R. C. Anderson, R. J. Spiro, and W. E. Montague (Eds.), *Schooling and the Acquisition of Knowledge.* Hillsdale, N.J.: Lawrence Erlbaum, 1977.

Goodman, K., and Y. Goodman. "Reading of American Children Whose Language Is a Stable Rural Dialect or a Language Other Than English" (Final Report, Contract No. 001–13—0087). Washington, D.C.: National Institute of Education, 1978.

Harste, J. C., C. L. Burke, and V. A. Woodward. "Children's Language and the World: Initial Encounters with Print." In J. A. Langer and M. Smith-Burke (Eds.), *Reader Meets Author: Bridging the Gap.* Newark, Del.: International Reading Association, 1982.

Langer, J. A. "Relation Between Levels of Prior Knowledge and the Organization of Recall." In M. Kamil and A. J. Moe (Eds.), *Perspectives in Reading Research and Instruction.* Washington, D.C.: National Reading Conference, 1980, pp. 28–33.

Langer, J. A. "From Theory to Practice: A Prereading Plan." *Journal of Reading* 25 (2), 152–156.

Langer, J. A. "Facilitating Text Processing: The Elaboration of Prior Knowledge." In J. A. Langer and M. Smith-Burke (Eds.), *Reader Meets Author: Bridging the Gap.* Newark, Del.: International Reading Association, 1982.

Langer, J.A. "Reading, Writing, and Reasoning: Making Connections." Paper presented at the International Reading Association, Anaheim, Calif., 1983, pp. 149–162.

Langer, J. A. "The Effects of Available Information on Responses to School Writing Tasks." *Research in the Teaching of English* (1984a) 18 (1), 27–44.

Langer, J. A. "Examining Background Knowledge and Text Comprehension." *Reading Research Quarterly,* (1984b) 4, 468–481.

Langer, J. A. and M. Nicolich. "Prior Knowledge and Its Effect on Comprehension." *Journal of Reading Behavior* (1981) 13 (4), 373–379.

Neisser, U. *Cognition and Reality.* San Francisco: W. H. Freeman and Co., 1976.

Pearson, P. D. and D. Johnson. *Teaching Reading Comprehension.* New York: Macmillan, 1978.

Piaget, J. *The Construction of Reality in the Child* (M. Cook, Trans.). New York: Basic Books, Inc., 1954.

Rumelhart, C. "Toward an Interactive Model of Reading." In S. Dornic (Ed.), *Attention and Performance VI.* London: Academic Press, 1977.

Both prior knowledge and knowledge to be acquired are to some extent structured; that is, they form a part of an existing pattern that needs to be understood in order to foster students' comprehension. If students are given specific aid in anticipating the structure of a complex text by means of an abstract yet simplified version of the text, will their comprehension of the text be improved? Jerrolds describes Ausubel's concept of the advance organizer, differentiates it from other types of advance information, reviews the research evidence of its value, and demonstrates how to build and apply an advance organizer.

The Advance Organizer: Its Nature and Use

Robert W. Jerrolds

David P. Ausubel is one of today's major learning theorists. He has written extensively about the process by which the learner extracts meaning from a complex written passage. Ausubel (1968) indicates that learning through conditioning, discovery learning, and rote learning all are means by which a person acquires new knowledge. They are, however, dynamically different from the process by which a person learns from the more sophisticated material found in some college and professional texts.

THEORETICAL BASIS OF THE ADVANCE ORGANIZER

Ausubel presents the following explanation of the dynamics of meaningful learning from texts.

> The model of cognitive organization proposed for the learning and retention of meaningful materials assumes the existence of a cognitive structure that is hierarchially organized in terms of highly inclusive conceptual traces under which are subsumed traces of specific informational data. The major organizational principle, in other words, is that of progressive differentiation

71

of trace systems of a given sphere of knowledge from regions of greater to lesser inclusiveness, each linked to the next higher step in the hierarchy through a process of subsumption (Ausubel, 1963, pp. 24–25).

Thus Ausubel says that potentially meaningful material is learned when it fits an existing cognitive structure, interacts with established elements of that structure, and is appropriately placed under a relevant and more inclusive concept in that cognitive structure.

Ausubel believes that the most effective way of increasing learning and retention of meaningful verbal materials is by manipulating the organization, stability, and clarity of the concepts relating to new material that already have been established in the learner's cognitive structure. He suggests that this cognitive structure manipulation can be best accomplished by the use of cognitive organizers. Therefore, he has formulated the concept of *advance organizer,* which is a set of related material presented prior to the new material and written on a higher level of abstraction, inclusiveness, and generality than the new material.

> The most efficient way of facilitating retention is to introduce appropriate subsumers and make them part of the cognitive structure prior to the actual presentation of the learning task. The introduced subsumers thus become advance "organizers," or anchoring foci, for the reception of new material. In effect they provide an introductory overview at the appropriate level of conceptualization (Ausubel, 1963, p. 29).

A cursory reading of this description of the advance organizer might lead one to believe that it is similar to long familiar devices such as overviews, precis, digests, briefs, synopses, abstracts, and introductions. However, Ausubel indicates that in most cases these do not work well for three reasons. First, they are not presented long enough in advance (presumably about 24 hours) to become incorporated into the cognitive structure to form an "ideational scaffold" to which the new, incoming ideas can be attached. Second, they are not written on a more general, inclusive, and abstract level than the new material; they generally are written on the same level as the material they introduce and simply duplicate some of the key information and leave out details. Third, overviews and such most often are not specifically designed to be related to the presumed idealitional content available in the learner's cognitive structure (Ausubel, 1968).

Ausubel's advance organizer is a set of material designed specifically to facilitate the incorporation of a given body of material into the cognitive structure. When the advance organizer has been established in the cognitive structure, the new, incoming ideas can be subsumed under its more inclusive, abstract, and general propositions. Through this previously established organizer, the new ideas are incorporated into the cognitive structure. In short, *the principal function of the organizer is to bridge the gap between what the learner already knows and what the learner needs to know before he or she can successfully learn the task at hand* (Ausubel, 1968, p. 148).

Although new facts and ideas may be incorporated into the cognitive structure, a second factor must operate if they are to remain available; that is, they must be maintained as separate entities from the higher level concepts under which they are subsumed. The advance organizer can serve this second function by specifically delineating similarities and differences between the new materials and established concepts.

As seen by Ausubel, a third factor affecting retention is that of seeming or real contradiction between the new material and the established concepts. Ausubel says that the individual, upon encountering such contradictions, will dismiss the new material as fallacious, will compartmentalize the new material and try to remember it by rote, or will attempt to reconcile the new material to the established structure.

> Organizers are also expressly designed to further the principle of integrative reconciliation. They do this by explicitly pointing out in what ways previously learned, related concepts in the cognitive structure are either basically similar to or essentially different from new ideas and information in the learning task (Ausubel, 1963, p. 82).

Ausubel (1968) says advance organizers work because they "draw upon and mobilize whatever relevant anchoring concepts are already established in the learner's cognitive structure" (p. 137); they provide for the anchoring of the new information under relevant propositions that have been established earlier; and they "render unnecessary much of the rote memorization to which students often resort because they are required to learn the details of an unfamiliar discipline before having available a sufficient number of key anchoring ideas" (p. 137).

RESEARCH REPORTS ON THE USE OF THE ADVANCE ORGANIZER

Although Ausubel is widely respected for the soundness of his theories in cognitive psychology, more than two decades of research have not established that Ausubel's position on the learning device called the advance organizer is well-grounded or not well-grounded. There is a considerable body of research that supports his tenets and a sizable number of studies that have failed to do so.

Barnes and Clawson (1975) examined the results of 32 studies of the effects of advance organizers. They reported that 12 of the studies basically found significantly superior results in using the advance organizer and that 20 of the studies did not. Barnes and Clawson also examined certain variables in these 32 studies to determine whether or not patterns in the ways advance organizers work could be detected.

When the variables—length of study, ability level of subjects, grade level of subjects, type of organizer, and cognitive level of the learning tasks—were analyzed separately, no clear patterns emerged regarding the facilitative effects of advance organizers (Barnes and Clawson, 1975, p. 651).

Luiten, Ames, and Ackerman (1980) submitted 135 studies to a metaanalysis and concluded that the advance organizer does produce positive results, even though the amount of improved learning and retention may be small.

The average advance organizer study shows a small but facilitative effect on learning and retention. The small effect may well be a function of the short duration of treatment of the typical study (all too often an experiment is concluded within one or two class periods). Moreover, the findings indicate that advance organizers facilitate learning in all content areas examined, albeit broadly defined, and with individuals of all grade and ability levels (Luiten, Ames, and Ackerman, 1980, p. 217).

Kozlow (1978) also did a metaanalysis of selected advance organizer research reports. His sample was 99 experiments found in 77 reports.

Of the 99 t-statistics computed for the experimental comparisons between advance organizer and control groups, 68 were positive indicating that the observed means for the advance organizer groups were higher than those for the control groups. Twenty-two of these positive t-statistics were statistically significant while none of the 29 negative t-statistics were significant. There were two t-statistics that were zero (Kozlow, 1978, p. 5047-B).

Mayer (1979) reviewed 44 published research studies involving advance organizers. He stated that 20 years of research on advance organizers had produced a great deal of data and conflicting claims. However, based on his review he concluded:

Twenty years of research on advance organizers has clearly shown that advance organizers can affect learning, and the conditions under which organizers are most likely to affect learning can be specified (Mayer, 1979, p. 161).

Stone (1983) located 166 reports on the use of advance organizers for possible use in a metaanalytic study. Out of that number, 29 met the requirements for that statistical treatment. "The 29 studies were broken down to yield as many effect sizes as possible. Because many studies gave results for several treatment or subject variables or included substudies, 112 effect sizes were obtained" (p. 195). Stone reported that, overall, the advance organizer produces increased learning and retention.

A second aspect of Stone's study was "to compare the results with some predictions from Ausubel's model of learning" (p. 195). Her results indicate that, overall, the predictions from the model were not confirmed.

Stone's somewhat contradictory results typify the results of the bodies of studies on advance organizers considered together. Disparate results of these studies are partially accounted for in the variety of subjects used in the experiments, organizers and modifications of organizers used, research designs and statistical treatments, subject matter of the advance organizers and the material to be learned, and length of time involved in the study, etc. In this writer's opinion, the greatest problems have been in the huge discrepancy among the different researchers' levels of sophistication in handling Ausubel's theoretical constructs and their translation of those constructs into appropriate advance organizers. Clark and Bean state:

> A primary reason for this lack of strong support is the absence of true objective descriptions and definitions of the organizers used and the concommitant poor control over their derivation and construction (Clark and Bean, 1982, p. 2).

These writers, like many others, claim that there is no operational definition of the advance organizer sufficient to insure that a particular advance organizer is adequately written.

Ausubel (1978) says he has clearly stated precise operational criteria for the advance organizer and explained in his books (Ausubel, 1963, 1968) how to construct one. In his research reports and other writing, he has illustrated the advance organizer repeatedly.

> Apart from describing organizers in general terms with an appropriate example, one cannot be more specific about the construction of an organizer; for this always depends on the nature of the learning material, the age of the learner, and his degree of prior familiarity with the learning passage (Ausubel, 1978, p. 251).

Despite the conflicting results of the research, there is a compelling logic in Ausubel's theoretical positions. Further, the learning device called the advance organizer is epistemologically entirely consonant with his theory. Perhaps most importantly, the advance organizer makes good sense to experienced secondary teachers. Alvermann (1984), a researcher who has made extensive use of different kinds of organizers in practical classroom situations, says, "When I introduce secondary teachers to different kinds of organizers, the one they want to use is Ausubel's advance organizer."

Most of the studies of the effectiveness of the advance organizer have been one-shot or short-term efforts. It would seem that such a trial provides the least possible chance for the advance organizer to be effective. Subjects of such experiments have been reading for years in their own style, whatever that may be. They have been exposed to summaries, introductions, and other devices that probably appear to the experimental subjects to be like the advance organizer, and they have found those devices to be of little or no help in dealing with the material they are trying to learn.

In education we seldom expect anything to aid learning unless the students have been taught how to use it and have had some drill or practice in that use. That the typical limited exposures of students to the advance organizer have revealed any positive results is good evidence of the potential power that the advance organizer could have under more appropriate conditions of teaching and extensive practice. The clear implication is that the advance organizer needs to be carefully prepared and taught.

WRITING AN ADVANCE ORGANIZER

Following is a passage written to be short but otherwise typical of the kind of content-area textual materials that a junior high school student would be expected to read. Following this representative passage, entitled "Life in the Sea," is an advance organizer especially written to facilitate the student's ability to understand and remember the content of the passage. In practice, the advance organizer, "Motion and Life," would be studied by the student at least a day in advance of reading the representative passage. The passage is presented first here so that the reader can see how the advance organizer was developed.

In writing the advance organizer, the author studied the passage very carefully. Each key idea, general idea, and unusual idea in the passage was identified. Facts that could be combined or summarized in a sentence or two were noted. Discrete sentences then were generated that were thought to be:

1. summaries of the entire passage; e.g., There are varying kinds of life in the sea. Life in the sea is interdependent.
2. summaries of subsections of the passage; e.g., Temperature affects life in the sea. Sea life must move or be moved.
3. comparisons of ideas in the passage with ideas the student probably is already familiar with; e.g., Like plants on land, those of the sea need chemicals and sunlight. There are streams in the sea just as there are rivers and other streams on land.
4. more inclusive than the content of the passage; e.g., Motion is essential to all life. Living things must have a constant supply of nutrients.
5. more abstract than the content of the passage; e.g., Living things are affected by their environment. One essential element in the nature of the sea is that it is always in motion.
6. more general than the content of the passage; e.g., There are certain conditions necessary for all life to flourish. Motion brings about changes in life.

The author then organized and combined all of these examples and the other discrete sentences into a short, unified passage. In the process of making these discrete sentences into a sensible introductory passage, every effort was made to produce a passage to which the ideas in the longer passage could be meaningfully related.

TYPICAL PASSAGE OF JUNIOR HIGH SCHOOL TEXT

Life in the Sea

All things that live in the world's oceans are placed in one of three categories by oceanographers, scientists who study the ocean. The three categories are plankton, nekton, and benthos. When the scientist talks about *plankton,* he or she is referring to those plants and animals of the sea that float on or near the surface of the water, having little or no ability to move themselves. When the oceanographer uses the word *nekton,* he or she is talking about animals that can swim about freely and easily in the water. The word *benthos* refers to plants and animals that live on the bottom of the sea. Some benthos walk or crawl about at the bottom of the sea, while others attach themselves permanently to the ocean floor.

To live and grow, plankton must have sunshine and certain chemicals. The various types of plankton can swim very little, if at all, but they float about easily. They must depend upon the water to carry them to the sunshine and chemicals or to bring the chemicals to them. The free-floating plankton actually may be carried thousands of miles from their original area by a fast-moving surface current. The plankton float on or near the surface of the water and absorb the sun's rays. They absorb the needed chemicals from the water. Even the simple up and down movement of the waves is important to the microscopic sea plants because this movement keeps them sliding past new water from which they absorb chemicals. The sea plants sometime drift or are pulled down to the murky deep water where sufficient sunlight cannot reach them. Unless the water moves them back toward the surface, they die.

The tiny plants floating in the sea become food for the tiny animals in the plankton group. The larger animals of the sea feed upon the smaller ones. Thus, indirectly, the most ferocious shark is dependent upon microscopic plants floating in the sea. If the proper chemicals are present in the water and other conditions such as sunlight and temperature are favorable, the little sea plants may double their size or number in five or six hours. If the helpless plants are carried by the currents into dark or otherwise unfavorable areas, the plants do not multiply rapidly and may even die. When the little plants die, they start a chain of events that leads to the death of the larger forms of sea life or to their moving away from the area.

Of the three groups of sea life, the nekton has the greatest freedom of movement. Fish, whales, squid, and other members of this group are able to move about freely in search of food or a generally more favorable environment. Some forms of nekton travel thousands of miles each year. They may travel with or against the ocean currents. Dolphins, sailfish, and barracuda can swim 25 to 30 miles an hour. When conditions grow unfavorable in one area, the nekton generally can move away to find a better place. Sometimes the unfavorable changes are so rapid or widespread that the nekton do not have time to escape. An entire ocean current may change courses and sweep them into an area that is too hot or too cold. Many fish have gas-filled bladders that enable them to stay at a given level in the water. Any sudden downward movement of water can carry the fish into deep water. A sudden surge of water may carry a fish upward to a death by explosion.

The third group of sea life, the benthos, move about little if at all. Coral, seaweeds, and oysters attach themselves to the ocean floor or objects on the ocean floor. Starfish and crabs creep about at the bottom of the sea. The sea bottom holds a great deal of bacteria. These were carried to the bottom on objects that sank. There they have plenty of moving water and solid surfaces on which to cling. If they have a sufficient food supply, they grow rapidly. Benthos in some form live in shallow shore waters; others live where the ocean is six miles deep; but all forms depend upon the moving waters to bring them food. If the waters bring unfavorable conditions, such as too much salt or too much dissolved oxygen, there is little or no hope of escape for the benthos.

The larger forms of life, the nekton and benthos, may in their turn contribute to the growth of the little sea plants. When a whale or other form of life dies, either it is eaten by other animals or it decays. If it decays, the forces operating in the sea cause it to break down into various chemicals. When these chemicals are brought near the surface by the movement of the water, the tiny plants can use the chemicals to make more food.

The amount of life in various parts of the sea is often surprising. There may be very little life in areas of clear, tropical seas. The water is so deep that the chemicals that sink to the ocean floor are not easily brought up high enough for the plants to reach them. If waters did not move in from other parts of the world, stirring these calm waters and carrying chemicals and plants, life might become scarce in these tropical regions of the high seas. Strangely enough there is much life in the cold polar areas. The rapid up and down movement of water in these regions brings the chemicals to the surface. Some kinds of sea plants do well in low temperatures. Scientists have found plants growing on ice floating in polar seas.

There is also an abundance of life in shallow water whether it is near dry land or over the top of an underwater mountain. In shallow areas there is much movement of the water as it strikes against the land forms beneath it and as rivers pour into the sea. Chemicals thus are stirred from the bottom and brought to the floating plants.

In the environment of the sea, three special factors greatly affect life. One of the most important of these is the presence of salt in the water. Sea water is about 3.5 percent salt. The constant worldwide movement of water keeps this percentage about the same in all oceans and in all parts of the oceans. Rivers, of course, do not have such a percentage of salt. Sometimes rivers at flood stage pour more fresh water into the sea than the nearby sea life can stand. The result is wholesale death to the surrounding life in the sea.

In tropical regions evaporation is very rapid. The evaporating water, of course, leaves the salt behind. When something happens to slow down movement of the water in such a region, the percentage of salt begins to build up, and certain forms of life die. In the Dead Sea and the Great Salt Lake, there is no movement of the water out to the oceans, and life has almost disappeared in these waters.

Another factor affecting sea life is the percentage of dissolved gases in the water. Many sea animals, especially fish, are very sensitive to the amount of dissolved gases the water contains. Dissolved oxygen varies greatly from one part of the ocean to another. Too much or too little of this oxygen will bring swift death to certain varieties of sea life. There is often rapid upward movement of the deep water off the coast of southwest Africa, carrying to the surface water that is extremely low in dissolved oxygen and that brings widespread destruction of nekton.

A third major factor affecting sea life is temperature. Although some forms of life exist in all the various temperatures of the oceans, the form varies. If there is a sudden change in the normal temperature of a region, widespread death of sea life will result. El Nino current off the coast of Peru may bring unusually warm water down the coast of South America, killing fish by the millions.

AN EXAMPLE OF AN ADVANCE ORGANIZER

Motion and Life

Life in the sea has many similarities to life on land. All living things must have nutrients, substances that enable them to live, grow, and reproduce. Plants, on land and in the sea, need certain kinds of chemicals and sunlight. Plants can take these chemicals and use sunlight in a special process to change the chemicals into food. Animals cannot manufacture their food from chemicals and sunlight; therefore, animals must get their food from plants and other animals.

When plants and animals die on land, their bodies are returned to the soil, where they break down into chemicals. In the sea, dead plants and animals decompose and the chemicals produced float in the water or sink to the ocean floor. In both cases, other forms of life absorb these chemicals, thus setting into motion the great cycles of life.

If the living thing on land or in the sea cannot get to the nutrient source, the nutrients must be brought to it. All life is directly or indirectly dependent upon plants, and plants generally are very limited in their ability to move about. Sea plants generally are moved about much more than land plants. All forms of life are dependent upon motion. For the continuation of life, it is essential that air and water be constantly moving. Life on the land gets many essential nutrients from the air. The various gases composing air would not stay in the right proportions if air did not constantly move. Land forms of life would die swiftly if these proportions were greatly changed. If air were not in constant motion, many places on the earth would become too hot while other places would become too cold to sustain life. The same types of problems would develop for life in the sea if the waters were not in constant motion.

Air moves in great streams over land and sea while great streams of water, many times the size of the Mississippi River, move through the world's oceans.

There are several forces that set air and water into motion and determine their direction and speed. One of these forces is the rotation of the earth on its axis. As the earth spins, the spinning movement causes great ocean and air currents to start moving in huge circles. The currents in the Northern Hemisphere move clockwise, while those in the Southern Hemisphere move counterclockwise.

Another force affecting the movements of air and sea is the gravitational pull of the moon and the sun. This pull causes the air in some places on the earth to be pulled upward and in other places to move downward. The gravitational pull causes tides in the sea, and tides cause waves. If a wave is near the shore and strikes bottom, the water in that wave will start to move forward as well as up and down. This movement stirs up the ocean bottom. Water in waves on the high seas does not move forward but only up and down.

Temperature is another powerful force affecting air and water movement.

Air and water near the equator become warm and are pushed away by the colder air and water moving in. As the warm air and water move further away, they become increasingly colder and eventually mix with air and water from the polar regions and start back toward the equator. Temperature also causes up and down movements. As cold air and water sink downward, they push warmer air and water upward.

Wind and water can set each other in motion. Because water cools and warms slower than does land, the oceans keep creating movements of air from colder to warmer areas. The frictional pull of the wind on water also causes the water to move in both currents and waves. When winds pull water out in currents from the shore, there is no water to follow. Replacement water must come from lower levels. This upwelling movement of water stirs up the ocean floor.

Like the land forms with which we are familiar, the sea bottom varies greatly. There are mountain ranges, level plains, and deep canyons. All these formations affect the movement of water in much the same way that such forms on land affect the movement of air; they may turn streams aside and cause waters to move up and down.

Forms of life on land and in the sea thrive in environments suited to them. Great changes in air movements can bring destructive droughts, floods, or frosts to a land area. Great and sudden changes in ocean movements bring destruction to life in the waters of the sea.

How Students Might Be Taught to Use Advance Organizers

Students could be given the advance organizer "Motion and Life" and the passage "Life in the Sea" and taken through the steps of using an advance organizer. First, the students would need to read the advance organizer with the aim of learning its content. Then, 24 or more hours later, they would need to read the passage with the intent of relating the new material to the content of the advance organizer. They would have to be able to see the relationship of the new material to the general, abstract, and inclusive content of the advance organizer. Finally, they would have to be able to keep the new information from becoming absorbed completely by the more general ideas of the advance organizer.

Specific instructions for learning the content of the advance organizer might be as follows:

1. Read this short passage carefully and try to learn what it says so that tomorrow you can use the material in this short passage to help you learn the material in a longer passage.
2. Study the material until you understand it. Think about the passage as a whole. Decide what it means, what the statements cover, and what limitations or restrictions they include.

3. Determine whether or not you should restate some of the general ideas of this passage in different words. It is easier to remember and deal with an idea if you can state it in your own words. Some of you may not see any way to restate the ideas and will want to leave them as they stand. Everyone should, however, try to restate the general ideas in her or his own words.
4. Check your restatements against the original to be sure that you have not changed the basic ideas. Be sure that your restatements cover everything in the original. Be sure your restatements do not go beyond the original.
5. After you have decided what is, for you, the most appropriate way to state the general ideas in this passage, study each of the general ideas so that you can remember them and relate them to what you are going to read tomorrow.

The next day the students could be taken through the process of reading the passage containing the new material to be learned and shown how to relate the new material to what they learned from the advance organizer.

They could be told that each new item of information should be related, if possible, to the general, inclusive, and abstract concepts in the advance organizer. The types of relationships the new material could have to the general ideas of the advance organizer should be delineated. The students should be told that:

1. a new item may elaborate one of the general advance organizer ideas; that is, it may take some element of an advance organizer idea and extend it.
2. a new item may describe one of the advance organizer ideas.
3. a new item may support one of the advance organizer ideas; that is, it may give additional evidence that the general organizer idea is true.
4. a new item may qualify one of the advance organizer ideas. It can do so by limiting the advance organizer idea to a certain time, place, or number of cases.
5. a new item may represent one of the advance organizer ideas; that is, it may say much the same thing as the advance organizer idea but in different words.
6. a new item may seem to contradict one of the advance organizer ideas.

There are many other ways that the new information may be related to the advance organizer ideas, but these are the most frequently found types of relationships.

Specific instructions for using the advance organizer to learn the material of the passage might be as follows:

- *A new item of information may be an elaboration of one of the general ideas we have learned.* We have the following statement from the new material: "When the little plants die, they start a chain of events that leads to the death of the larger forms of sea life or to their moving away from the area." One of the general ideas from the short passage we studied yesterday stated, "Animals cannot manufacture their food from chemicals and sunlight; therefore, animals must get their food from plants or other animals." Our new information takes part of the general idea we already have and extends it. In this case, it gives further information about the general idea.
- *A new item of information may describe one of the general ideas.* Let us look at this sentence, "If the proper chemicals are present in the water, and other conditions such as sunlight and temperature are favorable, the little sea plants may double their size or number in five or six hours." You may remember we had this general idea in the passage we read, "Forms of life on land and in the sea thrive in environments suited to them." Our new item of information describes in detail the general idea that forms of life thrive in environments suited to them.
- *A new item of information may support one of the general ideas.* We find this sentence in the passage, "El Nino current off the coast of Peru may bring unusually warm water down the coast of South America, killing fish by the millions." This fact supports the general idea we got from our other material, namely that great and sudden changes in ocean movements bring destruction to life in the waters of the sea.
- *A new item of information may qualify one of the general ideas.* We have the presentation of the fact, "If the helpless plants are carried by the currents into dark or otherwise unfavorable areas, the plants do not multiply rapidly and may even die." This statement indicates that there are special limitations on our general idea, "Plants can take these chemicals and use sunlight in a special process to change the chemicals into food."
- *A new item of information may represent a general idea.* Here is a sentence from our material, "Thus, indirectly, the most ferocious shark is dependent upon microscopic plants floating around in the sea." This statement says essentially the same thing as the general idea we looked at before, "Animals cannot manufacture their food from chemicals and sunlight; therefore, animals must get their food from plants or other animals." Thus, we have an example that represents a general idea.

- *A new item of information may contradict, or seem to contradict, one of the general ideas.* One of our specific facts is that scientists have found plants growing on ice floating in polar seas. This statement we can relate to our general idea that, if water were not in constant motion, many places on the earth would become too hot and other places would become too cold to sustain life. We can relate the two things because the specific fact seems to contradict one of the general ideas that we had acquired.

- In dealing with seeming contradictions, you should proceed in two steps: First, decide in what way or ways the item seems to be against one of the general ideas. Second, decide how the item can be brought into line with that general idea. In other words, how can it be made to fit the general idea? Even after you know the new items of information and their relationship to the general ideas you read the day before, you still have a major problem. That problem is that the general ideas can swallow up the new items of information. How can you insure that they will not be swallowed up by the general ideas and thus lost to you? You can proceed in two steps. First, recognize that the new facts are different from the general ideas. Second, determine ahead of time that you will maintain the facts in your memory as items you can sort out and use apart from the general ideas.

- Once you have the general ideas firmly in mind, as you read information closely related to those general ideas you tend to think of the new facts as being much the same thing as the general ideas. At least you tend to think of the new information as not being anything decidedly different from the general ideas. You must clearly recognize that the facts have an existence of their own. True, they are related to the general ideas, and you must understand that relationship. But if you do not recognize that the new information exists in its own right, that it is somehow different from the general ideas, you will remember little more than the general ideas. For example, one of the general ideas is, "All living things must have nutrients, substances that enable them to live, grow, and reproduce." Now we have the following new item of information, "There may be little life in clear, tropical seas because the water is so deep that chemicals sink to the bottom and are not easily brought up again." This sentence is telling us very much the same thing as the general idea. If we just assume that this sentence essentially is the same thing as the general idea, we will fail to remember that there are places in the clear tropical seas that are so deep that they support very little life. The point we want to remember is that, unless we recognize the specific new information as items in and of themselves, we are not likely to remember them. They will be swallowed up by the general ideas.

- It is easier to remember one general thing rather than all the parts of that thing or a number of specific facts. When you finish reading, you remember a great deal of the new information, but very quickly the new facts you have learned begin to fade into the old general ideas. Soon you can remember little other than the general ideas. To slow down this process of the general idea absorbing the new information, you must decide before you read that you will keep the new information alive in its own right. You can do so by saying to yourself how the new information is like the old general ideas and how it is not like the general ideas. This process will become easier as you practice.

- Suppose we have the following specific fact that we want to remember, "Even the simple up and down movement of the waves is important to the microscopic sea plants because this movement keeps them sliding past new water from which they absorb chemicals." This sentence is closely related to the following general idea, "For the continuation of life, it is essential that air and water be constantly moving." In order to remember the new information, we must note how this sentence is like the general idea, then we must note how it is different.

- We have the following sentence in our material, "The free-floating plankton actually may be carried thousands of miles from its original area by a fast-moving surface current." This sentence is very closely related to the following general idea, "Sea plants are generally moved about much more than land plants." We must note how the specific fact is like the general idea and how it is different from the general idea.

- When you read, it is easy to speed over the new information in material and assume that you understand the relationships and know what are general ideas and what are new items to be learned. If this method of reading to gain and retain new information is to be effective, it will be necessary to examine each new item and actually say to yourself what the relationship of that new information is to the general information you already have. Then you must see how the old and new ideas are alike and how they are different.

- In all these processes, you must decide the relationships in your own words. Saying to yourself what the relationships are will enable you to remember better what you have read.

THE POTENTIAL VALUE OF THE ADVANCE ORGANIZER

A frequent complaint about Ausubel's concept of the advance organizer is that classroom materials are not written the way he says they should be written. In the opinion of this author and a substantial number of researchers who have examined Ausubel's theory carefully, classroom texts should be. Until such a time as large amounts of textual materials are so written, the teacher will have to write the advance organizers for her or his own students. Since the teacher knows her or his students better than the textbook author who has never met those students, the teacher should be better able to write advance organizers that "fit" the cognitive structures of the students.

David P. Ausubel has presented a system describing how textual materials can be better learned and better remembered. The theory is eminently sensible. Research on this system for more than 20 years has provided substantial, but not unequivocal, evidence that the system can work. If textbook authors and teachers would employ the system in constructing a substantial body of textual materials, and if teachers would teach and provide practice in the use of the system over substantial lengths of time, there is good reason to believe that reading to learn at the junior high school level and beyond could be greatly improved.

About the Author

Robert W. Jerrolds is Professor, Department of Reading Education, at the University of Georgia.

References

Alvermann, D. E. Personal communication, October 10, 1984.

Ausubel, D. P. *The Psychology of Meaningful Verbal Learning.* New York: Grune and Stratton, 1963.

Ausubel, D. P. *Educational Psychology: A Cognitive View.* New York: Holt, Rinehart, and Winston, 1968.

Ausubel, D. P. "In Defense of Advance Organizers: A Reply to the Critics." *Review of Educational Research* (1978) 48 (2), 251–257.

Barnes, B. R. and E. U. Clawson, "Do Advance Organizers Facilitate Learning? Recommendations for Further Research Based on an Analysis of 32 Studies." *Review of Educational Research* (1975) 45 (4), 637–659.

Clark, D. H. and T. W. Bean. "Improving Advance Organizer Research: Persistent Problems and Future Directions." *Reading World* (1982) 22 (1), 2–10.

Kozlow, M. J. "A Meta-analysis of Selected Advance Organizer Research Reports from 1960–1977" (Doctoral disertation, Ohio State University). *Dissertation Abstracts International,* 1978.

Luiten, J., W. Ames, and G. Ackerson. "A Meta-analysis of the Effects of Advance Organizers on Learning and Retention." *American Educational Research Journal* (1980) 17 (2), 211–218.

Mayer, R. E. "Twenty Years of Research on Advance Organizers: Assimilation Theory Is Still the Best Predictor of Results." *Instructional Science* (1979) 8, 133–167.

Stone, C. L. "A Meta-analysis of Advance Organizer Studies." *Journal of Experimental Education* (1983) 51, 194–199.

*As noted by authors in this volume, there is growing recognition of the impor-
tance of taking time in teaching comprehension to explore and, if necessary, to
build students' background knowledge prior to reading a selection so that they
have a sound basis for anticipating, predicting, and understanding the meaning
of what they read. How may teachers, particularly at the middle- and upper-
grade levels, help students use their prior knowledge and experience to do this?
Nelson-Herber presents a series of instructional activities designed to tap students' resources in a way that "feeds forward to the context of the text."*

Anticipation and Prediction in Reading Comprehension

Joan Nelson-Herber

The significance for reading comprehension of readers' prior knowledge has received widespread attention during the past decade and has
been amply supported by research. It seems incongruous, then, that so
little instructional time is given to preparation for reading in classrooms
across the nation. This paper discusses the need for preparation for
reading assignments and, more specifically, focuses on the use of anticipation and prediction strategies for improving reading comprehension
in middle and secondary school classrooms.

Durkin's recent studies, reported in this text and others, support
what content reading specialists have been saying for years: that teachers spend very little instructional time in activating, reviewing, or developing relevant background information prior to reading; and that
comprehension is "taught" mostly by assignment and assessment, that
is, by assigning the reading task and then asking questions after the
reading has been accomplished. While Durkin's studies have focused
on reading instruction in elementary school classrooms, the same process of assignment and assessment may be observed in middle and

secondary school content classes. Teachers often assign textbook read-ings containing uncommon vocabulary, unknown facts, unfamiliar con-cepts, and unusual values without any preparatory instruction. Given our present understanding of the importance of prior knowledge, the fact that many students are not able to comprehend should be no surprise to educators.

MEANING RESIDES IN THE KNOWLEDGE AND EXPERIENCE OF THE READER

What do we know about prior knowledge and reading comprehension? Recent research provides evidence in support of the following generali-zations:

1. Prior knowledge is of central importance in the reading process and plays a critical role in text perspective and interpretation (Anderson et al., 1977; Pichert and Anderson, 1977).
2. Prior knowledge can be used to make ambiguous texts compre-hensible (Bransford and Johnson, 1972; Reynolds et al., 1982).
3. Relevant prior knowledge facilitates comprehension, increasing readers' recall and recognition of text (Bransford, 1984; Pearson et al., 1979).
4. Irrelevant, inaccurate, or conflicting prior knowledge can distort comprehension and interfere with the author's message (Lipson, 1984; Reynolds et al., 1982; Steffenson et al., 1979).
5. Prior knowledge can account for more variation in reading per-formance than either I.Q. or measured reading achievement (Johnston, 1981; Johnston and Pearson, 1982).
6. Prior knowledge can account for text difficulty to a greater degree than the frequently used measures of sentence length and word difficulty (Kintsch et al., 1975).

To put it simply, research supports the idea that the knowledge and experience a reader brings to the text determine, to a large extent, what the reader comprehends from the text.

Sometimes it is necessary, however, to use very unusual illustrations to help proficient adult readers recognize the importance of prior knowledge and experience in comprehension. The recent professional literature is replete with tricky sentences and contrived paragraphs designed specifically to demonstrate one effect or another. However, the importance of prior knowledge can be demonstrated with a simple sentence from a daily newspaper:

The bears were caught short by a drop in the prime and institutional panic.

It may seem like an unusual illustration, but it is a perfectly correct English sentence and would be perfectly comprehensible to any regular reader of the newspaper from which it was selected. Even all the words are familiar. However, anyone not familiar with stock market language and investment strategies would be unlikely to understand the author's message no matter how well he or she had learned the basic reading skills. To understand the message at all, the reader must have a schema for the message and must be familiar with the technical vocabulary. The reader must recognize the sentence as related to a stock market strategy and must know the special and unusual meanings of the words when used in this context. Even so, the reader may only get the general idea of the message. For example, he or she may understand that *some kind of investors were taken by surprise by a drop in interest rates and some action by institutions.* Notice that the reader with a little prior knowledge of the stock market may get the gist of the message but lose the richness of meaning that someone with a more elaborate stock market schema would comprehend. The sophisticated investor would recognize the term *bears* to mean investors who are interested in selling stock on the expectation that the market will move lower. Further, he or she would recognize that being *caught short* meant that the bears had sold stock that they did not own in hopes of buying it at a lower price before the settlement date and keeping the difference as a profit. She or he would recognize the *prime* as the interest rate at which banks and institutions can borrow money. And finally, he or she would know that when interest rates drop, institutions that are holding a lot of cash rush to buy stocks, thereby raising overall stock market prices.

It should be noted also that if the wrong schema were activated— e.g., *bears, caught, panic,* etc.—or if the reader brought incorrect prior knowledge to the message—e.g., *bears* as *buyers*—there would be even more variance in comprehension.

If the comprehension of such a simple sentence from a daily newspaper can be so profoundly influenced by the amount and quality of the reader's prior knowledge, is it any wonder that middle and secondary school students have difficulty comprehending sophisticated content-area textbooks to which they bring minimal prior knowledge of the subject? It must be obvious that comprehension of the demonstration sentence would not be improved by recycling the reader through basic reading skills. It should also be obvious that recycling students through basic reading skills because they encounter difficulty in comprehending content material for which they have little or no background knowledge is probably counterproductive. Unfortunately, instead of recognizing the nature of reading problems in middle and secondary schools, and providing appropriate advanced instruction, educators have fallen for the "back to basics" slogan and persistently have set up remedial reading programs that are locked into a deficit recycling model.

Each reader reconstructs meaning from text on the basis of his or her direct, vicarious, or analogous prior knowledge and experience. Efficient readers activate that knowledge and experience when approaching a reading task. They anticipate and predict meanings on the basis of what they already know about the reading content, and they monitor their reading comprehension to detect dissonance or conflict with what they already know. When dissonance or conflict occurs, that is, when it doesn't sound right or it doesn't make sense, they either reread the material to correct their understanding or resolve the conflict by constructing new knowledge or elaborating on old knowledge. In other words, they use prior knowledge as a base, both for reconstructing meaning from text and for constructing *new* knowledge from text. Without a minimum base of prior knowledge about a subject, readers experience difficulty and frustration in comprehending content material even when their reading skills are reasonably good. Basic reading skills are necessary but not sufficient for comprehension of content materials.

ADVANCED INSTRUCTION IS THE KEY

Reading instruction should occur at every level and in every classroom where reading is required to be successful. Instruction in middle and secondary school subject areas should include preparation for the reading assignment, guidance through the reading process, and support toward independence in reading the content materials of the subject (Herber, 1978). Instructional processes that simulate efficient readers' strategies can help the learner realize what efficient readers do. Students can be taught to use the reading skills they possess in combination with their knowledge and experience to reconstruct meaning from text and to build on what they already know in order to grasp the new ideas in text material.

Preparation for reading content materials is probably the most important and the most neglected part of the instructional process. Students can learn to use prior knowledge and experience to anticipate and predict meaning through instruction that activates related knowledge, previews key concepts and vocabulary, creates curiosity and expectation, sets purposes, and feeds forward to the context of the text.

SAMPLE TEACHING GUIDES

The sample teaching guides that follow are designed to show how teachers can prepare students for their reading assignments. Each of these guides has been used successfully in real classroom situations. Each has been found by the teachers who used them to be valuable in helping students to anticipate and predict meaning in content materials and to improve comprehension both of the assigned material and of related material read independently.

English Literature: Poetry

A poem has been selected for the first teaching guide because comprehension of poetry is heavily dependent on the reader's prior knowledge. Poetry operates both at the particular level and at the universal level. Poems require that readers use their prior knowledge not only to recognize what poets are saying, but what poets mean by what they say and how what they say relates to the whole world of experience.

Students in middle and secondary schools often are frustrated by poetry because they don't understand that the poet writes to describe or capture a universal idea or experience. They need prereading instruction that prepares them to anticipate and predict meaning on the basis of their own experience and to recognize how the ideas of the poet relate to world experience.

The following material has been used in a variety of settings to prepare secondary school students to read the poem "Ozymandias" by Percy B. Shelley, as well as other poems with the same general theme.

Ozymandias
by Percy B. Shelley

I met a traveler from an antique land,
Who said: Two vast and trunkless legs of stone
Stand in the desert. Near them, on the sand,
Half sunk, a shattered visage lies, whose frown,
And wrinkled lip, and sneer of cold command,
Tell that its sculptor well those passions read,
Which yet survive, stamped on these lifeless things,
The hand that mocked them and the heart that fed,
And on the pedestal these words appear:
"My name is Ozymandias, King of Kings.
Look on my works, ye mighty, and despair!"
Nothing beside remains. Round the decay
Of that colossal wreck, boundless and bare
The lone and level sands stretch far away.

Activating Related Knowledge

First, the students are asked to form into groups of four or five and work together to list as many words as they can think of that relate to both of the following ideas: *time* and *the desert.* The word *sand* is given as an example in that it relates both to time and to the desert. Different groups of students generate different word lists depending on their geographical locations and their own background of experience. The following lists were generated by an eleventh grade class in New England and by a tenth grade class in the Southwest:

Time and the Desert

New England		Southwest	
sand	heat	sand	changing
pyramids	wind	cactus	lizards
sphinx	ruins	sun	snakes
mummies	curse	moon	plants
ancient	tombs	heat	mirage
modern	archeologists	seasons	ruins
sun		pueblos	erosion
		nomads	

Obviously the groups had differing schemata for the organizing ideas. The New England group was responding with words related mostly to the ancient desert and the Southwest group with words related mostly to the living desert. Both groups recognized relationships with *time* that were both literal and inferential. Differences in lists show up even among groups in the same classroom.

After the lists are generated within the groups, they are shared with other groups in the class and key words are discussed in terms of their relationships with the organizing ideas. The purpose of the exercise is to activate students' prior knowledge of the organizing ideas and to share that experience among all the students. In addition, it gives the teacher the opportunity to assess students' knowledge related to the setting and tone of the poem and to enhance that knowledge when necessary.

Expanding and Refining Vocabulary

After the teacher has shown that he or she values the students' word list, they are quite willing to engage in a vocabulary activity with words that the teacher values. Students then are asked to remain in their groups and work together on a vocabulary exercise.

Recognizing Related Meanings

Directions: For each set of words below, cross out the word that does not belong with the others. In the space provided, describe how the other three words are related or why they belong together.

1. vast	boundless	limited	colossal
2. face	visage	front	rear
3. smile	sneer	laugh	frown
4. broken	whole	shattered	fragmented
5. column	mighty	pedestal	table
6. poet	artist	sculptor	scientist
7. emotions	passions	troubles	feelings
8. command	despair	abandon	hopeless

The exercise is designed to familiarize the students with the words that appear in the poem so they will recognize them when they read the poem. Working on the exercise as a group gives students the opportunity to hear the words pronounced, to see the words as they are being discussed, to recognize the relationships among the words, and to speak the words in the discussion. It should be noticed that several of the items are ambiguous in the sense that more than one answer is reasonable. Since this is a learning experience rather than a test, these kinds of items can be effective in focusing even more attention on the words and in requiring multiple recitation of the reasons for one grouping or another when students compare their responses. It should be pointed out to students, however, that on most well-designed multiple-choice tests there is only one best answer.

Drawing on Experience to Support Familiar Ideas

After gaining some familiarity with the vocabulary of the poem, students are asked to work in their groups to respond on the basis of their own experience to some statements of familiar ideas.

Think About It

Directions: Read each statement and decide whether or not you *really* believe it is true, based on your own experience. In your discussion of the statements, try to think of exceptions that might support a different point of view as well as examples that support the idea. For example, in the first item, does time *ever* wait for anyone? What about time-out in a football game? Does time ever *seem* to slow down or speed up? Is time real or have we created it? See if your group can come to an agreement on each statement.

1. Time waits for no one.
2. All people are mortal and someday will die.
3. Death is the great leveler.
4. An artist gets to know a lot about his or her subject.
5. Things are not always what they seem to be.
6. Pride goes before a fall.
7. All man-made things are temporal and someday will disintegrate.
8. A person's vision is temporal even though his or her perspective is eternal.

The exercise is designed to familiarize students with the ideas of the poet so that they recognize those ideas when they read them, interpret the poet's meaning, and apply the poet's ideas to the universe of experience.

Reading for a Purpose

Now that students have activated and/or developed "prior knowledge" of the setting, tone, vocabulary, and ideas of the poem, they are directed to read "Ozymandias" to see if the author of the poem agrees with the statements they have been discussing.

After the students read the poem, the statements may be used for discussion of the poet's ideas. For each statement, the students decide whether or not they think the poet agrees with it, and they find evidence in the poem to support their decision.

Though this amount of preparation for reading may seem excessive to some teachers of literature, most teachers who have learned to help students use these strategies are delighted with the changes in their students' attitudes toward reading literature and their ability to comprehend metaphor and abstraction. Moreover, the strategies can be designed for theme units wherein the same concept statements can be used for several pieces of literature to develop independence in reading.

For example, the statements used for discussion in "Think About It" above might be used to support students' reading of another poem. For homework after the lesson, the students might be asked to read the poem "Limited" by Carl Sandburg, to determine whether or not that poet agreed with the statements. Since the theme of "Limited" is similar to that of "Ozymandias," most of the statements can be supported with evidence from that poem as well.

Limited
by Carl Sandburg

I am riding on a Limited Express, one of the crack trains of the nation.
Hurtling across the prairie into blue haze and dark air go fifteen all-steel coaches holding a thousand people.
(All the coaches shall be scrap and rust and all the men and women laughing in the diners and sleeper shall pass to ashes.)
I ask a man in the smoker where he is going and he answers: "Omaha."

The same kinds of strategies for preparation for reading assignments can be used with different genres of literature as well as with science and social studies text materials. Prereading exercises can be designed to activate or develop students' experience related to the theme of the text material, to provide students with knowledge of the key concepts or technical vocabulary, and to lead students to anticipate or predict meaning on the basis of their own experience.

Science: Biology

During observation of a student intern, I watched a tenth grade class struggling unsuccessfully with a reading assignment only two pages long. The students had been asked to read the material and to write the answers to questions that the teacher had written on the chalkboard. Both the students and the teacher were frustrated and irritable because the students could not comprehend the material. Following the observation, the teacher and I discussed the students' difficulty and worked on some prereading strategies to develop and enhance the students' ability to comprehend the material. The density of concepts in the material made the reading extremely difficult for anyone not already familiar with the ideas contained in it (including me). Since the teacher already was familiar with the vocabulary, the facts, and the concepts being presented, she did not recognize the problem. Indeed, she had to draw a diagram to help me understand it. Once she recognized the problem, she decided to use a structured overview of the material to familiarize students with the vocabulary of the selection and the organization of the material presented (Barron and Earle, 1969). We also agreed that a vocabulary exercise based on the overview might be helpful. Our purpose was to develop in the students, in advance of the reading assignment, a sense of anticipation for what would be presented and how it would be organized.

Structured Overview

The next day, the teacher introduced the lesson, using the structured overview of the material. The teacher showed how the new material was related to what the students already knew. She pronounced each new vocabulary word and pointed out its relationship to other words in the text material. She built up the expectation that students would learn the classes of eumycophyta and examples of each, along with other information that they could use to complete the overview upon reading the material. Below is the overview.

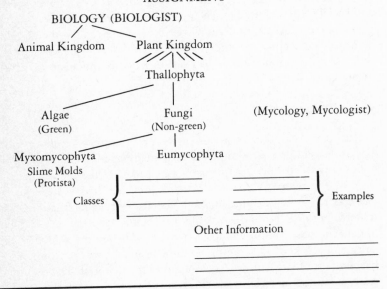

STRUCTURED OVERVIEW OF A BIOLOGY READING ASSIGNMENT

Refinement of Vocabulary and Concepts

Before the actual reading assignment, the teacher asked the students to move into groups of four or five and work together on the following vocabulary exercise.

Similarities and Differences

Directions: Some of the words in pairs listed below can be found in the structured overview. Based on your knowledge of the words from previous lessons and the way they are related in the overview, discuss with others in your group how the words in each pair are alike and how they are different. If you don't know for sure about any pair, guess where they may fit in the overview and then come back to them after reading the material to complete the overview and the vocabulary exercise.

biology—mycology

algae—fungi

achlorophyllous—chlorophyllous

myxomycophyta—eymycophyta

mycologist—biologist

protista—slime molds

autotrophic—heterotrophic

phycomycates—fungi imperfectae

Though the words are extremely difficult, the students were able to complete most of the exercise on the basis of the structured overview and their own knowledge from previous lessons.

Reading for a Purpose

Finally, the teacher asked the students to read the material to complete the structured overview and the vocabulary guide and then to answer the questions on the board. Given this preparation for the reading assignment, they were able to anticipate the organization of the material and to predict the appearance of facts and concepts based on their knowledge of the organization. They were able to answer the assessment questions with relative ease.

Social Studies: Public Health

As a final example, this lesson was taught by a special education teacher to a group of learning disabled students in a middle grade resource room (Stalcup, 1980). The reading selection was about the dangers of teenage smoking.

Activating Student Experience

As first preparation for the reading assignment, the teacher asked the students to say all the words they could think of related to smoking. The teacher listed their words on the chalkboard and they discussed how each word was related to smoking.

Expanding and Refining Vocabulary

During the discussion of students' word lists, the teacher added and explained a few words from the selection that the students needed to know.

Predicting from Experience

Next, the teacher introduced the following exercise:

Would You Say This?

Directions: Work together to read each statement and decide on the basis of what you already know whether or not you agree with the idea. If you agree with it, put a check in the first space. Then if you predict that the reading selection would support that statement, put a check in the second space.

1. _____   _____ Smokers don't live as long as nonsmokers.

2. _____   _____ More teenage girls smoke than do teenage boys.

3. _____   _____ Some teenagers smoke because it makes them feel older.

4. _____   _____ Some teenagers smoke because their friends do.

5. _____   _____ Some teenagers smoke because they don't think about the dangers of smoking.

6. _____   _____ Poisonous gases in cigarettes can damage a smoker's heart, lungs, and brain.

7. _____   _____ Babies of women smokers are at risk.

After energetic discussion of their own beliefs and opinions about the statements, the students predicted which of the statements would be confirmed by reading the article.

Reading for a Purpose

Finally, the teacher directed the students to read the text in order to confirm or reject their predictions on the basis of the evidence presented in the article.

Given this kind of preparation for reading, these "learning disabled" students were eager to read the material, and they were able to comprehend the facts, concepts, and values presented. Further, they gave every evidence of pleasure and satisfaction in doing so.

TEACHING AND LEARNING

Although these instructional strategies focus on particular reading se-lections, it is the process rather than the product of reading that is being stressed here. The strategies are designed to help students realize the value of prior knowledge and experience as a basis for reading and learning. They learn to anticipate and predict meaning, based on their own prior knowledge and experience, and to monitor their reading to detect dissonance or conflict with what they already know. When what they are reading doesn't "sound right" or doesn't "square with their experience," they seek evidence to correct their understanding or to resolve the conflict by constructing new knowledge or elaborating on old knowledge. Children do not come into the world knowing these processes; they must be learned. Some students learn them incidentally and become proficient readers on their own. Most students would benefit from instruction that builds positively on the basic reading skills and provides support for the transition to sophisticated subject-area reading materials.

In summary, the following ideas should be considered by middle and secondary school teachers as they plan their content-area reading as-signments:

1. Preparation for reading is an important part of the instructional process.
2. Simulation of the efficient reader's strategies helps the learner understand the reading process.
3. Generation of ideas around an organizing concept activates the learner's prior knowledge.
4. Prereading discussion of new vocabulary and/or the organiza-tional pattern of the material promotes anticipation and prediction of meaning.
5. Prereading discussion of known ideas related or analogous to content material promotes anticipation and prediction of mean-ing.
6. Instruction that activates prior experience, creates curiosity, sets purposes, and feeds forward to the content of the text should occur in every classroom where reading is required for success.

About the Author

Joan Nelson-Herber is Professor, Division of Professional Education, at the State University of New York at Binghamton.

References

Anderson, R.C., R.E. Reynolds, D.L. Schallert, and E.T. Goetz. "Frameworks for Comprehending Discourse." *American Educational Research Journal* (1977) 14, 367–382.

Barron, R. "Research for Classroom Teachers: Recent Developments on the Use of the Structured Overview as an Advance Organizer." In H.L. Herber and J.D. Riley (Eds.), *Research in Reading in the Content Areas: Fourth Year Report.* Syracuse, N.Y.: Syracuse University Reading and Language Arts Center, 1978.

Bransford, J.D. and M.K. Johnson. "Contextual Prerequisites for Understanding: Some Investigations of Comprehension and Recall." *Journal of Verbal Learning and Verbal Behavior* (1972) 11, 717–726.

Bransford, J.D. "Schema Activation and Schema Acquisition: Comments on Richard C. Anderson's Remarks." In R.C. Anderson, J. Osborn, and R.J. Tierney (Eds.), *Learning to Read in American Schools.* Hillsdale, N.J.: Lawrence Erlbaum Associates, 1984.

Herber, H. *Teaching Reading in Content Areas.* Englewood Cliffs, N.J.: Prentice-Hall, 1978.

Johnston, P. "Prior Knowledge and Reading Comprehension Text Bias" (Unpublished dissertation). University of Illinois, 1981.

Johnston, P. and P.D. Pearson. "Prior Knowledge, Connectivity, and the Assessment of Reading Comprehension." (Technical Report 245). Urbana: University of Illinois, Center for the Study of Reading, 1982.

Kintsch, W., E. Kozminsky, W.J. Streby, G. McKoon, and J.M. Keenan. "Comprehension and Recall of Text as a Function of Content Variables." *Journal of Verbal Learning and Verbal Behavior* (1975) 14, 196–214.

Lipson, M.Y. "Some Unexpected Issues in Prior Knowledge and Comprehension." *The Reading Teacher* (1984) 37, 8, 760–764.

Pearson, P.D., J. Hansen, and C. Gordon. "The Effect of Background Knowledge on Young Children's Comprehension of Explicit and Implicit Information." *Journal of Reading Behavior* (1979) 11, 201–209.

Pichert, J.W. and R.C. Anderson. "Taking Different Perspectives on a Story." *Journal of Educational Psychology* (1977) 69, 309–315.

Reynolds, R., M. Taylor, M. Steffensen, L. Shirey, and R. Anderson. "Cultural Schemata and Reading Comprehension." *Reading Research Quarterly* (1982) 17, 3, 353–356.

Stalcup, H. Unpublished lesson plan. Network of Secondary School Demonstration Centers for Teaching Reading in Content Areas. Binghamton, N.Y.: SUNY-Binghamton, Division of Professional Education, 1980.

Steffenson, M., C. Joag-Dev, and R.C. Anderson. "A Crosscultural Perspective on Reading Comprehension." *Reading Research Quarterly* (1979) 15, 1, 10–29.

There is considerable evidence that different types of questions elicit different types of response. If this is so, do the questions we ask in assessing reading comprehension require different types of responses that must be learned? Jones presents a variety of materials for teaching students how to recognize and respond to a number of different kinds of questions.

Response Instruction

Beau Fly Jones

Durkin's (1978–79) landmark findings concerning the lack of comprehension instruction in American classrooms already have been described in the introduction of this book. As important as these findings are, they do not fully address the range of problems of instruction. Achievement in school requires both comprehension and the ability to respond to questions about what is read. That is, when teachers ask students to summarize, to describe, or to compare and contrast, they expect students' responses to be organized in terms of commonly recognized (text) structures. Thus, a compare/contrast question requires a compare/contrast text structure, not a description of a sequence of events. Moreover, teachers expect a certain level of response: literal, inferential, application, and so on. Yet, these text structures and levels of processing requirements are almost never stated as part of the objective or task in most classrooms. The best students seem to figure out these requirements in a trial and error manner. However, the national outcry regarding the poor quality of speaking and writing suggests that the majority of American students are not fluent in responding to questions requiring written and oral discourse.

What is needed as a parallel to comprehension instruction is what I have termed *response instruction.* Broadly stated, this is systematic and explicit instruction to help students articulate, in oral and written dis-

The author wishes to thank the Chicago Public Schools and the Center for the Study of Reading for their support in developing the materials used in this article.

course, answers to questions about what they read. More specifically, response instruction involves teaching students how to structure their answers so that the answers cover the desired content, use an appropriate text structure, and reflect the intended level of response. Technically speaking, response instruction may include teaching students how to answer objective questions and analogies as well as how to answer questions requiring connected oral or written discourse. However, there already is research on response instruction for objective questions and research on testwiseness and analogies (Salomon and Auchenbach, 1984). Hence, this article will focus on response instruction for answers requiring connected discourse.

The article is organized to answer several questions:

1. What is the content of response instruction?
2. How should response instruction be taught?
3. Why should we provide response instructions?
4. When should response instruction be given?
5. Who should teach response instruction?
6. How should response instruction be scored?

After these questions are answered, there are three sample lessons.

WHAT IS THE CONTENT OF RESPONSE INSTRUCTION?

Generally, any information that helps students articulate answers to questions constitutes *response instruction*. Consequently, what is offered below is intended to be suggestive, not definitive. Since responses are answers to questions, it is important to consider what types of questions students must answer as well as the nature of the relationship between the questions and the text. Then we can consider ways to help students organize their answers.

Question Analysis

Armbruster, Anderson, Bruning, and Meyer (1983) have analyzed over 300 questions in social studies texts to develop a taxonomy of questions. Altogether, they define eight types of questions:

time *(When?)*
location *(Where?)*
quantity *(How much? How many?)*
name *(Who? Whose?)*

concept identification *(What? Which?)*
explanation *(Why? How?)*
description *(What is?)*
comparison *(Compare/Contrast? How did X change?)*

For each category of question, Armbruster et al. show systematically what information is *provided* in the question and also the pattern of ideas that is required in the answer.

Consider "Why-Conflict" questions, a subcategory of explanations, for example. These questions typically require that the student identify the goals and actions of the two or more parties in the conflict; the questions provide the definition of the conflict. The question, "Why was there trouble between the Indians and the colonists?" clearly defines the conflict between the Indians and the colonists. To explain the conflict fully, the student must explain how the colonists' actions interfered with Indian goals and vice versa. The authors argue that students in U.S. history and other fields typically are not taught how to analyze what a question is asking, find the relevant information or content in the text, and write an answer to the question. Providing explicit instruction in question analysis would be a major step toward response instruction.

Level of Thinking and Text Conditions

Raphael and Pearson (1982) argue that in analyzing questions, it is crucial to consider the relationship between the question and the answer, given the available information. Raphael and Pearson distinguish three text conditions: text explicit, text implicit, and script. In a *text explicit* condition, the answer is stated explicitly. In a *text implicit* condition, the answer is only implied; consequently, the student must use inferential thinking. In the *script* condition, according to Raphael and Pearson, the answer is not in the text; instead, the student must use prior knowledge. Regarding the latter, I prefer the term *text inadequate* because it allows the teacher to direct the student to consult additional texts, as well as prior knowledge, when the answer is not stated in the text or when it is stated so poorly that it is not usable. Raphael and Pearson found that teaching students to recognize these various conditions significantly improved comprehension. They argued that this instruction made students aware of the need for their answers to have different levels of thinking and helped them to analyze the nature of the available information as a first step toward formulating an answer.

Frames and Nonlinear Outlines

Once students have analyzed a question and have found the relevant information, the next step in response instruction would be to help students organize their answers. Undoubtedly, good teachers have found various ways to do this throughout the years. Two concepts are offered below because they have only just emerged from research. A *frame* is a set of content-specific questions or categories that an author or student uses to organize the text (Armbruster and Anderson, 1984). However, frame questions are not just any questions. They are *the* key sets of questions that are fundamental to understanding a given discipline. A typical frame underlying many narrative texts is the goal-action-outcome frame. This frame may be used to understand the behavior of one character in a story or the action of one group in an historical narrative. In this frame, the key questions are: What are the goals of group A? What actions did it take to achieve its goals? What are the results of the actions? Other questions that often are added to this frame for literary narratives are: What were the problems group A had in reaching its goals? What was the internal response of the group?

When students use frames to help organize the text or to answer questions, each frame question or category has an accompanying "slot" or category that the students use to fill in the answer to the questions. In the CIRCA (Collaboration to Improve Reading in the Content Area) project, involving the Chicago Public Schools and the Center for the Study of Reading, we have found it useful to teach students to use various types of *nonlinear outline structures* to accompany each frame. The outline structure should reflect the structure of the response.

To explain, researchers recently have developed a number of innovative systems for outlining, analyzing, and responding to questions. For example, Jones and Amiran (in Jones, Amiran, and Katims, 1984) have developed such a system, which they call *matrix outlining and analysis*. In this method, they teach students to outline responses to questions that ask for comparisons by using two-dimensional tables or matrices. Consider a question asking a student to "describe" (compare) colonial and local governments in early America before the American Revolution. The types of government would be the row headings of the matrix; the frame questions would be the column headings of the matrix. The three government frame questions are: Who governs? What powers do the leaders have? How do they get their powers? (See Figure 1a, p. 114). Once the matrix is completed, the student then can analyze the pattern of information in each column and row by specifying similarities and differences. Additionally, the student may use the matrix structure as the basis for organizing an oral or written response. Thus, a row generalization or probability statement may be a topic sentence that is supported by the information in the cells of that row. Through matrix outlining and analysis, it is possible to teach students to generate numerous high-level generalizations and to organize information for any number of paragraphs.

Similarly, Armbruster (1980) has developed an innovative system of outlining called *idea mapping* in which ideas are mapped in boxes according to certain rules she developed. Many of the frames in CIRCA are modifications of her definition of mapping. A frame that is frequently mapped in the CIRCA project is the problem-solving frame (see Figure 1b, p. 115).

To summarize, we have described several concepts and skills that would help students to respond to questions. First, it would be useful to teach students how to conduct *question analysis.* This means teaching students to analyze questions for the information they provide and for the information they require; i.e., the text structure that is implied or stated in the question. Second, students should be aware that questions require different *levels of thinking, given the text condition.* Third, students can use *frames* and *nonlinear outline structures* to help organize their answers.

HOW SHOULD RESPONSE INSTRUCTION BE TAUGHT?

Teaching Methods

One way to teach response instruction is by providing *explicit instruction,* as described by Pearson and Leys in this volume. Specifically, this means telling the students exactly what is expected on a step-by-step basis, providing guided practice, and then progressing to independent practice (Pearson and Gallagher, 1983). Explicit instruction is inherently *"top-down"* instruction in that the teacher begins instruction by providing general guidelines or rules followed by particular examples and practice.

In contrast, the teacher could sequence the same instruction by using a *"bottom-up"* approach. In this instruction the teacher begins by eliciting examples of the desired response from the class. Each example is examined for its merits. If one example is particularly good, it may be selected as a model response. Usually, though, the teacher works with the class as a group to formulate a response using the examples as a basis. Once good responses are obtained and the students are fairly familiar with the process of forming one, the teacher will elicit some general rules and guidelines followed by guided practice. Many of the methods articulated by content-area reading teachers involve bottom-up instruction with much emphasis on guiding the students as a group to figure out the best statement or response.

Modeling is another method of providing response instruction. In this method, the teacher ideally provides (1) one or more examples of models that illustrate various features of the expected responses, (2) comments that identify exactly what is good about each response, (3) sample thinking processes used to arrive at the response, and (4) guided practice with ample opportunities for editing, revision, and correction of errors.

Other Characteristics

It is crucial that response instruction should be *content driven* in two important ways. First, the content always should determine the prescribed text structure, regardless of its level of difficulty. That is, if the first chapter of the course focuses on questions about causal interactions, the teacher should not invent some description questions because descriptive text structures are easier to teach compared to cause/effect or explanation text structures. He or she should deal directly with causal analyses because that is the content in question. Second, the instruction should focus on teaching text structures as a *means* to understanding the content, not as an end in itself. It is very easy to lose balance here; one must constantly emphasize that text structures are merely a means of expressing ideas. Thus, instruction and correction of errors should constantly relate to the flow of ideas.

It is also crucial that response instruction involve a great deal of *interaction* with the students, regardless of the teaching method selected. That is, the teacher should frequently ask students to summarize, paraphrase, explain a point, defend an answer, or provide additional examples if the instruction is direct or involves modeling. The bottom-up approach is, of course, inherently interactive.

WHY SHOULD WE PROVIDE RESPONSE INSTRUCTION?

The answer to this question has to be somewhat anecdotal. In the course of doing experimental research, I was an observer in a high school that is recognized nationally as being outstanding in terms of student scores on the essay component of college entrance exams, college acceptance, and scholarships during college. What I saw surprised me at the time. On the day before a test, a teacher told the students what content to cover in the essay question and what paragraph structures to use throughout, paragraph by paragraph. I later learned that this training was part of a concerted schoolwide effort to train students to write a highly structured five-paragraph essay in all content areas. Similar procedures were followed for the junior term paper, including a 10-page handout specifying not only the content coverage and essay structure but also notetaking and studying procedures. Since then, I have discovered that there is a rather stable relationship between outstanding achievement among students and the type of response instruction prescribed above. Obversely, there seems to be an equally stable relationship between what Spady (1981) calls "vague-referenced" instruction (particularly regarding responses) and low achievement.

More recently, Bloom (1984) has been studying for several years the background of outstanding persons in all fields (musicians, chess players, scholars, etc.). He has found that what they have in common educationally is tutorial instruction, which is maximally high in providing *cues* as to what must be learned and the criteria for evaluation, *participation* (time on task), *correction of errors,* and *positive reinforcement.* It would seem that response instruction constitutes a substantial part of a tutoring model of instruction.

Additionally, Bloom has empirically established that the achievement level of students taught by the tutorial model is two standard deviations higher than that attained by traditional instruction. Currently, he is engaged in establishing what variables of instruction in typical classrooms might be altered to move the level of the average student toward the level of the most talented. Two variables that he has defined thus far are *enhanced cognitive entry level,* which teaches students the prerequisite content and skills they need for a given course, and *quality of instruction,* which seeks to provide high levels of instructional cues, participation, correction of errors, and positive reinforcement for whole groups.

Providing response instruction would generate the following:

1. high levels of cues, because the teacher tells the student directly what is to be learned and how to respond in order to attain the highest criteria of excellence
2. high levels of participation, because each student in the class responds to written questions, and responding is, by definition, participation

3. high levels of correcting errors, because the student is given the criteria for correcting errors in responses, is actively involved in an editing/revision process before submitting a final version, and often works to improve the version after it has been evaluated
4. high levels of reinforcement, because the teacher's role is that of helper and colleague in response instruction.

WHEN SHOULD RESPONSE INSTRUCTION BE GIVEN?

Elsewhere Jones, Friedman, Tinzmann, and Cox (1984) have argued that instruction for any given segment of text should involve three phases:

1. *Readiness instruction,* which seeks to preteach difficult vocabulary, relate the content to what is known, provide a purpose in reading, analysis of questions, and possibly estimate the likely response format on the basis of analyzing the question or surveying the features of the text such as titles and pictures
2. *Comprehension instruction,* which helps the student with "on-line" processing during reading as well as with constructing meanings from text after reading ("in-depth" processing)
3. *Response instruction,* which helps the student respond to questions about the text.

Thus, in one sense, response instruction actually may begin in the readiness phase if the students analyze questions before reading (e.g., a question asking the student to explain the effects of an event implies a compare/contrast text structure). Therefore, one purpose in reading would be to note the similarities and differences because the student must compare X before and after the event. The main thrust of response instruction, however, is after reading.

WHO SHOULD TEACH RESPONSE INSTRUCTION?

The answer to this question is unequivocal: everybody—teachers of students from kindergarten through graduate school in all subject areas. One of the reasons why instruction has become so fragmented in recent years is that content teachers often expect the reading teacher or the English teacher to provide all of the writing instruction. Yet, this is not possible because response instruction should be content driven, and teachers who teach reading, language arts, or English frequently are not sufficiently well versed in the content areas to teach the content and text structures needed for effective instruction. Essentially, a plea for response instruction is a plea to *integrate* the teaching of *writing* in the content areas with the concept teaching of *reading* in the content areas developed by Herber and others in this book.

HOW SHOULD RESPONSES BE SCORED?

Although there already are some excellent methods of scoring writing available, most of these were developed for the purposes of teaching composition, not a content subject. Scoring need not be complex; nor is there only one method. Perhaps the easiest method is to make brief outlines before teaching of the key points in the content, the key text structure elements such as the use of a specific text structure plus appropriate markers, and the level of response. These outlines should be the basis of teaching as well as of scoring. Moreover, while there are any number of ways to weight the various sets of scores, content coverage and level of thinking should receive the highest weights. An example of scoring an essay on the interaction of the Indians and Europeans in the New World is shown in Figure 2a (p. 116). A more systematic method developed for matrix outlining and analysis is shown in Figure 2b (p. 117).

About the Author

Beau Fly Jones is Director of Curriculum and Instruction at the North Central Regional Educational Laboratory, Elmhurst, Illinois.

FIGURE 1A. GOVERNMENT FRAME USING MATRIX OUTLINING AND ANALYSIS (from the *CIRCA Teacher's Manual, U.S. History, Grade 7,* reprinted with permission)

Political Essay, Part 1   Unit 2: Lesson 2

The Two Levels of Colonial Government

	Governing Unit	Power(s)	Source of Power(s)
F I R S T L E V E L	governor	(can veto laws)	(from the colony's owner)
	council	(passes laws for the entire cololny)	(from the colony's owner)
	assembly or legislature	(passes laws for the entire colony)	(elected by the colonists)
S E C O N D L E V E L	county and town officials	(make decisions on local problems; vote for government officials)	(elected by the colonists)
	people at town meetings	(make decisions on local problems)	(by living in the town) [not in the essay]
	justices of the peace	(make decisions that affect small areas of a colony)	(appointed by the governor)

**** END ****

EXPLANATION

1. You will use the government frame to record what you learn about government in the English colonies.

2. England set up two levels of government in its colonies; therefore, the government frame is divided into two parts.

3. The people who governed at the two levels are listed in the "Governing Unit" column of the government frame.

FIGURE 1B. FILLED-IN PROBLEM-SOLVING FRAME
(from the *CIRCA Teacher's Manual, U.S. History, Grade* 7, reprinted with permission)

Part 1, The First Presidency   Unit 4: Lesson 3

Questions for the Problem-Solving Frame

1. Who had the problem? (national government)

Problem

2. What was the problem? (a large national debt)

3. What caused this problem?	4. What were the negative effects?
(debts from the Revolutionary War such as loans from other countries, loans from American citizens, back pay due to soldiers, and overdue bills from merchants)	(America was a bad credit risk; other countries would not lend money to the new nation; Americans were fearful of investing their money in the government.)

Attempted Solutions

5. What actions were taken to solve the problem?	6. What were the results of these actions?
(Tariff Act passed)	(raised some funds but not enough)
(Hamilton proposed a financial plan to--	
1. pay war debts in full	(greatly improved the nation's credit rating, but many Americans and Europeans continued to distrust America's financial condition)
2. assume war debts of the states	
3. establish a National Bank	
4. pass an excise tax on whiskey.)	(led to the Whiskey Rebellion in Pennsylvania)

**** END ****

FIGURE 2A. SCORING PROCEDURES USED FOR AN ESSAY ON CAUSE-EFFECT RELATIONS (reprinted with permission)

Exploration   Test: TM-4

Paragraph Question (26.-31.)

Directions - WRITE a paragraph that summarizes the results of the economic interaction of the native Americans and the Europeans in the New World. The topic sentence has been written for you. Use the following steps to construct your paragraph:

Step 1.   SUMMARIZE the results of the economic interaction for the Indians in a sentence or two. INCLUDE at least two results.

Step 2.   SUMMARIZE the results of the economic interaction for the Europeans in a sentence or two. INCLUDE at least two results.

Step 3.   CONTRAST the results for the Indians and the results for the Europeans in a sentence.

REMEMBER that you can earn bonus points by including extra information and by constructing a well-written paragraph.

SCORING KEY

Step 1 Indian results - traded away their land - driven from their land - conquered by the Europeans	2 points for two results	1 bonus point for third result
Step 2 European results - found gold and silver - became wealthy and powerful - Spain established a large empire in Central and South America	2 points for two results	1 bonus point for third result
Step 3 Contrast of results - Indians hurt by conflict - Europeans helped by conflict	2 points	

Award one or two bonus points to a paragraph if it includes "something extra," such as supporting details, a generalization, or a connecting sentence.

FIGURE 2B. SCORING CARD USED WITH MATRIX OUTLINING AND ANALYSIS (reprinted with permission)

COMPARE-AND-CONTRAST ESSAY (CAC) CHECKLIST

INSTRUCTIONS. One checklist and grade sheet below will be used by your teacher to grade your CAC. As you write use the structure (S) column as a checklist to make sure that you have the correct number and types of sentences for each paragraph. After you have completed your essay, make a check (✓) in the column labeled (S) for each sentence that is present, accurate, and properly positioned. Each sentence does not necessarily have to be in the order listed as long as it is well-integrated in the paragraph structure. However, if the sentence is grossly out of order, make an "X" in the (S) column and do not count it as a credit. The number of checks will be the number grade you receive for Structure. Quality will be assessed by the teacher according to the criteria in the right column. Quality scores for each sentence go in the column marked (Q).

	S	Q	CRITERIA FOR GRADING QUALITY
INTRODUCTORY PARAGRAPH (1)			
Introductory sentences			Grabs reader's attention; sets stage (20)
Explanation of the title			Obvious (1); Original (2-3)
Thesis statement (col. gen.)			Specifics sims./diffs. (3); Discovery gen. (5)
Statement of purpose			Mention of attribute categories (1)
Transition sentence			Element from Intro (1); Element from Par. 2 (1)
FIRST MIDDLE PARAGRAPH (2)			
Topic sentence			Makes comparative statement (3); Specifies sims. (2); Specifies diffs. (2); Finds underlying com. ele. (5)
Detail, example or quote #1			Adequate (1); Good (2)
Detail, example or quote #2			Adequate (1); Good (2)
Wrap-up sentence(s)			Literal or paraphrase (1); Analytical (2-3)
Transition sentence			Element from 2 (1); Element from 3 (1)
*Use of signal words			Appropriate Use (1-2)
SECOND MIDDLE PARAGRAPH (3)			
Topic sentence			Makes comparative statement (3);
CONCLUSION (5)			
Restatement of thesis			Review (1); Paraphrased review (2)
*Col. relationship generaliz'tn			Obvious (1); Shows insight (2-3)
Causal inference			Obvious (1); Shows insight (2-3)
Supporting evidence:			Weak (1); Strong (2-3)
Probability statement			Obvious (1); Shows insight (2-3)
Supporting evidence:			Weak (1); Strong (2-3)
Closing statement			Appropriateness (1)
*Use of signal words			Appropriate Use (1-2)

*Optional

OVERVIEW OF A SAMPLE LESSON SUMMARIZING AN INTERACTION FRAME

Grade levels: 7–8   *Subject:* United States History

Question/task: Summarize the interaction frame for the International Essay on the French and Indian War.

Interaction frame: Much of history involves the interaction of *two or more groups of people.* A useful way to comprehend descriptions of these interactions is to use the interaction frame. In its simplest version, this frame involves asking the following questions: (1) What are the *goals* of each group? (2) What actions did each group take to reach its goals? (3) What was the nature of the *interaction?* (4) What were the *results* of the interaction for each group?

Text structure: Compare/contrast   *Time:* One class lesson

Materials: The materials for this lesson were taken from the CIRCA project, the Collaboration to Improve Reading in the Content Area. The collaborators are the Chicago Public Schools and the Center for the Study of Reading, University of Illinois, Urbana-Champaign. CIRCA materials consist of a *Summary Text,* which includes summary essays on each period of United States history, a *Teacher Manual,* which provides guidelines for in-depth instruction for each unit, and *Student Notebook.* These materials are used in conjunction with regular classroom textbooks. The materials shown are from the *Teacher Manual.*

Teaching procedures
1. Ask the students to *survey* the title and subtitles from the International Essay in the CIRCA *Summary Text* (not shown).
2. *Elicit* from the students:
- *predictions* regarding the content of the essay.
- a *rationale* for which frame to use (the interaction frame, because the essay deals with the interactions of the French/ Indians and English/Colonists during the French and Indian War).
3. Ask the students to *read* the essay, *correct* their predictions, and *add* any new information.
4. *Guide* the students to *map* the ideas from the essay into the interaction frame in Activity A (Figure 3a, p. 119).
5. *Guide* the students to *construct* a summary of the interaction frame (Figure 3b, p. 120).

Note that this lesson provides readiness instruction, comprehension instruction, and response instruction. Response instruction actually begins during readiness instruction when the teacher asks the students to use the title, subtitles, and graphics to decide which frame to use. The steps above are paraphrases of the actual instruction.

FIGURE 3A. INTERACTION FRAME FOR THE INTERNATIONAL ESSAY ON THE FRENCH AND INDIAN WAR
(reprinted with permission)

International Essay, Parts 1 and 2   Unit 2: Lesson 16

The French and Indian War: Conflict over the Ohio Valley

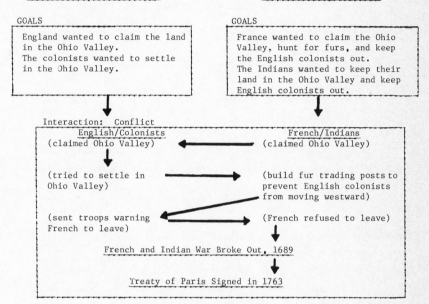

Allies: English/Colonists   Allies: French/Indians

GOALS

England wanted to claim the land
in the Ohio Valley.
The colonists wanted to settle
in the Ohio Valley.

GOALS

France wanted to claim the Ohio
Valley, hunt for furs, and keep
the English colonists out.
The Indians wanted to keep their
land in the Ohio Valley and keep
English colonists out.

Interaction: Conflict

English/Colonists   French/Indians
(claimed Ohio Valley)   (claimed Ohio Valley)

(tried to settle in   (build fur trading posts to
Ohio Valley)   prevent English colonists
                                         from moving westward)

(sent troops warning   (French refused to leave)
French to leave)

French and Indian War Broke Out, 1689

Treaty of Paris Signed in 1763

English/Colonial Results

England
-England won the war.
-England got the land in Canada
 and east of the Mississippi
 River.
-England became the major Euro-
 pean power in North America.
-Inference: England lost some of
 its power over the colonies.

Colonists
-Colonists grew more independent
 of England.
-Colonies became more unified
 with each other.
-New lands in the west were
 opened for settlement by the
 colonists.

French/Indian Results

France
-France lost the war.
-France lost Canada and all of
 the territory east of the
 Mississippi River.

Indians
-Indian tribes lost their land
 in the Ohio Valley.

**** END ****

FIGURE 3B. RESPONSE INSTRUCTION FOR SUMMARIZING AN INTERACTION FRAME (reprinted with permission)

International Essay, Parts 1 and 2   Unit 2: Lesson 16

Example Summary

The French and Indian War: Conflict in the Ohio Valley

The French and Indian War began over the ownership and use of the land and resources in the Ohio Valley. On one side of the conflict were the English and the colonists. On the other side were the French and the Indians.

What were the goals of each group?
The goal of England and the colonists was to claim the land in the Ohio Valley and establish settlements there. The goal of the French and Indians was also to claim or keep the land in the Ohio Valley and to keep the English colonists out.

(Why did the goals of the two groups of allies lead to a conflict?)
The shared goal, to claim the Ohio Valley, led to a conflict interaction because each pair of allies wanted to use the land in a way that interfered with the wishes of the other pair of allies. For example, if the English and colonists built settlements, less land would be available to the Indians for hunting or to the French for fur trapping. Therefore, the French and Indians wanted to keep the English colonists out of the Ohio Valley.

(What actions and responses did each group take to reach their goal?)
To reach their goals, the colonists tried to settle in the Ohio Valley and the French built fur trading posts to prevent the English colonists from moving westward. The English responded by sending troops warning the French to leave the Ohio Valley, but the French refused. Consequently, the French and Indian War began and eventually ended with the signing of the Treaty of Paris in 1763.

(What were the results of the war and treaty for England, France, and the Indians?)
As a result of the war and treaty, England won the war, took control of most of the land in North America, and became the major European power in North America. On the other hand, France lost nearly all of its land claims in North America and the Indian tribes who had supported them also lost their lands in the Ohio Valley.

OVERVIEW OF A SAMPLE LESSON USING MATRIX OUTLINING AND ANALYSIS

Grade levels: 4–8   *Subject:* Literature

Question/task: What techniques did the author use to reveal the character traits of the main character? Compare/contrast characters 1 and 2 with regard to character traits.

Text structures: Description; Compare/contrast   *Time:* Variable

Materials: The materials for this lesson are from the Chicago Mastery Learning Reading (CMLR) book *Applying Comprehension Instruction to Fiction and Nonfiction.* The first part of this book is devoted to a series of generic activities that systematically utilizes two progressions: (1) from speaking to writing, and (2) from description to compare/contrast. The series shown in Figures 4a and 4b seeks to apply the concepts of character traits from CMLR to literature. The instruction begins by reviewing typical character traits orally. Then two or more characters are identified. The class describes each character at length through discussion, and the teacher helps the students organize the information in the matrix. Then, the matrix is used as the basis for writing paragraphs.

Teaching procedures

1. *Review* the concept of character procedure traits, and *discuss* the difference between moods, character traits, and facts about a character. (This procedure is optional, but many students have difficulty with this task.)

2. *Identify* the characters to compare/contrast, and *write* them on the chalkboard in a matrix such as Figure 4a (p. 122).

3. *List* the traits for each character.

4. *Discuss* how each trait was revealed (e.g., author's statement, metaphor, dialogue, character's action, etc.), and *write* them in a matrix such as Figure 4a.

5. *Ask* the students to *describe* the traits of character 1 using the writing paradigm in Figure 4b (p. 123).

6. *Review* the signal words for compare/contrast paragraphs (see Figure 4c, p. 124).

7. *Ask* the students to *compare/contrast* traits of characters 1 and 2 using the writing paradigm in Figure 4d (p. 125).

FIGURE 4A. CHART OR MATRIX SHOWING CHARACTER TRAITS AND AUTHOR'S TECHNIQUES FOR EACH CHARACTER
(reprinted with permission)

Language Arts Activities   F-4-2
  for Fiction

CHARACTER TRAITS

4. Have the students list the character traits on a chart.

Pablo	José	Mary
brave	cowardly	honest
gloomy	cheerful	brave
impatient	friendly	cheerful
loving	mean	friendly
suspicious	irresponsible	neat
responsible	destructive	patient
self-reliant	bragging	modest
		loving

5. Have a discussion of the characters' similarities and differences

Analyzing Character Traits

1. Have the students analyze each character's traits by connecting the traits with the character's actions and the reasons for these actions. For example:

Character	Action	Reason	Trait
Dan	He leaves his pen.	He wants the detective to be misled.	tricky cunning
the detective	He sees the pen and assumes Dan is trying to be misleading.	He assumes that the witnesses will try to trick him.	smart alert

2. Continue this chart form with each of the actions the group wishes to discuss. All the major characters involved in each action should be analyzed.

Copyright © 1982, Board of Education of the City of Chicago, Chicago, Illinois
Published by Mastery Education Corp.

FIGURE 4B. INSTRUCTION FOR WRITING A DESCRIPTIVE PARAGRAPH (reprinted with permission)

Language Arts Activities   F-4-3
  for Fiction

CHARACTER TRAITS

Writing a Character Trait Paragraph

1. Have the students write a paragraph describing a character trait. Use the chart on F-4-1.

2. Explain that the paragraph should contain the following:

   • a topic sentence stating the character's name, the book title, and the trait

   • details showing how the trait was revealed--should be varied to include a character's action(s), a character's dialog or thought, and direct statement of the author.

3. Explain that the paragraph should look like this:

> Topic sentence defining the character, book title, and trait
>
>> Elaboration of the topic sentence (e.g., the author shows the generosity of a character by his/her direct statement and by the character's actions and dialog)
>>
>> 1. Example or quote showing the character's actions are generous (e.g., the character spends a lot of time making a gift for a friend)
>>
>> 2. Example or quote showing the character's dialog or thoughts are generous (e.g., the character says, "I really enjoy making things for other people.")
>>
>> 3. Example or quote of the author's direct statement (e.g., the author says that the character "was a kind and generous person")

4. Point out, where appropriate, that this paragraph is identical in structure to the paragraph about mood.

FIGURE 4C. FRAME OF COMPARE-CONTRAST SIGNAL WORDS
(reprinted with permission)

Language Arts Activities   F-4-4
   for Fiction

CHARACTER TRAITS

Comparing and Contrasting Character Traits

1. Have the students write a paragraph showing the similarities and
   differences between two characters.

2. List the compare-and-contrast signal words on the chalkboard.

in contrast (to)	like/alike
whereas	as
in opposition (to)	both/and
unlike	also
than	similar/similarly
while	identical
but	although
compared to	resemble
different/difference	share
however	the same as
on the one (other) hand	have in common

3. Explain that a compare-and-contrast character traits paragraph should
   contain the following:

   · an introductory sentence identifying the characters and title of
     the book

   · a general statement summarizing how the characters are similar and/or
     different

   · a more specific, but still general, statement telling how the
     characters are <u>similar</u>

   · details supporting the generalization regarding similarities

   · a second general statement stating how the characters are <u>different</u>

   · details supporting the generalization regarding differences.

FIGURE 4D. INSTRUCTION FOR WRITING A COMPARE-CONTRAST PARAGRAPH (reprinted with permission)

Language Arts Activities
  for Fiction   F-4-5

CHARACTER TRAITS

4. Explain that the paragraph should have the following structure:

> Introductory sentence identifying the characters and the title of the book

> Generalization summarizing how the two characters are alike (e.g., both are independent) and/or different (e.g., one is independent; the other is dependent)

> 1. Generalization stating how one knows both characters are independent (e.g., both think for themselves)
>
>> a. Example or quote from the book for character A
>>
>> b. Example or quote from the book for character B

> 2. Generalization showing how the characters are different (e.g., whereas character A is independent and thinks for himself, character B is dependent and relies on the opinions of others)
>
>> a. Example or quote from the book for character A
>>
>> b. Example or quote from the book for character B

OVERVIEW OF A SAMPLE LESSON TO COMPARE/CONTRAST VOCABULARY TERMS

Grade level: 6   *Subject:* Reading/Social Studies

Question/task: Learn a list of *related* geography terms. Be ready to compare/contrast their meaning.

Instructional strategy: Often when teachers ask students to learn a list of vocabulary terms, they do not state explicitly that students should be prepared to compare/contrast related terms, or tell them how to study for such a task. In the instruction that follows, response instruction is only one step out of a seven-step study procedure. In preliminary instruction, students are given the seven steps in two phases; a comprehension phase and an in-depth study phase. The *comprehension phase* has five steps: (1) read definition, (2) paraphrase it, (3) extract key words, (4) establish category label and sort the list of words into categories, (5) establish related words. The *study phase* involves (6) compare/contrast and (7) corrective review.

Text structure: Compare/contrast   *Time:* One class period

Materials: The materials for this lesson were taken from the *Vocabulary Learning Strategies* strand of Chicago Mastery Learning Reading. The lesson is from a long unit on categorizing geography terms. In this unit, students are given a long list of alphabetized words. Many words are *familiar.* The students are required to look up unfamiliar words and relate them to familiar words by establishing the category label and familiar unrelated words. At this point, they are ready to compare/contrast.

Teaching procedures

1. *Provide* the students with an alphabetized list of related geography terms: e.g., acid rain, bayou, butte, canyon, channel, conservation, continent, crater, delta, desert, drought, ecosystem, endangered species, erosion, food chain, gulf, island, isthmus. (Note that the list contains both familiar and unfamiliar words.)

2. *Explain* that each of these words are related to one of three categories: land formation, water formation, or ecology. *Explain* that students will categorize the related words into one of the three categories using the seven-step procedure.

3. *Explain* that the students will first work through four *comprehension steps*: *Read* the definition (which is provided). *Paraphrase* it (using five rules for paraphrasing provided in the materials). *Extract the key words. Establish the category label* (land formation, water formation, or ecology factor) and sort each of the alphabetized words into one of the three categories.

4. *Identify* closely related terms *within* each category (e.g., butte and plateau, bay and gulf, peninsula and island).

5. *Ask* the students to write compare/contrast summaries for each set of closely related words. Use the thinking/writing

FIGURE 5A. RESPONSE INSTRUCTION TO COMPARE-CONTRAST GEOGRAPHY TERMS (reprinted with permission)

Comparing and Contrasting   SA-5-3

CATEGORIZING

EXAMPLE

> **butte** - a hill that rises sharply from the flat area around it and has a flat top, steep sides
>
> **plateau** - a large, raised or elevated section of flat land
>
> <u>Ask yourself</u>: How are they the same?
>
> <u>Compare</u>:   Both a butte and a plateau are flat, and they are raised above the surrounding land.
>
> <u>Ask yourself</u>: How are they different?
>
> <u>Contrast</u>:   A plateau is a large section of land and a butte is not.
>
> Summarizing Sentence: A butte and a plateau are both a type of raised, flat land, but a plateau is larger than a butte.

Explanation: Both **butte** and **plateau** belong to the same category called land formations. They are alike because they are both raised, flat areas; however, they are different because a plateau is larger than a butte. Because you compared and contrasted the terms, you now have a working knowledge of the terms **butte** and **plateau**.

In the following activity, you will use the Compare and Contrast Strategy to help you distinguish or tell the likeness and difference between two similar things. Try using the categorizing and visualizing strategies to do this exercise. If you need help, look back at SA-4-1 through SA-4-3.

Copyright © 1984, Board of Education of the City of Chicago, Chicago, Illinois
Published by Mastery Education Corp.

FIGURE 5B. PRACTICE EXERCISE IN RESPONDING
(reprinted with permission)

Comparing and Contrasting   SA-5-3

CATEGORIZING

EXERCISE B INSTRUCTIONS

1. WRITE a Compare statement for each set of terms.

2. WRITE a Contrast statement for each set.

3. WRITE a summarizing sentence. Try using visualizing to help you
   write your summarizing sentence. The first pair has been done
   for you.

EXERCISE B PAIRS

1. bay/gulf

   Compare: A bay and a gulf are alike in that they are both bodies
            of water and they are both parts of an ocean, a sea, or
            a lake.

   Contrast: A bay and a gulf are different in that a bay is smaller
             than a gulf.

   Sentence: A bay and a gulf are both bodies of water that are a
             part of a sea or an ocean, but a bay is smaller than
             a gulf.

2. peninsula/island

   Compare: *A peninsula and island are alike in that both are an*

            area of land surrounded by water.

   Contrast: *The difference between the two is: an island is an area*

             of land that is completely surrounded by water. A

             peninsula is an area of land that is almost surrounded

             by water.

   Sentence: *A peninsula and an island are both areas of land*

             surrounded by water; but a peninsula is almost surrounded

             by water and an island is completely surrounded by water.

References

Armbruster, B.B. *"Mapping": An Innovative Reading Comprehension/Studying Strategy.* Paper presented at the annual meeting of the American Educational Research Association, Boston, April 1980.

Armbruster, B.B. and T.H. Anderson, "Content Area Textbooks." In R.C. Anderson, J. Osborn, and R.J. Tierney (Eds.), *Learning to Read in American Schools: Basal Readers and Content Texts.* Hillsdale, N.J.: Erlbaum, 1984.

Armbruster, B.B., T.H. Anderson, R. Bruning, and L.A. Meyer. *What Did You Mean by That Question? A Taxonomy of American History Questions* (Reading Education Report No. 308). Urbana: University of Illinois, Center for the Study of Reading, 1983.

Bloom, B.S. "Methods of Whole Group Instruction Which Are as Effective as One-to-one Tutoring." *Educational Leadership* (1984) 41, 4-17.

Durkin, D. "What Classroom Observations Reveal about Reading Comprehension Instruction." *Reading Research Quarterly* (1978-79) 15, 481–533.

Jones, B.F., M.R. Amiran, and M. Katims. "Teaching Cognitive Strategies and Text Structures Within Language Arts Programs." In J. Segal, S.F. Chipman, R. Glaser (Eds.), *Thinking and Learning Skills: Relating Basic Research to Instructional Practices* (Vol. 1). Hillsdale, N.J.: Erlbaum, 1984.

Jones, B.F., L.B. Friedman, M. Tinzmann, and B.E. Cox. *Content-Driven Comprehension Instruction and Assessment.* Rosslyn, Va.: Manual developed through InterAmerica Research Associates' Basic Skills Resource Center, funded by U.S. Army Research Institute for the Behavioral and Social Sciences, 1984.

Pearson, P.D. and M.C. Gallagher. *The Instruction of Reading Comprehension* (Technical Report No. 297). Urbana: University of Illinois, Center for the Study of Reading, 1983.

Raphael, T. and P.D. Pearson. *The Effect of Metacognitive Training in Children's Question-Answering Behavior* (Technical Report No. 238).

Urbana: University of Illinois, Center for the Study of Reading, 1982.

Salomon, M. and T.M. Auchenbach. "Effects of Four Kinds of Tutoring Experiences on Associative Responding in Children." *American Educational Research Journal* (1984) 11, 395–405.

Spady, W.G. "Outcome-Based Schools: The Obvious Need and the Emerging Response." *Educational Technology,* March 1981.

Part III
Interactive Comprehension Strategies

A frequent obstacle to the improvement of comprehension is the conception of instruction as something that is externally motivated by the teacher, is likewise targeted by the teacher to a specific objective, and is immediately measurable so that there is evidence that learning has or has not occurred. Such an instructional concept minimizes student-teacher and student-student interaction. This mechanistic interpretation of instruction also is being challenged by the newer cognitive psychology—one that views effective learning as essentially self-motivated; as consciously monitored by the learner toward multilevel goals, including that of the teacher; and as transferable to other learning situations.

The articles in this section illustrate teaching approaches designed to persuade the learner to assume more and more responsibility for the structuring of effective comprehension processes. Instruction moves from carefully modeled desired behaviors by the teacher to guided instruction and then to independent action by the students. Each approach emphasizes making the learner "aware of thinking" —a notion often currently referred to by the formidable term *metacognition*—through much classroom dialogue and discussion as the strategies are being developed. Since the learning involves generalizable strategic processes, the learning outcomes tend to be highly transferable and hence functional.

The concept of teaching reflected in these articles is one of a teaching-learning partnership. If the challenge of such a cognitive conception of the teaching-learning task in developing comprehension and thinking strategies is accepted, then the prospect for better comprehenders and thinkers in our schools is encouraging.

Teachers may propose reading strategies, but students dispose of them. Can students be taught not only to become aware of and understand effective comprehension and cognitive strategies, but to accept them and use them? Paris describes a learning-teaching model that features student-teacher and student-student interaction in a series of classroom dialogues and guided practice sessions that have been shown to help students become self-generated reading strategists.

Using Classroom Dialogues and Guided Practice to Teach Comprehension Strategies

Scott G. Paris

In most schools in the United States, reading instruction is surprisingly similar. More than 90 percent of American school children use basal readers and workbooks, and teachers' main instruction revolves around passages and exercises from these texts. Most teachers divide their students into small reading groups, based on children's abilities, and emphasize oral reading for young readers. Beginning readers also practice word attack skills, phonics drills, and sight vocabularies; older children spend more time on solitary drills such as silent reading and workbook exercises. Despite the widespread use of these methods, recent research has revealed that little instruction on comprehension skills occurs in these classroom routines (Durkin, 1978–79; 1981). Teachers may mention strategies occasionally, but they mostly follow advice in the teacher's manuals and ask questions about the content of the basal passages. Students are expected to acquire effective comprehension skills through practice without being taught specifically how to scan, reread, elaborate, or summarize information.

The problem, of course, is that practice is not sufficient for many

133

students. They never acquire effective reading strategies. This is a paradox because research has shown that strategies can be powerful aids to reading comprehension, studying, and learning (Brown, Armbruster, and Baker, 1984). The timing is even more puzzling because children from 8 to 15 years of age are capable of learning a great deal about problem-solving strategies (Gagne and Dick, 1983; Paris and Lindauer, 1982; Resnick, 1983). Why do teachers fail to teach children about cognitive strategies at just the right time in their development and schooling? The reasons may be due in part to the lack of information in professional training and published materials. Or teachers may think that children are not ready to learn about strategies in elementary grades. Or they may think it is too difficult to teach students these kinds of abstract reasoning. Whatever the reasons have been, it appears that our expectations were too pessimistic. Research during the past five years has shown repeatedly that students can be taught to use reading strategies through direct classroom instruction (Pearson and Gallagher, 1983). But before I present some practical teaching methods, I want to discuss some critical aspects of reading strategies and guided instruction.

READING STRATEGIES

There are many general reading strategies that we expect students to learn. Some occur before reading, some "on-line," and some are applied after the text is read. Consider the kinds of strategies that teachers would like to observe in 10- to 12-year-olds. Skilled readers might evaluate the task, examine the topic, and estimate the difficulty before reading. They might pause as they read to check on their understanding. They also probably will make inferences, reread parts, and summarize the main points when they finish. Brown, Palincsar, and Armbruster (1984) reviewed many reading curricula and identified six fundamental comprehension strategies:

1. understanding the purposes of reading
2. activating relevant background knowledge
3. allocating attention to main ideas
4. critical evaluation
5. monitoring comprehension
6. drawing inferences

These comprehension activities are important because strategic reading leads to self-directed learning, and it is not surprising to find consensus among various curricula. But, despite identification of relevant strategies, there are few methods recognized for teaching the skills to students.

The critical problem is how to make these invisible cognitive processes meaningful to students. Researchers have observed that children can be trained to use cognitive strategies to improve attention, memory, and communication by becoming aware of what the strategies are, how they work, and when to apply them (Paris and Lindauer, 1982). Children need to evaluate their own comprehension, plan sequences of actions, and regulate their reading behavior to adjust to changing conditions. These kinds of reflection on one's own thinking are called *metacognition.* Awareness of various strategies and the benefits of using them appropriately are important for learning how to use cognitive strategies independently. Independence is required so that students do not rely on teachers' help to analyze text and to solve comprehension difficulties. Strategic readers have the knowledge and motivation to use the strategies as self-directed aids for learning.

What kinds of metacognitive knowledge underlie the acquisition of reading strategies? There seems to be three categories of information that students need to acquire (Paris, Lipson, and Wixson, 1983). The first is called *declarative knowledge* and reflects "knowing that" propositions about reading. For example, children learn that titles provide cues to meaning and that there are differences between fiction and nonfiction. The second category of information refers to "knowing how," or *procedural knowledge.* For example, children learn how to skim by reading only occasional, "high-information" words. The third category of information is knowing when to apply strategies and why they are effective. Paris, Lipson, and Wixson (1983) refer to this as *conditional knowledge* to emphasize that it is important for students to understand the pragmatic value of reading strategies. Students have to be convinced that the actions are reasonable, worth the extra effort, and functionally effective. Without a thorough understanding, it seems unlikely that students will elect to use strategies without direct supervision. Thus, instruction that promotes students' declarative, procedural, and conditional knowledge also should promote their use of self-controlled reading strategies.

GUIDED INSTRUCTION

Knowing about reading strategies will not insure that students use them while they read. Teaching is more than telling; the information must be supplemented with a rationale for using strategies. This is where motivation blends with knowledge and where teaching and learning interact. The responsibility to use reading strategies must be shifted from teacher to student so that learning is self-regulated and not done merely for compliance or external rewards. Students need to internalize guidance that is provided initially by someone else so that they can provide their own criticism and motivation. The steps involved in shifting responsibility can include the following forms of instruction: informing, modeling, guiding, observing, correcting, and encouraging. Repeated cycles of such learning and teaching resemble coaching more than didactic "information giving." Indeed, this type of guided learning is how parents usually teach children routine skills such as cooking, fishing, and game-playing (Rogoff and Gardner, 1984). It is also the basis for reciprocal teaching, a method used successfully by Palincsar and Brown (1984) to teach study strategies to junior high school students.

How can teachers convey information to students about the benefits of strategies and the necessity to use them on their own? Most researchers agree that interactive learning facilitates persuasion. Students need to talk with each other about the tasks and options in order to see how various plans might be implemented. Through reciprocal teaching (i.e., situations in which students and teachers exchange roles) or peer tutoring, they can act as teachers as well as students. In this fashion they can adopt the role of an external monitor for someone else just as they need to act as an internal monitor for their own reading. As Vygotsky (1978) noted, this kind of interactive learning helps to shift the responsibility for recruiting and applying cognitive strategies from teachers to students.

Classroom dialogues are fundamental to this transfer because they give students opportunities to express their ideas. This allows teachers to listen to students' ideas so that they can gain an appreciation of students' concepts and attitudes about reading. Conversations in classrooms also help to "make thinking public" so that students can learn from one another. As they assert, defend, and question their ideas about their own reading and studying skills, they are being persuaded about the value of effective strategies. There are many ways in which teachers can stimulate Socratic discussions about thinking skills. We have found that these dialogues can be facilitated by using metaphors for strategies. For example, we have encouraged children as young as 7 to 8 years old to talk about what they need to do in order to "be a reading detective" or "plan a reading trip." These metaphors stimulate children to relate reading to other problem-solving tasks so they can generate similar plans and strategies for cognitive objectives such as reading, skimming, and studying. The metaphors facilitate communication about abstract skills. They make the strategies seem sensible and tangible because students can relate specific actions to each one. They also can perceive the need to use them by analogy.

In summary, teachers do not directly instruct students about reading strategies very often. This is paradoxical given the importance of strategies and the readiness of students to learn about them. Guided instruction appears to be an effective way to inform students about the existence of reading strategies. It also provides modeling, feedback, and persuasion so that students can internalize teachers' regulation of comprehension skills. Group discussions and direct instruction can provide information about declarative, procedural, and conditional aspects of strategies. Classroom dialogues also provide stimulation and motivation to use the strategies. In the following section, I discuss some ways in which we have taught reading strategies to children and sketch some lesson plans for different reading strategies.

INFORMED STRATEGIES FOR LEARNING

During the past five years, we have created a program for teaching comprehension strategies to third and fifth graders that we call Informed Strategies for Learning (ISL). We chose this name to emphasize that teachers provide information about strategies explicitly to students who in turn become informed about the metacognitive aspects of learning strategies. The program is based on group discussions and explicit instruction about the value of reading strategies. The fundamental purpose of each lesson is to inform students about reading strategies: what they are, how to use them, when to apply them, and why they are functional and necessary. These ideas are not often taught directly, and we found that both teachers and students were eager to talk about reading strategies. In our first study, Marjorie Lipson, an experienced teacher and colleague on the project, visited two third-grade and two fifth-grade classrooms each week for four months to provide the special ISL lessons. The regular classroom teachers observed and participated in the lessons, and we encouraged them to incorporate the ideas into their teaching. To help them understand and anticipate our instruction, we gave them 2-to-3-page lesson plans in advance of each week's instruction.

As we designed ISL, it became evident immediately that the first problem we had to tackle was how to translate abstract ideas about cognitive strategies into comprehensible notions for 8- and 10-year-olds. We chose metaphors because they provide easy vehicles for communication and offer concrete bases for depicting and discussing strategies. For example, a corral of horses illustrated how "rounding up your ideas" is similar to summarizing the main points of a story. We were pleasantly surprised to observe how quickly students grasped the analogies and how easily they extended the concepts to reading. The tangible actions of using strategies were also easy to communicate and to recall with cues such as "rounding up ideas," "searching for clues," and "planning your reading trip."

Our choice of metaphors as an instructional device was fortunate because it represented active agents (e.g., detectives) using specific strategies to solve concrete problems. The correspondence to strategies for reading, and indeed for writing, studying, and learning, is direct and obvious. We also realized that the metaphors were fun. They stimulated teachers and students to think analogically. I was pleasantly surprised to observe a class discussing planning to read and to hear one fifth grader say, "It's like my Dad told me about sailing. You have to have a rudder on the boat to make it go where you want. That's what a reading plan is like—a rudder on a boat that steers you where you want to go."

But what was the actual instruction like? Each lesson began with a focus on the bulletin board. These were large colorful displays that were changed each week with a new module. Students were asked to read the title and to observe the metaphor. Discussion was directed immediately to the analogy with reading and the implications for how we read. For example, planning an automobile trip is like planning to read because you need to know your destination before you start, you need a good map, and you should observe your progress and speed along the way. These kinds of similarities were promoted by several focal questions, written on each bulletin board, that directed children to ask themselves questions as they read (e.g., "What is my reading goal?"). Following this introductory discussion, each comprehension strategy was modeled for students as they read a chart story, overhead projection, or worksheet. As the teacher showed students how to use the strategy, the teacher also discussed how, when, and why it helped reading comprehension.

The remainder of each lesson was devoted to guided practice. Students were given reading assignments, mostly worksheets to be read silently but also group tasks that could involve oral reading. Now students were required to generate and apply the strategies on their own, seeking help from the teacher or peers only when they became confused or thwarted. Each lesson concluded with feedback provided in group discussions so that students could share their perceptions of the benefits and problems associated with each strategy. This is a very important phase of ISL because it promotes whole-class discussions of the skills students are expected to learn. Students share their feelings with each other and the teacher—an experience that is altogether too infrequent in many classrooms. These dialogues also permit teachers to assess the difficulty of the lessons as well as the effectiveness of their instruction immediately and informally. We found that whole-group instruction promoted cooperation among students and removed the stigma and boredom of reading groups. The poorest readers were often the most vocal participants in discussions because they could talk about reading even if they had difficulty actually reading. An additional difference between ISL lessons and traditional reading groups is the focus on direct instruction of skills and questions about skill learning as opposed to content learning. Parenthetically, I should add that we varied the content of the passages used in ISL lessons to include poetry, news articles, fiction, history, science, etc. We also stressed the application of strategies in all reading situations and not just school tasks.

Our initial study was quite successful. The children in our four experimental classrooms showed significant gains in awareness and use of reading strategies compared to four control classes (Paris and Jacobs, in press; Paris, Cross, and Lipson, in press). Children who understood reading strategies and goals and how to plan and regulate their reading consistently received higher scores on comprehension tests. The ISL lessons promoted awareness and use of strategies as measured by interviews and actual reading performance. For example, students in experimental classes were significantly better at using context to fill in missing words in a cloze task and they were much better at detecting errors in passages.

The success of our project encouraged us to expand ISL and to revise the lessons so that they could be used easily by regular classroom teachers. We revised ISL to include complete lesson plans and materials for third-grade and fifth-grade teachers. Our most recent version of ISL includes 20 instructional modules grouped into units of five related skills or concepts. The first group emphasizes evaluating the task and planning how to read. The second group focuses on levels of meaning. The third group emphasizes strategies for reasoning during reading. The fourth group teaches students how to monitor and repair comprehension breakdowns. The fifth group reviews and integrates the four previous skills and concepts. We found that a sequence of instruction with periodic reviews helps students to appreciate a conceptual and strategic orientation to reading.

Bulletin boards depicting the metaphors for each module served as concrete reminders to students to use the strategies. The metaphors were used in the lessons and repeated in the worksheets so that students felt comfortable with the analogies and vocabulary (e.g., roadsigns for reading or tracking down the main idea). We used a "fading technique" to shift responsibility to students (Pearson and Gallagher, 1983). Each module included three lessons; each one required approximately thirty minutes. The first lesson introduced the strategy and provided explicit modeling on how to use it. The second lesson required students to apply it with less guidance, and the third, or bridging, lesson required students to use the strategy in other content-area assignments. In a sense, practice was informed and guided until students could use the strategies independently.

In addition to the lesson plans and materials, we also provided teachers with periodic inservice workshops in which they learned about the theoretical principles of metacognition, reading strategies, and informed instruction. They also learned about instructional formats such as group discussions, metaphors, and guided practice that are alternatives to traditional reading groups. Much of this information was new to many teachers who had to learn about comprehension strategies themselves in order to teach them to their students. The workshops also provided opportunities for teachers to discuss how ISL worked in their classrooms. We tried to model the positive features of group discussions and problem-solving in the workshops, and quite often teachers modified our lesson plans and materials to fit their teaching styles and the needs of their students. We encouraged that kind of flexibility and were pleased that all of our 50 volunteer teachers continued with the program the entire year.

The principles of guided instruction on comprehension strategies that we developed can be extended to many other cognitive strategies and age levels. In fact, many of the teachers in our projects spontaneously developed related methods for teaching strategies in mathematics and composition. We think that the lessons were most successful when teachers used them creatively and adapted them to their own teaching styles. Thus, we encourage teachers to apply the principles of informed instruction that have worked well for us but to modify them according to the content area and level of the students. In order to illustrate how the principles of ISL can be implemented in different grade levels, I have sketched three lesson plans on guided instruction and cognitive strategies. Several strategies are listed for each lesson to illustrate the rich potential of the metaphors, but a teacher might choose to instruct only one strategy per lesson.

Example Lesson Plan: Grade 3, "Plan Your Reading Trip"

Target Skills

- Declaring a reading purpose
- Generating alternative strategies
- Monitoring comprehension

Dialogues

Use questions such as the following to stimulate discussions about reading strategies among students.

1. How do you prepare for a vacation? What do you need to do before you take a trip?
2. How is planning to read like planning a trip?
3. Are there different places that you can end up after you read? Name some different purposes for reading.
4. Would you read in a different way if you had to remember lots of details or just the general idea?
5. What are some things that you can do while you travel or read that help you get where you are going?
6. What can you do to get back on the right road if you get lost while you read?

Guided Practice

Use worksheets to reinforce the use of strategies, but fade instructional support so that students learn to generate and apply the strategies.

1. Construct a worksheet on a short passage that places road signs throughout the text. As students confront the signs, they must obey them; e.g., "Stop" (say the meaning in your own words), "Dead End" (go back and reread the parts you did not understand), "Slow" (adjust your reading rate). Students may help generate these signs and the messages for reading as part of classroom discussions. It is important, however, that students practice using the strategies.
2. After students finish the worksheets, discuss their responses to the signs and whether or not they thought it was helpful to obey them. Stress the effort needed and why each strategy is effective. Besides providing feedback, these discussions permit students to observe how their peers use strategies differently. It also allows

them to observe a variety of good responses to the same directions.
3. In a subsequent lesson, construct a worksheet with blanks or asterisks at various locations in a passage and ask students to write
in their own road signs and then follow their own directions.
Thus, they will generate and apply relevant strategies as they read.

Example Lesson Plan: Grade 7, "Sherlock, Magnum, and You"

Target Skills

- Gathering clues to meaning
- Evaluating evidence
- Predicting text information
- Making inferences
- Summarizing the main points

Dialogues

Use questions such as the following to generate discussions about
study skills.

1. What does a detective do when given a case to solve? How is
studying like being a detective?
2. If you wanted to study a chapter in a social studies book, what
kinds of clues would you look for? How do titles, pictures, names,
and key events help you recall other parts of the chapter later?
3. A detective must sift through many facts to find the relevant ones.
How do you distinguish important from irrelevant information
when you study?
4. Oftentimes a detective is thrust into the middle of a case and must
reconstruct events leading up to the crime or anticipate what is
about to happen. Do you ever look back or look ahead as you
read? Would it help you understand what you are reading? How?
Why?
5. What is a *deduction?* How do detectives use deductions to solve
crimes? Can you use the same process of deduction to identify the
main points of a passage? Why would this help you study and
remember information more easily?

Guided Practice

1. Provide students with a long passage (about 1,000 words) to read
and study. Ask them to gather clues, evaluate evidence, make

inferences, and identify the main points as they study. After 15 minutes of silent reading and studying, ask the class a series of questions about the passage so that students can observe their own comprehension.

2. Then ask students how they studied and which strategies they used. Make sure you ask why they chose particular strategies and why they believe the strategies helped.
3. As part of a homework assignment, require students to write down the strategies that they use to study material for a test the same night that they actually study. Collect these records and return them with the tests at a future date. Use the test scores and study records as the basis for another group discussion on the usefulness of strategies and the need to act like a detective while reading and studying.

Example Lesson Plan: Grade 11, "Movie Critic"

Target Skills

- Evaluating an author's writing style
- Understanding an author's point of view
- Judging the aesthetic quality of writing

Dialogues

Use questions such as the following to stimulate discussions.

1. What criteria do movie critics use when they judge films and television shows? Do you use the same criteria? What determines if you like a film? Can you use the same criteria to evaluate writing?
2. Style can vary as much as content in a film or in writing. What devices can authors or filmmakers use to express their personal styles and feelings?
3. Explain how different styles of writing might be used to express romance, anger, intellectual arrogance, or religious beliefs. How does the aesthetic character of writing vary among exposition, narration, and poetry?
4. Filmmakers and authors often present a hidden message to their audiences. How can you determine the author's point of view about the subject, setting, and characters?

Guided Practice

1. Assign students the task of reviewing a movie and writing a critical review such as one found in a newspaper. Use the classroom discussion to identify the main criteria for the review and critique.
2. Discuss the reviews in class and point out students who use the criteria effectively. Emphasize the variability in opinions and interpretations even when the same criteria are used.
3. Ask students to write an essay on the same topic and then distribute the papers to fellow students. The task is to review and critique the writing styles of their peers. When they have written their reviews, assign them to small groups to discuss each other's reviews and the criteria that they used to evaluate clarity and style.
4. As a final option, students could review and critique their own writing from a previous assignment.

CONCLUSION

These lessons are brief examples of the ways in which metaphors and group discussions can facilitate instruction on strategies for reading, studying, writing, and learning. The lessons are designed to make abstract cognitive strategies sensible and tangible by emphasizing concrete actions that foster comprehension. The metaphors, bulletin boards, and worksheets are graphic illustrations and reminders to use the strategies, but the important point is for students to appreciate the usefulness of the strategies for their own learning. When students combine information about cognitive strategies with motivation to use them, the students assume responsibility for their own learning by acting as both teacher and student. This equips students with knowledge, skills, and attitudes that will promote continued learning.

About the Author

Scott G. Paris is Professor, Department of Psychology, at the University of Michigan.

References

Brown, A.L. "Metacognitive Development and Reading." In R. Spiro, B. Bruce., and W. Brewer (Eds.), *Theoretical Issues in Reading Comprehension.* Hillsdale, N.J.: Erlbaum, 1980.

Brown, A.L., B.B. Armbruster, and L. Baker. "The Role of Metacognition in Reading and Studying." In J. Orasanu (Ed.), *A Decade of Reading Research: Implications for Practice.* Hillsdale, N.J.: Erlbaum, 1984.

Brown, A.L., A.S. Palincsar, and B.B. Armbruster. "Instructing Comprehension-Fostering Activities in Interactive Learning Situations." In H. Mandl, N. Stein, and T. Trabasso (Eds.), *Learning from Texts.* Hillsdale, N.J.: Erlbaum, 1984.

Durkin, D. "What Classroom Observations Reveal About Reading Comprehension Instruction." *Reading Research Quarterly* (1978-79) 14, 481–533.

Durkin, D. "Reading Comprehension Instruction in Five Basal Reading Series." *Reading Research Quarterly* (1981) 16, 515–544.

Gagne, R.M. and W. Dick. "Instructional Psychology." *Annual Review of Psychology* (1983) 34, 261–295.

Palincsar, A.S. and A.L. Brown. "Reciprocal Teaching of Comprehension-Fostering and Monitoring Activities." *Cognition and Instruction* (1984) 1, 117–175.

Paris, S.G., D.R. Cross, and M.Y. Lipson. "Informed Strategies for Learning: A Program to Improve Children's Reading Awareness and Comprehension." *Journal of Educational Psychology,* in press.

Paris, S.G. and J.E. Jacobs. "The Benefits of Informed Instruction for Children's Reading Awareness and Comprehension Skills." *Child Development,* in press.

Paris, S.G. and B.K. Lindauer. "The Development of Cognitive Skills During Childhood." In B. Wolman (Ed.), *Handbook of Developmental Psychology.* Englewood Cliffs, N.J.: Prentice-Hall, 1982.

Paris, S.G., M.Y. Lipson, and K.K. Wixson. "Becoming a Strategic Reader." *Contemporary Educational Psychology* (1983) 8, 293–316.

Pearson, P.D. and M.C. Gallagher. "The Instruction of Reading Comprehension." *Contemporary Educational Psychology* (1983) 8, 317–344.

Resnick, L.B. "Toward a Cognitive Theory of Instruction." In S. Paris, G. Olson, and H. Stevenson (Eds.), *Learning and Motivation in the Classroom.* Hillsdale, N.J.: Erlbaum, 1983.

Rogoff, B. and W.P. Gardner. "Guidance in Cognitive Development: An Examination of Mother-Child Instruction." In B. Rogoff and J. Lave (Eds.), *Everyday Cognition: Its Development in Social Context.* Cambridge, Mass.: Harvard University Press, 1984.

Vygotsky, L.S. *Mind in Society.* Cambridge, Mass.: Harvard University Press, 1978.

The concept of metacognition—*thinking about how one thinks—has received increasing attention in recent years as a means whereby students can help clarify their reading comprehension processes. If classroom dialogues are focused on three or four specific processes of comprehension, will they prove useful in developing comprehension strategies? Palincsar and Brown cite several illustrative classroom dialogues designed for this purpose.*

Reciprocal Teaching: Activities to Promote "Reading with Your Mind"

Annemarie Sullivan Palincsar

Ann L. Brown

In response to our query of junior high students, "How do you read when you want to be sure to understand and remember what you have read?" we received an array of enlightening (if not enlightened) responses, from "I stare real hard at the page, blink my eyes, and then open them and cross my fingers that it will be right here" (pointing to upper portion of scalp), to a solemn "You must read with your mind."

Many strategies for instructing students to understand and remember what they read (i.e., to "read with their minds") are presented in this volume, and Wittrock (1983) has identified no fewer than 32. In this article, we advocate four particular strategies as well as a means of instruction. We will comment on those features of our instructional procedure that seem particularly facilitative and will describe two modifications of the instructional procedure that can be applied in classroom settings.

The four strategies include question-generating, summarizing, predicting, and demanding clarity. These particular strategies were selected because they meet a number of criteria:

1. They are strategies spontaneously engaged in by successful readers (Brown and Lawton, work in progress).
2. They serve as a means of both comprehension monitoring and comprehension fostering.
3. Each strategy can be used in response to a concrete problem of text comprehension.

Summarizing is an activity of self-review. It requires that the reader identify and integrate important information in the text. Question-generating is a means of self-testing; i.e., can I locate the kind of information about which questions might be asked and can I formulate an answer to these questions? Predicting serves several functions. In addition to its broadly recognized role of purpose setting, the reader cannot make meaningful predictions without activating relevant background knowledge and/or knowledge of text structure (Collins and Smith, 1982). Finally, demanding clarity might be likened to taking a driver using cruise control off the open highway and placing the driver in Boston as a tourist using a stick shift. In teaching students to demand clarity, we are asking them to be alert to unfamiliar vocabulary and unclear referents (street signs), disorganized or inconsiderate text (fellow drivers) and difficult concepts (rotaries). Of course, one can't stop there; the reader must also employ fix-up strategies (Brown, 1980; Collins and Stevens, 1982) to maneuver out of the situation; e.g., rereading or seeking further information.

The instructional technique we used to teach these four strategies is called *reciprocal teaching.* The Latin derivation of the word *reciprocal* is *reciprocus,* which means "going backward and forward." This definition gives an unfortunate picture of not going anywhere, but a less literal definition of the word is, "one party acts by way of return or response to something previously done by the other party." In our work the two parties are represented by the teacher and the student. Certainly such an interchange is facilitated if the two parties are holding discourse on the same subject. For our purposes, this subject is represented by the text. Finally, the extent to which this interchange between the two parties is productive is influenced by the extent to which the two parties share a common goal. Our goal has been the acquisition and/or refinement of the four strategies.

When this procedure is first implemented, the teacher does most of the acting. The teacher models the processes of summarizing, question-generating, predicting, and clarifying. The students are respondents to the extent that they are asked to answer the questions generated by the teacher and elaborate on the teacher's summary, predictions, and clarifications. As the days of instruction proceed, the students are given opportunities to assume the role of teacher; i.e., to initiate and lead the discussion of the text segment. The adult teacher remains actively involved, but his or her response is determined in large measure by the offering of the student as teacher. The adult teacher may need only to inform the student teacher that he or she is doing well. The teacher may need to elicit more information or return to modeling the activity. The following pieces of dialogue are presented for illustrative purposes. The first segment illustrates the teacher leading the dialogue and the students acting primarily as respondents.

Teacher: The title of this story is *Genius with Feathers.* Let's have some predictions. I will begin by guessing that this story will be about birds that are very smart. Why do I say that?

First student: Because a genius is someone really smart.

Teacher: But why would I say *"birds* that are very smart?"

Second Student: Because they have feathers.

Teacher: That's right. Birds are the only animals that have feathers. Let's predict now the kind of information you might read about very smart birds.

Third student: What kinds of birds?

Teacher: Good question. What kinds would you guess are very smart?

Third student: Parrots or blue jays.

First student: A cockatoo like the bird on *Baretta.*

Teacher: What other information would you want to know? (No response from students.)

Teacher: I would like to know what these birds do that is so smart. Any ideas?

Second student: Some birds talk.

Fourth student: They can fly.

Teacher: That's an interesting one. As smart as people are, they can't fly. Well, let's read this first section now and see how many of our predictions were right. I will be the teacher for this section. (All read the section silently.)

Teacher: Who is the genius with feathers?

First student: Crows.

Teacher: That's right. We were correct in our prediction that this story would be about birds, but we didn't correctly guess which kind of bird, did we? My summary of the first section would be that it describe the clever things that crows do, which make them seem quite intelligent. Is there anything else I should add to my summary?

First student: How they steal corn?

Teacher: That's a detail that described one of the ways in which they are clever. For our summary we will not include details. I think I found a word that needs clarification. What does *resourceful* mean?

All students: (No response.)

Teacher: If I say that you are a resourceful person, I mean that you are able to deal with problems and difficulties easily. Being resourceful is another way in which crows are intelligent. I would like to make a prediction now. The section's last sentence says, "One major reason they have mastered survival against heavy odds is their amazing communication system." My prediction is that the next section will describe this communication system. How do you think crows communicate with one another?

All students: Caw-caw.

First student: With a special song.

Teacher: Let's read on. Who will be the teacher for this section? (Dialogue follows that shows the student Jim leading the discussion and the teacher providing corrective feedback.)

Jim: How do crows communicate with one another?

Teacher: Good question! You picked right up on our prediction that this is about the way crows communicate. Who do you choose to answer your question?

Jim: Barbara.

Barbara: Crows have built-in radar and a relay system.

Jim: That's a good part of it. The answer I wanted was how they relay the messages from one crow to the other crow.

Teacher: Summarize now.

Jim: This is about how crows have developed a system.

Teacher: Of what? You must include the whole main idea.

Jim: Of communication.

Teacher: That's right. The paragraph goes on to give examples of how they use pitch and changes in interval, but these are supporting details. The main idea is that crows communicate through a relay system. Jim?

Jim: Any clarifications?

Second student: Does *relay* mean to transpose?

Jim: (Looks at teacher.)

Teacher: Well, to *transpose* means to change. For example, in music I would transpose a song by playing it in a higher or lower key. To *relay* just means to pass on. In a relay race, the runners pass on a baton from one person to another until the race is over. Any more clarifications?

Jim: I'm a little unclear about something in this paragraph.

Teacher: What would that be?

Jim: I just want to make sure about being great mimics. Does that mean that crows are smart and pick up things very quickly?

Teacher: That's part of it. Dave, what do you think a *mimic* is?

Dave: Somebody who imitates somebody else's voice.

Third student: Like that guy on television, Rich Little.

Teacher: Rich Little does impersonations. He mimics or imitates not just the person's voice but also the way the person walks and talks. To *mimic* is to imitate or copy. That was a good point to clarify. Jim?

Jim: It says in this section that crows can use their communication system to play tricks, so I predict the next section will say something about the tricks crows play. I would like Sue to be the next teacher.

Teacher: Excellent prediction. The last sentence of a paragraph often can suggest what the next paragraph will be about. Good, Jim.

We compared reciprocal teaching with a procedure in which students were given practice using texts to find the answers to comprehension questions (Brown and Palincsar, 1982). We have implemented the procedure in small (n=6) settings (Palincsar, 1982; Palincsar and Brown, 1984), and we have explored its use with larger (n=17) groups (Palincsar and Brown, in progress). To summarize our results, we have found the reciprocal teaching of summarizing, question-generating, predicting, and demanding clarity to be a very effective means of improving comprehension as measured by both norm-referenced and criterion-referenced measures. We have found that students maintain the acquired skills at least several months after the intervention has been discontinued. Additionally, students have generalized improvement in reading comprehension beyond the experimental setting to the standard classroom (i.e., social studies and science classes). It is important to note that in all of our work the students were middle school and junior high school students who were able to decode grade-appropriate material at an instructional level (i.e., at least 80 words per minute correct with 2 or fewer errors per minute), but whose comprehension skills were not commensurate with their decoding ability. In many cases, these students were performing two years below grade level on standardized tests of reading comprehension and consistently scoring below 50 percent on informal measures of comprehension. What follows is a description of those features of the instructional situation that appear to facilitate acquisition of strategies.

USE OF THE RECIPROCAL TEACHING PROCEDURE

Ascertaining Where to Begin Instruction

We have observed that, even at the junior high school level, some students, when presented with one sentence, are unable to ask a question about the information contained in that sentence. With these students, particularly in a group setting, it is unlikely that modeling is the most efficient way to begin instruction. Modeling should be preceded by instruction that, in the case of question-generating, might proceed in the following manner:

1. Posing "real-life" situations in which the student must ask a question; e.g., "You want to go to the matinee show at the theater but are unsure of the time of the matinee. You call the theater and ask. . . ."
2. Presenting bare-bone sentences containing an obvious piece of information and prompting the student to use a particular "ques-

tion-word" that asks about the information contained in the sentence, e.g., "Ask a question about the information in this sentence: 'The falcon is a female hunting bird.' Begin your question with the word 'what.'" In time, the "question-words" can be faded out.
3. Presenting brief paragraphs in which one sentence clearly contains main-idea information. Ask the student to identify (e.g., underline) the main-idea information, and then ask a question about this information. We have found that at this point, when the students indicate a degree of proficiency with each of the strategies, we can initiate the reciprocal teaching dialogue during which instruction continues principally through modeling, corrective feedback, and a healthy dose of praise to maintain interest.

Providing the Student with Incentives to Acquire and Apply Strategies

We have found that time is well spent sharing with students why they are being taught a particular strategy, in what situations the strategy may be employed beyond the immediate instruction (e.g., preparing for tests or writing a book report), and what benefits can be derived by employing the strategy. The manner in which we have measured and shared these benefits is to have the student take short comprehension assessments during which they read 450-word passages and then answer (from recall only) a series of 10 comprehension questions. The students complete five of these assessments before we begin the reciprocal teaching procedure, and then they complete one each day after instruction. Of course, these assessments also give the teacher the opportunity to evaluate whether or not instruction has been effective. For those students whose performance on the assessments does not improve, it is helpful to attend more closely to their participation in the reciprocal teaching procedure. Are they getting adequate opportunities to participate? Is there evidence that they are showing mastery of one or more of the strategies? Do they need to return to more basic instruction regarding the strategies?

We also have found that student interest is piqued by using text material that they need to learn in the content areas; e.g., the history or science text. While students regard this as an opportunity to do their "homework" in class, it is one very effective way of promoting the transfer of the strategies beyond the basal reader.

Providing Adequate Opportunity to Acquire Proficiency with Strategies

While we have been delighted with the progress students can make toward becoming active readers who look for and construct meaning from text, we readily acknowledge that this can be a slow and sometimes tedious process. Repeatedly we have observed that at least 12 days of instruction, which occur over successive school days, are required before the majority of students demonstrate stable improvement in comprehension. Furthermore, our instruction has extended over a 20-day period, often the equivalent of nearly two full school months. While we have no empirical evidence to suggest that there is a magic number of days in a specific interval of time during which instruction must occur, we have considerable experience to support that strategy training should not be abandoned before a substantial instructional period.

Relinquishing Teacher Responsibility and Maintaining Teaching Responsibility

One of the facets of the reciprocal teaching procedure that we and the teachers with whom we have worked have enjoyed is the opportunity to see our teaching styles reflected by the students. We encourage the students to reinforce one another for a job well done, to select the next teacher, to ask for further information from one another, and to take responsibility for the transition from one section of the text to the next. There are several benefits resulting from this approach. Students indicate a new found appreciation for the demands of teaching: the struggle involved in helping a student who doesn't get the point or the frustration of asking a question that does not elicit the information you are seeking. In many cases, behavior problems remedy themselves as group management becomes, in large part, a student responsibility.

The teacher focuses his or her expertise on guiding students in the acquisition, refinement, and application of the strategies. The reciprocal teaching procedure encourages individualization of instruction in a group setting. For example, the ability to construct a question by merely reading a sentence from the text with the proper inflection so that the sentence sounds question-like may be all that is expected of a particular student. At the same time, another more advanced student may be encouraged to ask a question that integrates information across several paragraphs. This sensitivity to the match between what the student is capable of and the instruction necessary to improve the student's skill is one that is honed with experience. Several teachers have indicated that listening to the tape-recorded reciprocal teaching sessions, particularly during the initial days of instruction, helped them to develop this skill. They became aware of opportunities for instruction that eluded them in the actual session.

EXTENSIONS OF THE RECIPROCAL TEACHING PROCEDURE

Application of Comprehension Monitoring/Fostering Strategies in the Content Areas

The following is a description of how six seventh-grade developmental reading teachers incorporated the teaching of summarizing, question-generating, predicting, and clarifying into a series of study sessions devoted to earth science. The examples are drawn from one of these sessions.

General Procedure

The teacher wrote the chapter title "Wind and Water Change the Earth's Surface" on the chalkboard, and the class wrote three pieces of information that they predicted they would learn from this section.

Sample Predictions

1. How water erodes the earth and forms rivers.
2. How wind blows sand and makes deserts change.
3. How wind blows away loose and dry soil.

The class discussed their predictions. The teacher related their predictions to content covered earlier in the class. Then the teacher assigned a segment of text to be read silently. For each segment, the students wrote a brief summary, one question that they would expect to see on a test of this section, and one idea or word that they found difficult to understand or expected a younger student would find difficult.

Sample Summaries

1. This section was about how water has moved the earth's crust and how rocks and mountains have been shaped for thousands of years.
2. This section was about erosion and how it changes the earth's surface over many years.
3. This section was about erosion and how it takes place.

Sample Questions

1. What does erosion do?
2. Where are sand dunes found?
3. What happened to the people who lived in the dust bowl in the 1930s?

Sample Clarifications

1. I think that *grains* needs to be clarified.
2. I don't think younger students would understand the word *erosion*.
3. They didn't tell enough about the sand dunes and how they happen.

Following each section, the teacher led a discussion during which the students shared their summaries, asked one another the questions they had posed, and clarified those words and ideas that were unclear. The teachers then constructed the science tests by selecting the best of the students' questions generated during the study sessions. The students who wrote the questions were given credit by indicating their names beside their respective question(s).

Peer-tutoring Using the Reciprocal Teaching Procedure

We have only begun to investigate the possibility of using the reciprocal teaching procedure in a peer-tutoring situation, but our preliminary work suggests that junior high school students can be prepared to assume the role of tutor in conducting the reciprocal teaching procedure. Initially we placed our students in peer-tutoring situations because we were curious to discover what they would choose to teach their tutees, given only the instructions, "Teach your tutees how to become better readers." We found that those students who had participated successfully in the reciprocal teaching procedure remained faithful to the procedure.

We then selected the more capable members of several developmental reading classes as determined by teacher-nomination, measures of decoding, and measures of comprehension. The teachers taught these students the four strategies using the reciprocal teaching procedure. In addition, the teachers focused more on the procedure itself, calling attention to the need to:

1. review with the tutees what the four strategies are
2. model the strategies

3. give the tutees the opportunity to practice the strategies
4. inform the tutees how they are doing or how they might improve their use of the strategies.

After 10 days of such instruction, the tutors began to work with their tutees. The following dialogue is representative of one such peer-tutoring session:

Tutor: Ranger, could you ask a good question?

Tutee: Yes. What kind of silk thread does the spider spin out?

Tutor: Now that was picky. Here's a question I would ask. On the spider's body, what section does the silk come from? What's your answer?

Tutee: The hind end.

Tutor: Now could you summarize, Ranger?

Tutee: What it's mainly talking about is where the tubes are on the spider and where the thread comes out to make the webs.

Tutor: Yes. The text is talking about the different locations of how spiders get silk out of their bodies. Predictions? Nothing you could predict? What about how they spin the webs from the silk? I'll do the next one.

This transaction is fairly representative of a peer-tutoring session and typifies the modeling with which tutors were fairly successful. During these sessions, the adult teacher circulated among the pairs of students and evaluated progress, praised the tutors and their tutees, and provided further instruction for those students with whom modeling would not be sufficient.

In the tutoring investigations, we continued to use the daily assessment that the adult teacher corrected while the tutors graphed the scores and shared them with their tutees. It is our observation that carefully monitored peer-tutoring may well be one successful component in a strategy training program that is supplemented by instruction and modeling by the adult teacher.

SUMMARY

Theories of learning suggest that efficient learning from text requires flexible use of a repertoire of comprehension-fostering and monitoring activities. We have suggested four complementary activities selected to address specific problems in text comprehension. These strategies include summarizing, or self-review; question-generating, or self-testing; predicting, or setting the stage for further reading; and demanding clarity, or noting when a breakdown in comprehension has occurred.

We have advocated a means of instruction whereby teacher and students engage in a dialogue about the text. This dialogue facilitates on-line diagnoses of comprehension difficulty, expert modeling of the strategies by the teacher, and structured practice in acquiring and refining the strategies. Furthermore, we have advocated that students be "informed learners"; i.e., informed regarding the nature of the strategies, their efficiency, and their range of utility.

Although we are the first to acknowledge that the reciprocal teaching procedure requires skillful teaching—"teaching with your mind"—we hasten to emphasize that such teaching efforts have been rewarded by significant gains in the ability of students to "read with their minds."

About the Authors

Annemarie Sullivan Palincsar is Professor, Departments of Counseling, Educational Psychology, and Special Education, at Michigan State University.

Ann L. Brown is Professor, Department of Psychology, at the Center for the Study of Reading, University of Illinois, Urbana-Champaign.

References

Brown, A.L. "Metacognitive Development and Reading." In R.J. Spiro, B.C. Bruce, and W. Brewer (Eds.), *Theoretical Issues in Reading Comprehension.* Hillsdale, N.J.: Lawrence Erlbaum Associates, 1980.

Brown, A.L. and J.D. Day. "Macrorules for Summarizing Texts: The Development of Expertise." *Journal of Verbal Learning and Verbal Behavior* (1983) 22(1), 1–14.

Brown, A.L. and A.S. Palincsar. "Inducing Strategic Learning from Text by Means of Informed, Self-Control Training." *Topics in Learning and Learning Disabilities* (1982) 2(1), 1–17.

Collins, A. and E.E. Smith. "Teaching the Process of Reading Comprehension." In D.K. Ditterman and R.J. Sternberg (Eds.), *How and How Much Can Intelligence Be Increased?* Norwood, N.J.: Ablex, 1982.

Collins, A. and A. Stevens. "Goals and Strategies of Inquiring Teachers." In R. Glaser (Ed.), *Advances in Instructional Psychology* (Vol. 2). Hillsdale, N.J.: Lawrence Erlbaum Associates, 1982.

Linden, J. and M.C. Wittrock. "The Teacher of Reading Comprehension According to the Model of Generative Learning." *Reading Research Quarterly* (1981) 16(1), 44–57.

Palincsar, A.S. *Improving the Reading Comprehension of Junior High Students Through the Reciprocal Teaching of Comprehension-Monitoring Strategies.* Unpublished doctoral dissertation, University of Illinois, 1982.

Palincsar, A.S. and A.L. Brown. "Reciprocal Teaching of Comprehension-Fostering and Monitoring Activities." *Cognition and Instruction* (1984) 12, 117–175.

Wittrock, M.C. *Generative Reading Comprehension.* Paper presented at the meeting of the American Educational Research Association, Montreal, Canada, April 1983.

Part IV
Integrative Comprehension Strategies

While the articles in this section differ in the particular strategies advocated, they nevertheless share a common concern for the integration of process and content; that is, the need to view the reading act as one in which the processes of acquiring meaning are inextricably bound up with the substance of the meaning being acquired. This view, often described as "holistic," decries the teaching of isolated reading skills and deplores the failure of content-oriented teachers to recognize that they, too, have an inescapable responsibility to help students unlock the meaning of the texts they assign. The articles that follow explore ways in which the interaction of the students' thinking and the text may be strengthened.

The first article deals with the use of certain characteristics of text structure to aid comprehension: Strickland and Feeley explore children's concept of story in a number of ways to enhance the effectiveness of relevant reading and writing activities. The articles by Niles, Herber, and Sardy describe further integrative strategies that are especially appropriate for improving thinking and study processes in the middle and upper grades.

One outgrowth of schema theory is active interest in the nature and development of children's concept of story. Will emphasis upon this concept help children improve their ability to understand stories and to create stories of their own? Strickland and Feeley present a model for integrating the teaching of story that employs the modalities of reading, listening, speaking, including creative dramatics, and writing.

Using Children's Concept of Story to Improve Reading and Writing

Dorothy S. Strickland

Joan T. Feeley

Research suggests that there is a relationship between children's knowledge of the structure of stories and their ability to comprehend and produce stories on their own. This article explores that relationship and its application to classroom practice. It is divided into three parts. Part one provides an overview of the research on the nature and development of children's concept of *story* and the investigations into the structure of stories. Part two presents a variety of strategies suggesting the many ways that knowledge of story structure can be strengthened and extended in the classroom. Part three describes a specific strategy devised by the authors that attempts to incorporate into a single framework some of the best in the current thinking and practice related to developing children's concept of story.

CONCEPT OF STORY AND STORY STRUCTURE

How children acquire a concept of story and use it in the processes of reading and writing has been a topic of considerable interest and inves-

163

tigation in recent years. Stories represent a particular kind of narrative discourse, identifiable by structure, content, and language. The use of story is characteristic of both adults, who use story frames to summarize events, and children, who use story in dramatic play, in retelling events, and in every other phase of their communication. Some researchers, interested in the development of story in children, have studied the evolution of story concepts in the children themselves (Applebee, 1978; McConaughy, 1980). Others have focused their investigations on the internal structure of stories (Mandler and Johnson, 1977; Rumelhart, 1975; Stein and Glenn, 1977; and Thorndyke, 1977).

Researchers studying children's concept of story have noted certain developmental trends. As in the learning of any concept, young children formulate a general sense or idea of what stories are all about, focusing on beginnings, endings, and obvious attempts. For example, McNeil (1984, p. 15) reports a kindergarten child's retelling of "The Lion and the Mouse" as follows: "A lion got trapped in a net and mighty mouse came and saved him." These early notions of story are gradually modified and refined as children continue to encounter new stories in a variety of situations.

Perhaps the first evidence of the developing sense of story in children is their use of language to create a special or private world. This is thought to be the forerunner to the child's use of language to create a world of make believe, involving dramatic play and leading to the gradual acquisition of the specific conventions that constitute a sense of story. As children mature, their stories increase in length and complexity. The characters, settings, and actions become further removed from the immediate environment. Children gradually gain greater control over the events in their stories, moving from a loose collection of related events to tightly structured narratives that link a set of events to each other and to a common theme (Applebee, 1978). A fifth grader produced a much more detailed retelling of the "The Lion and the Mouse" than did the kindergartner, including all attempts and reactions and even the theme or moral, "Sometimes little can help big" (McNeil, 1984, p. 19). According to McConaughy (1980), this older child is approaching an adult idea of story because of the attention to cause and effect and inferencing beyond the text.

Whaley (1981) found that when reading stories, older children were better at predicting events than younger children. She concluded that the expansion of a story sense in older students enabled them to predict more of the story structures. Mandler (1978) found that children seem to organize their recall according to an ideal story structure. They tap into their existing concept of story as they attempt to remember new stories. Younger children tend to emphasize the outcomes of specific action sequences rather than specific events and their causes. As children mature, their story retellings appear to move away from a simple, ideal concept of story toward a more complex adult model.

Analyses of children's written stories reveal the same developmental patterns. Sutton-Smith (1981) reports that young children organize their stories around basic pairs of actions, such as chase and escape, and tend to repeat these actions in their written stories. For example, three first graders who had made doughnuts with their class that morning were composing a follow-up written piece (Long and Bulgarella, 1985). Instead of recording how doughnuts were made, they decided to write about a man who made doughnuts that came alive, "Kinda like Raggedy Ann and Andy" (p. 167). To avoid being eaten up, the doughnuts run away. Because one child in the group wanted a happy ending, both the doughnuts and the man go to a "cellabrashun" where they had "wine and cake . . . and they both had a good time" (p. 171). As children mature in written expression, multiple pairs of actions with supporting elements become apparent, suggesting a movement toward the elaboration of event structures. For instance, two fourth-grade boys we observed in a local elementary school had developed a superhero named "Machine Gun Joe," a tough army sergeant who saved Americans around the world, from Olympic athletes in Korea to kidnapped ambassadors in Italy. Each episode was connected by a staccato reprise: "It was a mean job, but somebody had to do it!"

In summary, the research focusing on the development of story in children suggests that virtually all children are exposed to story to some degree; that they begin to develop a concept of story at an early age; and that as they mature their concept of story expands. A related body of research focuses on the nature and internal structure of the stories themselves. The works of Mandler and Johnson (1977), Rummelhart (1975, 1977), Stein and Glenn (1977), and Thorndyke (1977) suggest that stories have an underlying structure that can be described in terms of their narrative parts and interrelationships. Although various researchers label the major story elements differently, the following components are generally included:

- *Setting*—introduces the main character, time, and setting
- *Beginning*—an initiating event that leads the main character to formulate his or her own major goal
- *Goal setting*—includes reactions to the beginning and the formation of a major goal
- *Attempt*—actions of the characters to achieve the goal

- *Outcome*—success or failure of the attempt
- *Internal response*—subgoals, thoughts, and feelings of the character, leading to actions
- *Ending*—long-range consequence of actions; final response of story character

These subdivisions comprise the elements of the overall schema or framework of a story, which consists of setting, characterization, and plot. Any story can be broken down into its various components, thus providing an operational model for story comprehension and production.

Researchers studying the development of story in children and those studying the structure or grammar of stories have linked their findings to children's development of reading and writing. The role of prior knowledge and experience in reading and writing suggests that learners who have had many experiences with stories and have developed a strong schema for stories make use of that framework as they read and write. Listeners and readers are said to use their knowledge of story structure to guide them in anticipating the events in a story. They make predictions based on what will occur next in a story, a process believed to be essential to reading comprehension. Prior knowledge of what a story is helps facilitate recall of a text (Mandler and Johnson, 1977; Stein, 1979). Story schema actually acts as a guide or road map for retrieving story information. It may help a student to decide when a portion of a story is complete or incomplete and may help fill in or infer information that may have been forgotten.

The learner's preexisting concept of story is equally as important in producing stories as it is in comprehending them. Several researchers who have analyzed children's written stories found story narratives to be the most prevalent structure (Britton et al., 1975; Applebee, 1978; Sutton-Smith, 1981). Story schema may be activated during the first stage of the writing process when ideas are being conceived (Britton et al., 1975). The author draws upon the story elements of setting, character, and plot during the writing of the story, and these may serve as a framework for revision as well.

STRATEGIES FOR DEVELOPING CHILDREN'S CONCEPT OF STORY

Researchers and curriculum specialists have sought to apply what has been learned about the relationship between children's knowledge of story and the development of literacy. These efforts have produced a variety of strategies for using story structure. Although there is some disagreement about whether or not the direct teaching of story structure is either necessary or helpful, there is universal agreement about the need to expose students to an abundance of stories in a variety of ways and to expand that exposure to include activities that strengthen their concept of story (Strickland, 1984). Actually, explicit knowledge about story grammar may be most important for teachers as they plan literature experiences for their students. The following descriptions are representative of the many ways in which story grammar can be applied to extend and enhance story comprehension in the classroom.

Questions and Discussion

Schweiger (1984) offers a set of questions that may be adapted to any story and used as a basis for discussion:

1. Setting
   - Where and when did the story take place?
   - Who are the main characters?
2. Initiating events (actions)
   - What got the story started?
   - Why does the main character have a problem? What does the character need?
3. Goals
   - What is the problem of the main character?
   - How can the character solve the problem?
4. Major events (actions)
   - What did the main character do first to solve the problem?
   - Did it work? Did the character reach his or her goal?
   - What did the character do that did not work?
   - Did the character try something else? What was it?
5. Conclusions
   - What finally happened in the story?
   - How did the story end?
6. Reactions
   - Was there a lesson in the story?
   - Would you have acted differently?
   - Would you read the story again? Would you recommend it to a friend? (Schweiger, 1984, p. 6)

Questions such as these help readers to focus on key elements in the story and to analyze them in relation to each other and to their own views of the world. In each case, the questions may be expanded to tap

students' ability to make inferences, draw conclusions, and apply information in the story. For example, students may be asked to compare
the setting in the story with the location in which they live. They may
discuss possible underlying motives of the characters: what drives them
to behave the way they do? They may substitute their own versions of
various elements of the story and suggest possible outcomes to accompany them. They may compare this story with others having similar
themes.

Creative Dramatics

Galda (1982) used creative dramatics to help young children develop their reading comprehension and sense of story. "To play about
a story children must understand characters and their motivations,
events as cause and effect, and the logical order of beginning, middle,
and end" (p. 54). Galda suggests that the teacher select a favorite fairy
tale, fable, or make-believe story with vivid imagery and dynamic characters; *Little Red Riding Hood* and *The Three Billy Goats Gruff* are good
examples. The story is read aloud to the children, followed by questions
and discussion requiring the students to evaluate the story and discuss
the characters. For example, children may be asked why they thought
Little Red Riding Hood was a good story or why they thought the troll
wanted to eat the Billy Goats Gruff. The result is twofold. Children are
allowed to share their feelings about the story and to focus on the
characters and their reactions to the sequence of events in the story.

If the students appear to have enjoyed the story, the teacher may
invite them to role-play it. Students then are given whatever guidance
they may need in selecting their roles and playing them out. According
to Galda, when players discuss things such as roles, props, and story
settings, they become more aware of aspects of the story that they
individually might not have noticed (p. 53).

Story Retellings

Cambourne (1984) developed a retelling strategy that necessarily
makes use of children's story schema as they make and confirm their
own predictions and compare them with the predictions of others. This
retelling strategy has the potential for involving the learner in reading,
writing, speaking, and listening simultaneously. Moreover, a wide
range of language functions may be highlighted simply by modifying
the purpose, audience, mode of retelling, or the kind of text to be
retold.

To prepare for this activity, the teacher must organize the class in small groups. Multiple copies of the story are made and stapled so that only the title is visible. The stapled copies are distributed and students are asked to write one or two sentences on what a story with such a title might be about. Next, they are asked to list some words or phrases that they would expect to encounter if their prediction were to come true. The members of each small group share and compare what they have written.

After setting a purpose for reading, the teacher instructs the students to unstaple their stories and read silently. They are told in advance that after the reading they are to pretend to write to someone who hasn't read the story and tell them about it. Students may use the reverse side of the paper to write their retellings. They are not allowed to look back at the story.

Another share-and-compare session follows the retelling, during which students work with partners to compare and contrast what each included and omitted and discuss the reasons why. Additional sharing may focus on the words and phrases each student used that are different from those used in the story but mean the same thing. Finally, each student may point out the elements of the other's retelling that they would choose to borrow and include in their own story.

A MODEL FOR IMPROVING STORY READING AND WRITING

We have seen how story structure can be used to guide and facilitate the discussion of stories, act as a framework for the reconstruction of stories through creative dramatics, and serve as a mechanism for facilitating and confirming recall during the retelling of stories. The following model for improving story reading and writing has the potential to make use of all of these strategies in one comprehensive plan. The plan moves systematically from students' exposure and discussion of stories, to their recounting and reconstructing those same stories, and finally, to the production of similar but original stories.

Step One

During this initial phase of the plan, students are exposed to a variety of stories within a particular genre. For example, teachers of younger children might wish to focus on simple make-believe animal stories or fairy tales. Teachers of older students might wish to focus on tall tales or mystery stories. Stories that contain vivid imagery and dynamic characters work best. Over a period of days, several stories may be read aloud to the class. "Book talks" about books in the same genre also may be given. For a book talk, the teacher introduces a particular book or group of books to the class. For each book, the title and a brief synopsis is given without giving away the story. If the children are familiar with other works by the same author, this may be pointed out as well. The books are then made available to the children for their personal reading. The key emphasis during this phase of the model is to immerse children in stories of a particular type. The discussions surrounding these stories and the particular genre they represent serve as a logical point of departure for the activities that follow.

Throughout the reading aloud by the teacher and the independent reading by the children, group discussion and personalized reading conferences are focused on the elements of the story. Questions related to setting and characterization, initiating events, goals, major actions, conclusions, and the reader's personal reactions and responses are used when appropriate to further story comprehension and appreciation. A series of questions might focus on what the characters look like, how they behave, and what motivates them. The questions should be framed so that students are encouraged to use their knowledge of stories to make predictions about the text. For example:

- "Now that the three bears have returned home, what do you think will happen?" (predicting how the main characters might solve a problem)
- "Do you think that Frances' mother is really going to allow her to eat nothing but bread and jam every day?" (predicting behavior of a main character)
- "Now that the author has described Paul Bunyon, can you close your eyes and see him? Tell what you see" (predicting images)
- "Why do you suppose that the department store executives acted so surprised when Mrs. Gordon introduced herself as the detective on this case?" (character motives)

Step Two

After the teacher reads the story aloud to a group, one or more of the following activities may be used to extend students' understanding and enjoyment.

Further Discussion Through Story-Based Questions

The questions below focus on major events or actions in the stories —a post-reading/listening activity that requires looking back, reflecting, re-creating, and creating alternatives.

- "What do you suppose would have happened if Goldilocks had arrived before the three bears left home?" (predicting outcomes based on a change in the initiating event)
- "What did Frances try that did not work? What else did she try?" (major problem-solving events)
- "What are some examples of exaggerated events in the story of Paul Bunyan?" (recalling major events)
- "What mysterious thing happened in the department store to get this story started?" (initiating event)

Creative Dramatics

Various forms of creative dramatics may also follow a favorite story. This may involve students in pantomime as the story is read aloud a second time. Or, they may role-play various characters in the story, act out specific scenes, or dramatize the story from beginning to end. To prepare for the dramatization, students must focus on various aspects of characterization, setting, and the sequence of events. Questions such as the following help children prepare for the dramatization:

- "What kind of person was Paul Bunyon? How did he look, talk, walk?" (characterization)
- "What did the three bears' home look like? How can we arrange things to look something like that?" (setting)
- "What happened first in *Bread and Jam for Frances?* What happened next? How did the story end?" (sequence of events)
- "Mary Gordon was a no-nonsense detective. How did she behave as she went about her work?" (characterization)

Story Retelling

Stories may be retold in oral or written form. Oral versions may be told before the group or retold into a tape recorder and made available for individuals to listen to at their leisure. Written versions may be shared and compared with others retelling the same story in written form. Story elements may be used as a framework for comparison:

- Were any characters left out or added?
- Were the characters and setting described so that you could really see them?
- Were all the events included? Were they in the right in order?
- Was the ending retold as it happened in the story?

As students compare and contrast elements in their retelling, they may wish to compare how each used language in different ways to say the same thing.

Step Three

A series of writing activities, moving from whole group to small group and independent writing is the final stage of the model. Teacher and students may select a favorite story to retell in written form with the teacher or one member of the group acting as scribe. As in the activities described above, the teacher uses prompts based on story schema to help the story unfold.

- Where and when did the story take place?
- Who were the main characters?
- How did the story get started?
- What problems did the characters encounter?
- How did they try to solve their problems?
- What worked? What didn't work?
- How were the problems solved?
- How did the story end?

The writing activities evolve through four steps:

1. Whole group writing of favorite story. Teacher acts as scribe.
2. Whole group writing of original but similar story. Teacher acts as scribe.
3. Small groups collaborate to write and share original story with one member of each group acting as scribe.
4. Individuals write original stories on their own and share with the group.

In each case, students use story schema to guide them through the writing process. All of the sharing and discussion surrounding each particular story helps to strengthen students' understanding of the nature of the genre itself and serves as an invaluable set of prewriting experiences. The collaborative writing in large and small groups allows for much-needed rehearsal. It promotes fluency and self-confidence with the process. As groups and individuals use story-based prompts to review their work stories, they are making use of a key strategy for revising stories.

The model presented above gives students an opportunity to put to use and develop all that they know about thinking, talking, reading, and writing about stories. It assists teachers in making connections between reading comprehension and writing. The model is multilevel; that is, it allows teachers to work with a variety of different levels of ability at once. The model provides an instructional framework with sufficient structure to give teachers guidance; however, it also offers sufficient flexibility for teacher and student decision-making along the way. Teachers and students make decisions about the story genre they choose to explore, the stories within the genre they choose to read, the means by which they choose to extend understanding and appreciation of the stories, and the stories they choose to write in groups or individually.

About the Authors

Dorothy S. Strickland is Professor, Department of Curriculum and Teaching, at Teachers College, Columbia University.

Joan T. Feeley is Professor, School of Education, at William Patterson College.

References

Applebee, Arthur N. *The Child's Concept of Story.* Chicago: The University of Chicago Press, 1978.

Britton, J., T. Burgess, N. Martin, A. McLeod, and H. Rosen. *The Development of Writing Abilities.* London: Macmillan Education Ltd., 1975.

Cambourne, B. "Retelling as a Pedagogical Strategy: Summary Thoughts." Detroit: Presentation at Miscue Update Conference, 1984.

Galda, L. "Playing about a Story: Its Impact on Comprehension." *The Reading Teacher* (1982) 36, 52–55.

Long, R. and L. Bulgarella. "Social Interaction and the Writing Process." *Language Arts* (1985) 62, 166–172.

Mandler, J.M. "A Code in the Node: The Use of Story Schema in Retrieval." *Discourse Processes* (1978) 1, 1–13.

Mandler, J. M. and N.S. Johnson. "Remembrance of Things Parsed: Story Structure and Recall." *Cognitive Psychology* (1977) 9 (1), 111–151.

McConaughy, S.H. "Using Story Structure in the Classroom." *Language Arts* (1980) 57, 157–165.

McNeil, J.D. *Reading Comprehension: New Directions for Classroom Practice.* Glenview, Illinois: Scott Foresman, 1984.

Rumelhart, D. "Notes on a Schema for Stories." In D. Bobrow and A. Collins (Eds.), *Representations and Understandings: Studies in Cognitive Science.* New York: Academic Press, 1975.

Rumelhart, D. "Understanding and Summarizing Brief Stories." In D. La Berge and S.J. Samuels (Eds.), *Basic Processing in Reading: Perception and Comprehension.* Hillsdale, N.J.: Lawrence Erlbaum, 1977.

Schweiger, B. "Story Grammar." *Collage* March/April (1984) 5–8.

Stein, N. and C. Glenn. "An Analysis of Story Comprehension in Elementary Children." In R. O. Freedle (Ed.), *Discourse Processing: Multidisciplinary Perspectives in Discourse Comprehension.* Hillsdale, N.J.: Ablex, 1977.

Stein, N. "How Children Understand Stories: A Developmental Analysis." In L. G. Katz (Ed.), *Current Topics in Early Childhood Education* (Vol. 11). Norwood, N.J.: Ablex, 1979.

Strickland, D. "Building Children's Knowledge of Stories." In J. Osborn, P. Wilson, and R. Anderson (Eds.), *Reading Education: Foundations for a Literate America.* Lexington, Mass.: Lexington Press, 1984.

Sutton-Smith, Brian. *The Folkstories of Children.* Philadelphia: University of Pennsylvania Press, 1981.

Thorndyke, P. W. "Cognitive Structure in Comprehension and Memory of Narrative Discourse." *Cognitive Psychology* (1977) 9 (1), 77–110.

Whaley, J. F. "Story Grammar and Reading Instruction." *The Reading Teacher* (1981) 34, 762–771.

Effective comprehension requires attention-study processes as well as the study of content. How may study processes be taught to secure a better integration of the processes with the content of reading? Niles offers several examples of how intervening questions (i.e., those to which students are asked to respond during the course of study of a text) may be appropriately used in reading for study.

Integration of Content and Skills Instruction

Olive S. Niles

Books and other print materials are a principal source of the knowledge students are expected to acquire during their school experience. It is important that they acquire this knowledge but just as important that they understand *how* they acquired it so that they may go on absorbing knowledge and getting pleasure from print on their own as long as they live. This means that they must understand the process of reading and study that they are using as they work with the print materials in each of the disciplines they study.

The content of reading and the process of reading are inextricably interrelated. Without content, of course, the process is meaningless. Furthermore, content (or the form in which it is presented) affects, may even control, the process. Without skill in the process, however, content often may be impossible for the student to acquire.

Reading can be taught and learned by dividing the process into subskills (using context clues, reading for main ideas, drawing inferences, following sequence, analyzing imagery, and the like). Teachers and students may work with each of these subskills separately, eventually combining them as they are needed in processing the many different kinds of materials the mature reader encounters. In fact, this is the way reading usually has been taught and learned.

But many researchers now believe it is better to reverse this procedure and begin with the whole process, looking at the parts only to the extent that this is necessary in order to understand the whole. This holistic approach does not eliminate attention to subskills, which may, indeed, be taught separately in the early stages of learning to read or when students exhibit a need to improve some particular part of the process. However, the holistic approach puts the teaching and learning of subskills in a place subordinate to the process as a whole.

Reading involves an active partnership between the reader and the writer, as they both deal with the material as a whole. The competent reader consciously brings to the act all that he or she already knows about the subject involved, constantly predicts what the writer will present, confirms these predictions or revises or rejects them, and finally arrives at meaning. Comprehension is the result of this interaction to which both writer and reader contribute. Readers do not absorb meaning; they help to create it.

The content of reading and the process are best taught simultaneously. This is the text from which many a sermon has been preached over the years. The sermon will not be repeated here except to point out two considerations sometimes overlooked:

1. Teachers do not have time in an era of exploding knowledge to teach process and content separately.
2. The motivation of students to learn process is improved if the task immediately relates to what they consider the real business of education, the content they are expected to learn.

Recent trends, however, have tended to ignore the close relationship of content and process. The whole basic skills movement, behavioral objectives, classroom management systems for individualizing instruction, and most of the competency testing procedures all have emphasized teaching and testing subskills out of context. Secondary school reading programs and remedial programs in both elementary and secondary schools are still predominantly taught in reading classes or learning laboratories, divorced from the mainstream of instruction. To be sure, as measured by both formal and informal tests, improvement in the reading process itself as a result of this isolated instruction often has been demonstrated. To what extent this improvement has been transferred to the learning of content, where it really counts, is not known. So many factors are involved—some of them attitudes rather than skills—that this transfer is extremely difficult to measure.

If content and process are to be taught simultaneously, thus capitalizing on the relationship, content teachers will have to assume most of the responsibility. So far, many of them have successfully resisted the implications of such an assignment. They have done so mainly because of their insecurity and their belief that teaching reading is a very complicated, difficult task. Also, most secondary teachers and many intermediate grade teachers are content-oriented. They tend to teach as they were taught. We know now that even for them this was not necessarily a good way; most of them would have been better students and teachers if more attention had been paid to *how* to learn and somewhat less to content *per se.*

A first step in correcting this situation could be to help content teachers understand the importance of each of the three basic parts of any good lesson in any subject: prestudy, during-study, and poststudy or evaluation. In earlier days, though not so very long ago, teaching focused on poststudy. The teacher told the class what to study: "Read the next chapter and be prepared to discuss it tomorrow." This procedure, which Herber calls *assumptive teaching,* placed the responsibility entirely on the students so far as the process to be used was concerned. Teachers simply assumed that the students already had mastered the process and could make any necessary adjustments to the material at hand.

There has been considerable discussion of the types of questions teachers use, especially in this poststudy teaching session (Hunkins, 1972; Sanders, 1966; Turner, 1983). Although some taxonomies have contained more elaborate classifications (Lapp and Flood, 1978), four kinds of questions usually have been identified: literal; interpretive, or inferential; critical, or evaluative; and creative, or associational. These kinds of questions require that students relate what they have read to their own experience or to previous reading and viewing and come up with answers related to their personal, individual perceptions. Investigation showed that a high percentage of teachers' questions were of the literal type. Such questions tap only students' ability to recall, not their ability to think. Hence, teachers and writers of texts were urged to include more of the other types of questions. These distinctions among kinds of questions are still valid and useful for evaluating students' comprehension. However, more recently (Herber and Nelson, 1975) the use of questioning as a way to teach the process of reading has itself been questioned, though the usefulness of questions to provide practice with skills already learned is acknowledged.

Recently some other types of postreading activities have been suggested; for example, the graphic postorganizer (Moore and Readence, 1980) and semantic mapping (Pearson and Johnson, 1978; Armbruster and Anderson, 1980).

Not too long ago, research began to insist that prereading activities at all levels are an important part of teaching (Adams and Bruce, 1982; Anderson, Spiro, and Anderson, 1978; Pearson and Johnson, 1978; Stevens, 1982; Moore, Readence, and Rickelman, 1982). Schema theory has emphasized the fact that what students bring *to* their study (information, attitudes, language background, concepts, experiences, cultural background) strongly affects what they take *from* it. If it is true that reading is, indeed, a transaction between the reader and the text (or the writer), it is clear that an active rather than a passive process is involved and that the reader must be prepared to participate in this transaction. The text must be viewed as a blueprint from which readers create their own meanings, which may be more or less similar to what the writer intended. Ausubel (1968, p. vi) stated the main point very clearly: "The most important single factor influencing learning is what the learner already knows. Ascertain this and teach him accordingly." Many suggestions for prereading activities and strategies have appeared, the best known being the first steps of the SQ3R design (Robinson, 1962) and its various modifications, such as PQ4R described by Thomas and Robinson (1977). Langer (1982), Vacca (1981), and Thelen (1982) have described similar procedures all emphasizing prereading.

Thus, prereading and postreading procedures have been studied quite actively and many approaches devised for their improvement, some sensible and useful but a few others so detailed and teacher/pupil time-consuming that it seems unlikely that they will be widely used. Some, also, are useful only with certain kinds of material. What content teachers seek are simple, widely applicable procedures that they can understand quickly and implement without tedious preparation or the production of voluminous study guides or other written materials.

The part of the lesson that has so far received the least attention is the during-reading segment. Recent studies of what is called *comprehension monitoring,* a metacognitive process by which readers evaluate the success of their efforts to comprehend, seem to be leading to more attention to what happens during reading and to how this process of monitoring can be improved (Wagoner, 1983; Baker and Anderson, 1982). It seems reasonable to believe that it is during the time when students actually are studying that the teacher has the best opportunity to guide them and to demonstrate the kinds of interaction with text a given piece of content material requires if it is to be thoroughly comprehended, appreciated, and recalled. The rationale for emphasis on during-study activities is presented by Herber (1978). It is also described as one approach to content-area reading instruction by Moore and Readence (1983). Several procedures for dealing with students' during-reading process have been devised; for example, Three Level Guides (Herber, 1978); Selective Reading Guide-O-Rama (Cunningham and Shablack, 1975); Pattern Guides (Olson and Longnion, 1982); ConStruct Procedure (Vaughan, *Journal of Reading,* 1982); and various note-taking, summarizing, and outlining procedures. All of these, however, seem to be focused more on helping students master a specific content than on helping them understand the process for arriving at this mastery.

A procedure that is simpler to prepare than most of these others appeals to content teachers because it seems a "natural" way to teach and not very different from the way they usually teach. It requires, however, that the teacher prestudy the material himself or herself and think of questions and hints to use *during* the students' study to make them realize what they are doing and thus understand the process as well as master the content. It is particularly important that students learn to predict what will follow and to recognize and respond to the top-level organizational structure of the piece; i.e., chronological order, cause-effect, comparison-contrast, etc. Various researchers have categorized these structures in different ways. The important point is not the particular categories but rather the fact that students are trained to look for structure and to use it to help them read and recall (Bartlett, 1978; Meyer and Freedle, 1979; Meyer, Brandt, and Bluth, 1980; Taylor, 1980).

Intervening *during* study with the use of adjunct questions is supported by limited research (Vaughan, *Secondary School Reading,* 1982), which seems to show that questions *in* text are more valuable than either questions *before* text or questions *after* text. In any case the procedure leads to teacher-student-text interaction at the point where this is probably most meaningful. Adjunct questions must include "process questions" (see examples below). Merely asking questions about content may help students master specific content but will not further their understanding of the process.

Intervening in the students' during-reading activity requires that the teacher preselect stopping points where students can reflect upon what they are doing and why they are doing it. The questions to be asked should make students concern themselves both with the results of the reading process (comprehension) and with the process itself. Essentially what happens is that the reading experience is slowed down so that students have time to observe the transaction that is occurring between themselves and the text. One way to do this is for the teacher to read aloud to the students as they progress through some material and, by pausing and questioning at appropriate points, force attention to the kind of thinking the students should be doing. A second way is to instruct students to read silently to a certain point (probably better, in this case, than oral reading to students because silent reading normally occurs in content reading) and then ask them to stop and respond orally to both "process" and "content" questions. A third procedure involves the preparation of study sheets that instruct the students to stop at key points and respond to questions, either by discussing them in a small group of peers or by writing answers to the questions, answers later to be shared with the teacher in a follow-up session. Probably the most effective procedure is the second, partly because it allows the teacher to evaluate student response immediately and, thus, clarify issues that arise, and partly because it requires less time-consuming prior preparation on the part of the teacher than the third procedure. Not that it does not require preparation. Few teachers can make on-the-spot decisions concerning the appropriate issues to raise with students; they have to think it through in advance. The most difficult part may be locating those stopping places where discussion will most efficiently make students aware of reading as a process and of their role in the transaction with the text. Hunt (1982, p. 349) describes the process: "The question, then, is what methods we might use to slow down and interrupt the process of reading for our students so that they (and their teachers) can reflect on the transaction between themselves and the text, modify and enrich it, reassemble and reperform it—that is, gain some measure of control over it."

This procedure, as described above, obviously relates to a whole piece of text such as students encounter daily in content reading. Though it focuses on the whole process of reading, it may serve to alert the teacher to the need for some direct teaching of a specific subskill with which students are having difficulty. It may even mean departing from the content text temporarily and providing some practice in easier materials. For example, if a question that calls for students to infer a main idea causes difficulty, the alert teacher will deal with this problem directly by providing explanation and practice in inferring main ideas. Emphasis on the whole may lead to temporary emphasis on the parts.

Since demonstrating is usually more effective than describing, some sample during-reading lessons are presented. They involve different content and different levels of difficulty. Lack of space dictates that prereading and postreading activities related to the during-reading part of the lessons be omitted. For the same reason the excerpt from the social studies text is abbreviated; certain parts have been omitted except for their accompanying subheads, which are all presented as in the original. In the left columns, stopping points with related questions and hints are indicated. Asterisks identify process-oriented questions. In the right columns, the text itself is presented.

Crystal Moment
by Robert P. Tristram Coffin

Read the title. *How would you describe a crystal? The poet is using a metaphor. Metaphors always imply comparison. What could make a "moment" like a "crystal"?

Read lines 1–4. *What rhyme scheme has the poet used? Where does each thought end?

How does the poet feel about the "moment in September"?

Read lines 5–22. *What does the buck do in its attempt to escape? *What do you predict the outcome will be?

*An *image* is a word or group of words intended to help the reader see, hear, touch, smell, or taste something the writer is describing. What images does Coffin use to help you *hear* the baying of the hounds and to help you *see* the buck swimming?

Read lines 23–28. *Sometimes writers leave out a word or words and use a comma in their place. The poet has done this in line 23. Reword the sentence that begins "Pursued. . . ." Do not use the words "pursued" or "pursuers."

*Did the chase end as you predicted? Explain.

In what sense are life and death "upon one tether"?

Is the poet's sympathy with the buck or with the hounds?

1 Once or twice this side of death/Things can make one hold his breath.

3 From my boyhood I remember/A crystal moment of September.

5 A wooded island rang with sounds/Of church bells in the throats of hounds.

7 A buck leaped out and took the tide/With jewels flowing past each side.

9 With his high head like a tree He swam within a yard of me.

11 I saw the golden drop of light In his eyes turned dark with fright.

13 I saw the forest's holiness/On him like a fierce caress.

15 Fear made him lovely past belief/My heart was trembling like a leaf.

17 He leaned towards the land and life/With need upon him like a knife.

19 In his wake the hot hounds churned,/They stretched their muzzles out and yearned.

21 They bayed no more, but swam and throbbed,/Hunger drove them till they sobbed.

23 Pursued, pursuers reached the shore/And vanished. I saw nothing more.

25 So they passed, a pageant such
As only gods could witness
much.

27 Life and death upon one
tether/And running beautiful
together.

What Does the Circulatory System Do?

Read the title. *What does *circulatory* mean? It is related to *circle.* What happens to something that circulates?

Read paragraph 1. Why do doctors no longer bleed sick people?

Read the first sentence of paragraph 2. *What do you predict the writer will tell next?

Read all of paragraph 2. *What is done to make you particularly notice one of the words? Which word?

*What does plasma carry through the body as the blood circulates? What are *nutrients?* You may need a dictionary. Writers do not always furnish context clues to help you. There are none here.

Read paragraphs 3–5. What three things are found in the second part of the blood? What does each of them do?

*The writer has made it easy for you to remember the parts of the blood by the way he organized the material. Show that you understand what the writer did by completing the outline below.

Parts of the Blood
I. Plasma
   A. Yellow fluid, mostly water

Long ago, people thought that they could cure a sick person by causing the person to bleed. Doctors in the Middle Ages thought a sick person had bad blood. They thought that when a person was bled, the bad blood was let out of the body. The man in the drawing is receiving this often-harmful treatment. Today, we realize that the blood, which circulates through the body, nourishes the body cells and keeps them healthy.

Blood consists of two parts. The blood in the test tube in the picture is separated into its two parts. The yellow fluid—*plasma*—is mostly water. Nutrients, some oxygen, and waste products are dissolved in the blood plasma. You might notice yellow fluid oozing out from a scab if you scrape yourself.

The thick, red mixture at the bottom of the test tube consists of blood cells that make up the second part of your blood. The picture shows a close-up view of blood cells. The smooth, disk-shaped cells are *red blood cells* that carry most of the oxygen in your blood.

Find the round, rough-surfaced cells in the picture. These white

B. Carries nutrients, oxygen, and waste products

II. Blood cells
   A. Red cells
      1. Smooth, disk-shaped
      2. _____
   B. White cells
      1. _____
      2. _____
   C. _____
      1. _____
      2. _____

blood cells protect you from disease. *White blood cells* surround and destroy harmful organisms that might make you ill.

Notice the tiny specks in the picture of the blood cells. These specks—or *platelets*—form from pieces of cells. The platelets release a substance that helps a blood clot to form if you cut yourself. The blood clot acts like a plug to keep your blood from draining out of your cut blood vessel.

The Industrial Revolution Led to Sweeping Changes in English Life: Conditions in Eighteenth-Century England Favored Rapid Industrial Change

Read the title and subtitle. *What do you predict will be the two main patterns of thought in this chapter? What clues helped you identify these patterns?

Read paragraph 1. *What sentence summarized paragraph 1?

Read paragraph 2. Between 1750–1850 what two major changes had occurred? What is this period called?

*What device did the writer use in paragraph 2 to call your attention to the most important facts?

If an Egyptian farmer of four thousand years ago had visited England in the early eighteenth century, he would have found many things familiar. At that time, most Englishmen lived on farms or in small villages and worked the land with crude tools and the aid of horses and oxen. The women spun thread with a distaff and spindle, just as the ancient Egyptians had, and wove cloth in their own homes. The world's methods of raising food and making cloth had not changed much since the days of the Pharaohs.

If, however, the same Egyptian farmer had visited England a century later, he would have been a total stranger to the country's agricultural and manufacturing methods. Great factories had begun to dot the landscape and new cities were growing up around them. Large numbers of farmers had left the fields to work in the factories, and those who stayed behind were able to produce much more food because of improved farm machinery and large-scale operation. People now wore ready-made clothing turned out by machinery rather than by hand labor. New and faster means of transportation were available, too. Because these changes came about so rapidly (approximately 1750 to 1850) this period of English history is known as the *Industrial Revolution.* It marks two important changes: 1. from making goods by hand to making them by machine; 2. from working in the home to working in a factory away from home.

Read the first sentence of paragraph 3. *What do you predict will follow?

Read all of paragraph 3. What made England a leader in the Industrial Revolution? Be careful: read the whole paragraph.

*What group of words in paragraph 3 leads you to expect the writer will discuss some of the "many factors"?

What brought about these sweeping changes? The most obvious answer is that new machines appeared in England between 1750 and 1850 that made hand labor seem very slow and inefficient. Why, you may ask, did not all European countries make use of the new machines since the scientific principles on which they were built were known to the scholars of many countries? The answer is that many factors in addition to scientific principles are necessary to bring about an Industrial Revolution. As we shall see, of all the countries of eighteenth-century Europe, England was best equipped to become the first great industrial nation:

- *A revolution in agriculture meant a large number of unemployed workers.*
- *England had the capital to invest in new industries.*

Read paragraphs 4–6. *What two patterns of thought are combined in these paragraphs?

*There is a great deal of detail in these paragraphs. How much of this detail do you think you should try to remember? Considering the three paragraphs as a whole, what is the main idea?

New machinery increased the production of cloth. A vital role in the Industrial Revolution was played by the inventors who applied scientific principles to practical needs. The impact of their inventions was first felt in the textile industry, which had always been important in England. One of the earliest inventions, John Kay's flying shuttle (1733), greatly increased the speed with which cloth could be woven. But the usefulness of the flying shuttle was limited by the fact that the spinners, who were still twisting yarn with a simple spinning wheel, could not work fast enough to keep up with the weavers. This bottleneck was overcome a few years later when James Hargreaves devised a means of turning eight spindles with just one spinning wheel. He called his machine the *spinning jenny.* A barber named Richard Arkwright improved the spinning jenny by adding rollers through which the yarn was drawn into thread. His machine was called a *water frame* because its rollers were turned by a water wheel.

The yarn produced by the spinning jenny was too soft and uneven, however, and that produced by the water frame was too coarse. Samuel Crompton combined the good points of both machines with some ideas of his own to produce a spinning machine called a *mule.* An improved version of the same machine is still used today. In 1785 Edward Cartwright applied the use of water power to his *power loom,* thus enabling a weaver to produce as much as twelve men had been able to do with hand looms.

A number of other inventions also helped expand the textile industry. In 1794 an American inventor, Eli Whitney, developed the *cotton gin* ("gin" is a shortened form of "engine"), which enabled one man to pick the seeds out of as much as a thousand pounds of raw cotton a day. A few years later a machine was developed to stamp brightly-colored designs on cloth.

Read all the bullets except the last. List five factors that produced the Industrial Revolution in England.

Read the last bullet. *What pattern of thought do you predict will follow?

- *The steam engine provided power for the new machines.*
- *Coal and iron helped English industries grow.*
- *Roads, canals, and railways increased the flow of trade.*
- *Machines changed people's way of life.*

Read the last three paragraphs. In what ways was the life of the factory worker unlike that of a medieval serf?

*What summarizing sentence states the main point of the last three paragraphs?

Was the lot of the nineteenth-century factory worker worse than that of the medieval peasant? You will remember from the story of the Middle Ages that the serf on the manor was forbidden to leave the land and that he led a life of drudgery and toil. While factory workers were free men, in many ways their lives were more miserable than those of the serfs. At least the serf had the security of his land on the manor. The factory worker lived in daily fear of being replaced by a machine or laid off if the factory closed. The serf could rely on his garden or livestock if the crop failed, but the factory worker had only his job to keep him housed and fed.

While the serf's cottage was only a sod hut, it was often better than the crowded, unsanitary tenement. Certainly a serf's work in the fields was healthier and more pleasant than work in a gloomy, damp coal mine or in an unventilated, smoky factory.

A comparison of the two ways of life must take into account the worker's morale and self-respect. The medieval peasant felt that his crop and his garden were the result of his own efforts, just as the craftsman felt pride in his skill at weaving. But the factory worker who spent his day monotonously tending a machine had no responsibility for planning or turning out a finished article and therefore had no reason for pride in his work. As you readily see, in many ways the lot of the "free" factory worker in the nineteenth century was more unhappy than that of the serfs.

Readers of this article must not assume that the kind of during-reading procedure described and illustrated should be applied to all or even most of the reading that students do in their texts. From a purely practical point of view, it would be impossible because of time constraints. But beyond this consideration, it would be frustrating to students to have their reading constantly slowed down and interrupted. Teachers must trust that transfer will take place and that, having been shown how to "think" as they read, students will continue to do so when they read independently. If the process is taught with the use of "real reading," that is with the textbooks they use every day, there is a better chance that transfer will occur than would be the case if the process were taught with unrelated materials. Teachers are advised, therefore, to select pieces of material from the students' own texts, pieces with which they think students might have some difficulty in comprehension or recall and certainly material containing important information worth the time and effort spent in careful study. Then they should conduct during-reading activities on a fairly consistent schedule early in the year, perhaps once a week with the intervals between such sessions lengthened as teachers begin to see that transfer is occurring.

There is a fine line between the desirable teacher/student interaction the procedure described above encourages and overdependence on the teacher. The goal, of course, is transfer to the students' independent study. We have not yet found a foolproof way to guarantee this outcome.

The procedure can be used with almost any kind of material, even something as different in appearance as an algebra text. Mathematics has its own language and organization, which students must learn to read. Also, it is appropriate for use at any grade level in which student textbooks are extensively used, usually beginning in grade four. The present writer would argue that the procedure should be started early, before students have formed bad habits as they adjust to the major difference between the generally narrative style of basal readers and the generally expository style of content books (Wood and Mateja, 1983).

The integration of content and skills instruction will follow when the same teacher teaches both; the material used is the "real stuff" of students' textbooks; and the activities *during* reading receive as much attention as the *prereading* and *postreading* parts of the lesson.

About the Author

Olive S. Niles is Professor, Department of Reading, at Lowell University.

References

Adams, M. and B. Bruce. "Background Knowledge and Reading Comprehension." In J. A. Langer and M. Trika Smith-Burke (Eds.), *Reader Meets Author/Bridging the Gap: A Psycholinguistic and Sociolinguistic Perspective.* Newark, Del.: International Reading Association, 1982, pp. 2–25.

Anderson, R. C., R. Spiro, and M. Anderson. "Schemata as Scaffolding for the Representation of Information in Connected Discourse." *American Educational Research Journal* (1978) 15, pp. 433–440.

Armbruster, B. B. and T. H. Anderson. *The Effect of Mapping on the Recall of Expository Text* (Technical Report No. 160). Champaign, Illinois: University of Illinois Center for the Study of Reading, 1980.

Ausubel, D. *Educational Psychology: A Cognitive View.* New York: Holt, Rinehart, and Winston, 1968.

Baker, L. and R. I. Anderson. "Effects of Inconsistent Information on Text Processing: Evidence for Comprehension Monitoring." *Reading Research Quarterly* (1982) xvii, pp. 281–294.

Bartlett, B. J. "Top-Level Structure as an Organizational Strategy for Recall of Classroom Text." Unpublished doctoral dissertation, Arizona State University, 1978.

Cunningham, D. and S. L. Shablack. "Selective Reading Guide-O-Rama: The Content Teacher's Best Friend." *Journal of Reading* (1975) 18, pp. 380–382.

Herber, H. L. *Teaching Reading in Content Areas.* Englewood Cliffs, N. J.: Prentice-Hall, 1978.

Herber, H. and J. Nelson. "Questioning Is Not the Answer." *Journal of Reading,* April 1975, pp. 512–517.

Hunkins, F. P. "Questioning Strategies and Techniques." Boston: Allyn and Bacon, 1972.

Hunt, R. A. "Toward a Process-Intervention Model in Literature Teaching." *College English* (1982) 44, pp. 345–356.

Langer, J. A. "Facilitating Text Processing: The Elaboration of Prior Knowledge." In Judith A. Langer and M. Trika Smith-Burke (Eds.), *Reader Meets Author/Bridging the Gap: A Psycholinguistic and Sociolin-*

guistic Perspective. Newark, Del.: International Reading Association, 1982.

Lapp, D. and J. Flood. *Teaching Reading to Every Child.* New York: Macmillan, 1978.

Meyer, B. J., D. M. Brandt, and G. J. Bluth. "Use of Top-Level Structure in Text: Key for Reading Comprehension of Ninth-Grade Students." *Reading Research Quarterly* (1980) xvi, pp. 72–103.

Meyer, B. J. and R. Freedle. *The Effects of Different Discourse Types on Recall.* Princeton, N. J.: Educational Testing Service, 1979.

Moore, D. W. and J. E. Readence. "A Meta-Analysis of the Effect of Graphic Organizers on Learning from Text." In M. L. Kamil and A. J. Moe (Eds.), *Perspectives on Reading Research and Instruction* (Twenty-ninth Yearbook of the National Reading Conference). Washington, D. C.: National Reading Conference, 1980.

Moore, D. W. and J. E. Readence. "Approaches to Content Area Reading Instruction." *Journal of Reading* (1983) 26, pp. 397–402.

Moore, D. W., J. E. Readence, and R. J. Rickelman. *Prereading Activities for Content Area Reading and Learning.* Newark, Del.: International Reading Association, 1982.

Olson, M. W. and B. Longnion. "Pattern Guides: A Workable Alternative for Content Teachers." *Journal of Reading* (1982) 25, pp. 736–741.

Pearson, P. D. and D. Johnson. *Teaching Reading Comprehension.* New York: Macmillan, 1978.

Robinson, F. P. *Effective Study.* New York: Harper and Row, 1962.

Sanders, N. M. *Classroom Questions: What Kinds?* New York: Harper and Row, 1966.

Stevens, K. C. "Can We Improve Reading by Teaching Background Information?" *Journal of Reading* (1982) 25, pp. 326–329.

Taylor, B. M. "Children's Memory for Expository Text After Reading." *Reading Research Quarterly* (1980) xv, pp. 399–411.

Thelen, J. "Preparing Students for Content Reading Assignments." *Journal of Reading* (1982) 25, pp. 544–549.

Thomas, E. L. and H. A. Robinson. *Improving Reading in Every Class: A Sourcebook for Teachers* (second ed.). Boston: Allyn and Bacon, 1977.

Turner, T. N. "Questioning Techniques: Probing for Greater Meaning." In J. Estill Alexander (Ed.), *Teaching Reading.* Boston: Little, Brown, 1983.

Vacca, R. T. *Content Area Reading.* Boston: Little, Brown, 1981.

Vaughan, J. L. "Use the ConStruct Procedure to Foster Active Reading and Learning." *Journal of Reading* (1982) 25, pp. 412–422.

Vaughan, J. L. "Instructional Strategies." In Allen Berger and H. Alan Robinson (Eds.), *Secondary School Reading: What Research Reveals for Classroom Practice.* Urbana, Ill.: National Conference on Research in English and ERIC Clearinghouse on Reading and Communication Skills, 1982, pp. 67–84.

Wagoner, D. A. "Comprehension Monitoring: What It Is and What We Know About It." *Reading Research Quarterly* (1983) xviii, pp. 328–346.

Wood, K. D. and J. A. Mateja. "Adapting Secondary Level Strategies for Use in Elementary Classrooms." *Reading Teacher* (1983) 36, pp. 492–496.

Content field teachers have long been frustrated by the expectation that they teach not only their subject matter but also the reading skills needed for its comprehension. Is there an alternative to a skill approach that will help solve this problem? Herber shows how instructional guides developed to integrate reading-thinking processes may be used to promote the understanding of content material at three comprehension levels—literal, interpretive, and applied.

Levels of Comprehension: An Instructional Strategy for Guiding Students' Reading

Harold L. Herber

The centrality of comprehension to the process of education is evident in instructional concerns expressed by both practitioners and researchers. Practitioners discuss the importance of their students being able to comprehend printed materials. They look to researchers as well as to other practitioners for ways to improve their students' reading performance.

Researchers study the comprehension process and related methods and materials to help teachers attain their instructional goals. Cooperative efforts of practitioners and researchers toward improving comprehension instruction are increasing.

The purpose of this article is to present an instructional strategy for improving reading comprehension, a strategy that has evolved from the work of both practitioners and researchers. It focuses on how content-area teachers can manage reading instruction and how they can mediate and model reading comprehension.

MANAGING READING INSTRUCTION

Including reading instruction in one's curriculum is generally perceived by content-area teachers to be an onerous problem. This is particularly true when teachers are uninitiated in instructional strategies for teaching reading. Teachers have two basic questions: "What reading skills do I teach?" "How do I teach the reading skills?" These two questions translate into one large management problem: finding ways to integrate instruction in course content with instruction in related reading-reasoning processes.

The management problem seems overwhelming to content-area teachers when, in response to their question "What reading skills do I teach?" they are presented with an extensive set of terms representing reading skills. These terms are found in professional texts written by authors whose theoretical orientation is toward a specific-skills model of reading. According to this orientation, a combination of specific skills constitutes the reading process. The skills range from those needed to identify and acquire new vocabulary, and comprehend narrative and expository materials, to those needed for efficient study of printed materials and for high-level reasoning about what is being read. Each skill can be identified and taught, individually and in combination with others. In the professional texts written from this orientation, these skills are identified as essential for successful reading in various content areas and are recommended to teachers as the focus for instruction.

To teachers who do not have the academic or experiential background either to understand the meaning of these specific skills or to know that alternative theoretical orientations exist, what is proposed seems to be an impossible task. Teaches who follow the admonitions and attempt to balance the teaching of specific skills with the teaching of course content become frustrated because of management problems. They are not quite certain how to teach the skills, nor are they certain what materials to use for the instruction. Those who are persistent enough to follow the authors' prescriptions for teaching the specific skills have difficulty finding time to do so without giving short shrift to the course content they are responsible to teach. For example, teaching a lesson on finding the main idea of a passage in a history class takes time away from the study of history. Even when the teacher uses the regular history text as the resource for the lesson, the concentration is on the skill rather than on the content and the latter is lost in favor of the former. Multiply this experience with teaching main idea by the number of specific skills recommended for the teacher to teach and you have an indication of the complexity that causes a severe management problem. So, while content-area teachers view reading instruction as important, for most of them the management problem remains: how to teach reading skills and course content at the same time.

An alternative answer to the question "What reading skills do I teach?" lies in considering a different theoretical orientation to the process of reading. Viewing reading as a holistic process rather than as a set of discrete skills can lead to strategies that make instruction in reading more easily managed within the context of instruction in course content. Professionals who subscribe to the holistic model of reading believe that reading is a natural-language process. *Meaning* resides in the reader; so what the reader brings to the text determines what he or she takes from the text. When the text is written in language familiar to the reader, he or she is able to give meaning to it. Instruction in this meaning-acquisition process does not require that language be broken down into discrete parts to assure understanding of the whole. Rather, instruction requires sufficient preparation of the reader before reading so he or she can make connections between what is already known and what is being presented in the language of the text. The reading instruction provides sufficient support of the reader so the reader will make connections, attribute meanings, and develop understandings.

The holistic model of reading and the instruction it promotes hold distinct advantages for the content-area teacher who is looking for the answer to the question "What reading skills do I teach?" It is not necessary to use artificial text for instructional purposes. Rather, teachers can use the natural text that is found in resources commonly assigned for study in subjects taught in the school curriculum. This makes possible the instructional integration of course content and related reading process. As students are shown how to read this natural-language text, they also are taught the substance of the course in which the text is used. So, teachers teach their students how to read the textbooks they are required to read. This is much more manageable than teaching special lessons on specific reading skills from special text, especially when the instruction takes time away from the study of the content of the curriculum.

The second question that reflects the management problem for content-area teachers is "How do I teach the reading skills?" Again, the answers are found in the logical extensions of the two models previously discussed. The specific-skills model generally promotes *direct instruction* through lessons that focus on skills found in materials especially constructed for such lessons. The holistic model generally promotes *functional instruction* through lessons that focus on the content of the required texts being read.

An example of direct instruction was given earlier, a lesson on reading for the main idea. The notion of "direct teaching" of reading comes from the focus of attention for the lesson. Reading skills are the focus. Lessons are designed to teach specific skills directly; materials are selected because they can serve as a vehicle through which the skills can be taught. Frequently, special materials are purchased or constructed for use in such lessons. Alternatively, content-area texts sometimes are used for instruction in and practice on specific skills. But regardless of the materials being used, the focus of the lessons is directly on the reading skills. Learning and using the substance of what is read is of secondary importance. Thus, the direct teaching of specific reading skills in a content-area class tends to separate the learning of reading skills from course content. Direct teaching of reading skills in a content-area class reduces the time available for teaching the content and intensifies the management problem.

Functional instruction of reading, with particular focus on comprehension, is illustrated later in this article. The notion of "functional teaching" comes from the functions served both by the reading/reasoning processes to be taught and by the teaching itself. The reading/reasoning processes are implicit in the section of the textbook assigned for the study of a particular concept in the course, and they function to facilitate students' understanding of the required reading. The teaching guides students' application of the reading/reasoning processes implicit in the required reading and, thus, develops students' understanding of what is being read. Because functional teaching uses textbooks required for a content area, and because it facilitates students' study of concepts from the required curriculum, it promotes the instructional integration—rather than separation—of reading processes and course content. This economizes time and reduces the management problem.

MEDIATING COMPREHENSION INSTRUCTION

To most practitioners and researchers, comprehension is central to the reading process. Helping students understand what is read is the goal of reading instruction. Finding ways for content-area teachers to manage comprehension instruction has been an important objective in the development of all-school reading programs (Herber and Nelson-Herber, 1984). Many have attained the objective through the functional teaching of comprehension within the holistic model of reading (Herber and Nelson, 1984). Central to attaining the objective was finding ways to mediate the development of comprehension.

The first step was to define comprehension in a way that reflected the full range of the process while making it seem instructionally manageable. Gray's (1960) description was promising, "Reading the lines . . . reading between the lines . . . reading beyond the lines." Smith's (1963) descriptors of her notion of comprehension stimulated a search for labels for Gray's three phases. Smith (1963) described *literal* comprehension, *interpretive* comprehension, *critical* comprehension, and *creative* comprehension. Herber (1965, 1970, 1978, 1985) used *literal* to describe the acquisition of basic information or details from what is read. Literal comprehension is "reading the lines," or determining "what the author says."

Smith's notions of *interpretive* and *critical* comprehension were considered overlapping and Herber used the term *interpretive* to describe the acquisition of ideas from what is read as the reader looks for relationships across details presented by the author. Interpretive comprehension is "reading between the lines" or determining "what the author means by what he or she says."

Embedded in Smith's notion of *creative* comprehension was the reader's application of prior knowledge to the author's ideas and the generation of broader, more abstract, more general concepts or principles. Herber used the term *applied* to describe this aspect of comprehension. Applied comprehension is "reading beyond the lines" or "applying your ideas to the author's ideas and coming up with new ideas."

Herber gave the term *levels of comprehension* to the combination of his three descriptors. While in the early discussions of levels of comprehension Herber (1965, 1978) suggested the possibility of a hierarchical relationship among the three levels, subsequent research and program development in schools led to two important refinements: first, the levels are more interactive than hierarchical (Herber, 1978); second, the levels are more accurately considered a description of an instructional strategy to develop a reader's comprehension than a description of comprehension itself (Herber, 1985).

The interactive aspect of the three levels is consistent with Rumelhart's (1976) interactive model. It also seems more consistent with the assumptions of holistic models of reading. Recent research into reading comprehension confirms the appropriateness of the descriptors and the practicality of the instructional strategy they form. For example, Pearson and Johnson (1978), drawing on their own research and that of others, have created a taxonomy of comprehension questions and answers that is similar to Herber's levels. They refer to *textually explicit* comprehension, which is akin to the literal level and involves the reader in identifying explicit information from the text. They refer to *textually implicit* comprehension, which is akin to the interpretive level and involves the reader in identifying ideas that can be inferred from the text. They refer to *scriptally implicit* comprehension, which is akin to the applied level and involves the reader in relating ideas from prior knowledge to information or ideas drawn from the text.

The construct of levels of comprehension becomes an instructional strategy when the levels are represented in instructional materials called "reading guides" or "levels guides." Reading-guide materials are designed to assist students as they read and respond to text at each level of comprehension. The specific nature of their design is discussed in the next section of this article. Illustrative examples of levels guides are presented at the end.

These materials are used to guide students not only as they read text but also as they discuss what they have read with other students and with their teacher. In performing this guiding function, they serve as *mediators* (Shoemaker, 1977), a particularly apt simile. That is, the levels guides *provide a link* between readers and text that promotes understanding of text and facilitates communication among the readers. Guides for the literal and interpretive levels of comprehension mediate between students and text, facilitating students' acquisition of essential information and their analysis of implicit ideas. A guide for the applied level of comprehension mediates among students, their prior knowledge, and ideas implicit in text, enabling them to synthesize across information sources and to generalize new or expanded concepts.

The levels guides *mediate discussions* among students as they draw information, ideas, and generalizations from the text and their prior knowledge. This mediation is particularly important because students often work in small groups as they respond to the guides. The guides give focus and purpose to students' interactions and increase the efficiency and productivity of their work. The guides also mediate between students and the teacher, giving focus to that communication and increasing the "safety" factor (Nelson-Herber, in press) for students who need assistance in developing their communication skills.

MODELING READING COMPREHENSION

Metacognitive studies suggest the importance of helping students develop an awareness of their own thought processes as they read (Brown, 1981). Helping students become aware of "what their minds feel like" as they comprehend their textbooks moves them closer to the point where they can function as independent readers. Instructional materials that guide students' reading can develop this awareness by attempting to model or to simulate the comprehension process. While comprehension of text is far too complex a process to be explained fully by the simple construct of three levels of comprehension, it is possible to say with some confidence that comprehension does at least involve the three factors previously mentioned: acquisition of information; development of ideas from that information; synthesis of text-based and reader-based ideas into new or broader generalizations (Pearson and Johnson, 1978). Guides designed around the construct of three levels of comprehension can serve to make students aware of these three factors. When such guides are used with textbooks required in various content areas, students also develop an understanding of the concepts being taught through those texts. Thus, they learn course content and related reading/reasoning processes simultaneously.

Construction of the guides is particularly important to the integrated learning of content and process. Items in the guides are framed as declarative statements rather than as questions (see examples at the end of the article). That is, the literal-level guide contains statements that may (or may not) reflect information presented in the reading selection to which the guide is related. Similarly, the interpretive-level guide contains statements that may (or may not) reflect ideas that can be inferred from information presented in the reading assignment. The applied-level guide contains statements that may (or may not) reflect generalizations that can be supported from ideas in both the text and the readers' prior knowledge. Items in the guide for each of the levels are created by teachers as they ask themselves the question appropriate for each level: what is the important information in this assignment (literal); what ideas is the author trying to convey (interpretive); what generalizations seem appropriate for this material, given students' prior knowledge and experience (applied). In essence, then, items for the guides are really answers to these questions posed by the teacher.

Directions for the guides ask students to identify statements that can be supported by information in the text (literal and interpretive levels) as well as by their prior knowledge and experience (applied level). Students are asked to identify specific information and ideas they have drawn on to support their acceptance or rejection of statements. As they discuss their responses to the statements with other students in their small groups, they share the supporting evidence. Thus, students consciously experience the marshaling of information and ideas in response to a reading assignment; they consciously experience what it is like to comprehend text material; and, at the same time, they engage in the study of ideas important to the curriculum in which they are enrolled.

The belief is that the use of guides, comprised of declarative statements of the sort just described, serves to model the process of comprehension in a broad and general way. The response to the guides constitutes a kind of simulation of comprehension that students consciously experience both as they respond to the guide and as they discuss their response with other participants. For example, as students respond to literal-level statements, they experience what it is like to sort through an assignment in text to find the significant information. As they respond to interpretive-level statements, they experience what it is like to study relationships across information presented in text and to infer meanings from those perceived relationships. Finally, as students respond to applied-level statements, they experience what it is like to bring prior knowledge to text, to relate it to information and ideas drawn from the author, and to develop generalizations from the relationships.

Students do not actually create a product of the comprehension process. Because the statements (which *are* the product of the teacher's comprehension process) have been created for students to react to, students have only to judge whether or not they fit the text under consideration. By marshaling evidence to support or reject the statements, however, students do develop an awareness of how such statements can be formulated by drawing from information and ideas presented in text and by drawing from prior knowledge. Students do develop a consciousness about the comprehension process, to the point where they can talk about it with their teachers and peers (Herber and Nelson-Herber, 1984).

In this manner, these guides constitute a simulation of comprehension. As such, they constitute a "prequestioning" strategy for guiding students' development of comprehension and for preparing students subsequently to answer questions that reinforce and provide practice on the comprehension processes they have acquired. Herber and Nelson (1975) discuss how the interactive use of declarative statements and questions can lead to students' independence in comprehension.

SAMPLE GUIDES

Below are levels guides for three subject areas: social studies, literature, and mathematics.[1] The social studies material was used with a sixth grade class that was studying means of survival and how they are obtained. The organizing idea for the lesson was, "Survival requires food, clothing, and shelter. These basic needs can be obtained by money, goods, and

---

1. Sample levels guides are reproduced by permission of TRICA Consultants, Inc., Homer, New York.

services." Note that all of the items in the guides are declarative state-ments. Examine the statements in the guides to see how they fit the text, how they fit the directions at each level, and how they fit with one another both within each level and across the three levels.

The literature material was used with an eighth grade class that was starting a poetry unit. This particular guide was one of four used as students read and discussed four different poems, each related in some way to the organizing idea, "Time has both quantitative and qualitative dimensions and every person experiences both dimensions differ-ently." Even though the guides are for the reading of poetry rather than exposition, their purpose, function, and interrelationships are similar for the reading of social studies material. Some variations occur to accommodate the literary form and the different content, and you can see these variations. You also can see the carefully developed relation-ships between the guides for the three levels (items 3, 4, and 5) and the poem, among statements within each level, and among statements across the three levels.

The mathematics lesson shows how the application of levels of com-prehension is adapted to the reading of word problems. This particular material was used in a lesson related to the organizing idea, "The areas of rectangular regions can be calculated if their dimensions are known." This guide reflects an adaptation of the levels-of-comprehen-sion construct studied by Riley (1976) for use with the reading of word problems. The adaptation presents a variation of the literal level first, followed by a variation of the applied level, followed by a variation of the interpretive level. Take careful note of the kinds of items presented in each of the levels and how the adaptation seems to fit the special needs imposed on the construct by mathematics and word problems. Herber (1978) and Riley (1976) discuss this adaptation in more detail for those interested in pursuing the matter further.

Example: Grade 6, Social Studies

Survival

1. Some people are poor. Some people are rich. Some people live in cold places and some in warm places. There are many other differences among people that you could talk about. 2. However, there is one thing that is the same for everyone all over the world. That one thing is the wish to live, or *survive*. What people *need* for survival also is the same for all people. They need three things. They need food, clothing, and shelter. 3. When people do not have enough *food* to eat, they become sick and die. Even though different people eat different food, their *need* for food is the same. 4. When people do not have enough *clothing* to protect their bodies, they may not

survive. The *need* for clothing is the same even though different people wear different clothing. 5. When people do not have enough *shelter,* they may not survive. The kind of shelter people have is different in different places. However, the need for some kind of shelter is the same. 6. There are differences among people in the ways they get their food, clothing, and shelter. Some people buy these things with *money.* Some people barter for them with *goods* that they grow or make. Some people work for them by giving some kind of *service.* 7. Many people use *money* to buy what they need. They have a job that gives them money for their work. They use that money to pay for their food, clothing, shelter. 8. Some people work for themselves and are not paid money. They trade what they make for what they need. They barter their *goods* for their food, clothing, and shelter. 9. Some people have no money to buy what they need and they do not have goods to barter. They find someone who will pay them for their work with food, clothing, shelter. By giving a *service* to other people, they meet their own needs. 10. People are both the same and different. Their needs are the same but they meet those needs in different ways. Do you suppose this is one reason our world is such an interesting place?

Level 1

Check the statements that say what the author says in the story. The statements may use the same words as the author. They may use different words but say the same thing. Be ready to give reasons for your choices. Numbers in parentheses refer to the numbered paragraphs.

_____ 1. There are many differences among people. (1)

_____ 2. All people have the wish to survive. (2)

_____ 3. All people need food, clothing, and shelter. (2)

_____ 4. Different people eat different food. (3)

_____ 5. Different people wear different clothing. (4)

_____ 6. Different people have different kinds of shelter. (5)

_____ 7. Some people use money to buy what they need. (6, 7)

_____ 8. Some people use goods to *barter* for what they need. (6, 8)

_____ 9. Some people meet their needs by giving a service to other people. (6, 9)

_____ 10. People have differences but they meet their needs the same way. (10)

Level 2

Check the statements that express ideas you can find in the story. Be ready to identify information from the reading selection that supports your choices.

_____ 1. Even if you wear very nice clothes, you won't live long if you don't eat.

_____ 2. A person does not have to have money to survive.

_____ 3. A little seems like a lot to someone who has nothing.

_____ 4. A person with an extra piece of clothing always can eat.

_____ 5. Money, goods, and services can buy each other or can buy food, clothing, or shelter.

Level 3

Check the statements that express ideas you can find in the story and in your own experience. Be ready to give reasons for your choices.

_____ 1. You have to give something to get something.

_____ 2. What people want is not always what they need.

_____ 3. Life would be boring if everyone and everything were the same.

_____ 4. People who have should help people who have not.

Example: Grade 8, Mathematics

Rectangular Regions

Problem: Lorenzo and Maria are buying sod for their back yard and connecting dog run. Here is a sketch of the area.

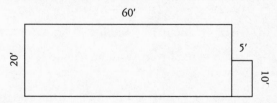

If sod costs $.75 a square foot, how much will it cost to cover the area with sod?

Level 1

Check all items that correctly identify information contained in the problem and what is to be found.

_____ 1. Lorenzo and Maria are improving their property.

_____ 2. Their dog run is square.

_____ 3. The dog run is smaller than the yard.

_____ 4. The back yard is rectangular.

_____ 5. The back yard is square.

_____ 6. Lorenzo and Maria have a dog.

_____ 7. A square foot of sod costs less than a dollar.

_____ 8. What is to be found?

    _____ a. The cost of the sod for the dog run.

    _____ b. The cost of the sod for the yard.

    _____ c. The total cost of the sod.

    _____ d. The cost of each square foot of sod.

    _____ e. The size of the house.

    _____ f. The color of the house.

    _____ g. The area of the dog run.

    _____ h. The area of the yard.

    _____ i. The length of fence around the dog run.

Level 2

Check the following items that identify operations needed to solve this problem.

_____ 1. length multiplied by width.

_____ 2. length multiplied by width added to length multiplied by width.

_____ 3. square feet multiplied by cost per square foot.

_____ 4. area times cost.

_____ 5. length times width plus length times width times cost.

_____ 6. length times width times cost plus length times width times cost.

_____ 7. l · w = a.

_____ 8. l · w · $ = cost.

_____ 9. (20 × 60 × $.75) + (5 × 10 × $.75) = _____.

_____ 10. (30 × 60) + (10 × 5) × $.75 = _____.

Level 3

Check the following statements that express ideas about mathematics that you found in your problem.

_____ 1. Areas of quadrilaterals can be found by multiplication.

_____ 2. Areas of rectangular regions can be found by multiplication and addition.

_____ 3. Areas of quadrilaterals can be found by addition.

_____ 4. Finding the cost of covering an area is a two-step process.

_____ 5. Other.

Example: Grade 8, Literature

Time: The Sprinters

Can a person beat time? Will time always be faster? What feelings come as people struggle against time? This poem may have an answer.

1. Before you read this poem, note the definitions of these words:
   pummeling—pounding rapidly
   pistoning—pushing with great force
   outpace—move faster than someone or something else
   mock—make fun of something or someone

2. One person in the group should read the poem aloud to the rest of the group. They may listen and follow along or just listen. (Poem *The Sprinters* by Lee Murchison is read.)

3. Some of the items listed below refer to runners; others refer to watchers; others to time. Decide to which category each item belongs and then place the letter of that item under the heading below to which it best belongs.

a. gun explodes them
b. fly in time's face
c. the ticking glass
d. try to smash
e. the beat that runs
f. the beat that streaks away

g. tireless
h. pound the stands
i. loving him
j. grace-driven stride
k. mocks the clock
l. bands that lock us in

Runners	Time	Watchers
____	____	____
____	____	____
____	____	____
____	____	____
____	____	____
____	____	____

4. Now check the following ideas you think this poem supports. Be reading to give reasons for your answers.

_____ a. Time is a barrier to be broken.

_____ b. No matter how fast a person moves time is always faster.

_____ c. People love winners more than losers.

_____ d. Records are made to be broken.

_____ e. A kind of violence and wildness is part of any attempt to do the impossible.

5. Each of the following statements may present ideas related to time. Place a check (✓) on the numbered line if you agree with the statement *and* if you think the author of the poem would agree with it. Be ready to discuss reasons for your choices.

_____ 1. Nothing is slower than time wished away; nothing is faster than time held dear.

_____ 2. People work for today and dream for tomorrow.

_____ 3. Time is a fence to be climbed, a chain to be broken.

_____ 4. What you do with your life is more important than how long you live.

_____ 5. Different people experience the same thing differently.

CONCLUSION

The essence of good teaching is showing students how to do what you require them to do. This includes showing them how to comprehend content-area material. The reading guides discussed in this article are an excellent vehicle for "showing how." Both their use and the results of their use bring considerable satisfaction to students and to their teachers.

About the Author

Harold L. Herber is Dean of the School of Education at Syracuse University.

References

Brown, A. "Metacognitive Development and Reading." In R.J. Spiro, B.C. Bruce, and W.F. Brewer (Eds.), *Theoretical Issues in Reading Comprehension.* Hillsdale, N. J.: Lawrence Erlbaum Associates, 1981.

Gray, W.S. "The Major Aspects of Reading." In H. Robinson (Ed.), *Supplementary Educational Monographs,* No. 90. Chicago: University of Chicago Press, 1960.

Herber, H.L. *Developing Study Skills in Secondary Schools.* Newark: International Reading Association, 1965.

Herber, H.L. *Teaching Reading in Content Areas.* Englewood Cliffs, N.J.: Prentice Hall, Inc., 1970, 1978.

Herber, H.L. "Developing Reading and Thinking Skills in Content Areas." In J. Segal, S. Chipman, and R. Glaser (Eds.), *Thinking and Learning Skills: Relating Instruction to Basic Research.* Hillsdale, N. J.: Lawrence Erlbaum Associates, 1985.

Herber, H.L. and J. Nelson. "Questioning Is Not the Answer." *Journal of Reading* (1975) 18, 512–517.

Herber, H.L. and J. Nelson. "A Network of Secondary School Demonstration Centers for Teaching Reading in Content Areas." Basic Skills Improvement Program, Title II, Final Report, Syracuse University, 1984.

Herber, H. and J. Nelson-Herber. "Planning the Reading Program." In O. Niles and A. Purves (Eds.), *Becoming Readers in a Complex Society.* Chicago: NSSE, 1984.

Nelson-Herber, J. "A Safe Place to Learn," in press.

Pearson, P.D. and D.D. Johnson. *Teaching Reading Comprehension.* New York: Holt, Rinehart, and Winston, 1978.

Riley, J.D. "An Investigation of the Effects of Reading Guides and a Directed Reading Method upon Word Problem Comprehension, Problem Solving Ability, and Attitude Toward Mathematics." Unpublished doctoral dissertation, Syracuse University, 1976.

Rumelhart, D.E. *Toward an Interactive Model of Reading* (Technical Report No. 56). Center for Human Information Processing. La Jolla: University of California, 1976.

Shoemaker, M. "Evaluation of Reading Instruction in Content Areas." Unpublished paper, Syracuse University, 1977.

Smith, N.B. *Reading for Today's Children.* Englewood Cliffs, N.J.: Prentice-Hall, 1963.

How should authors and readers relate to each other? Sardy argues that students should be taught to respond to text materials not as an authoritative document to be merely digested, but as a set of ideas to be carefully examined, queried, and adapted to their own purposes and expectations. She details the assumptions and procedures of the Directed Thinking about Reading (DTAR) for challenging students to analyze and reflect upon their reading and thus attain an understanding of the text that is personally meaningful.

Thinking About Reading

Susan Sardy

The process of learning to think about reading is very much the same as learning to think about any other problem. In each case, the learner's mind is assailed by a variety of stimuli. The reader also must act to select, repress, soften, emphasize, correlate, and organize, all under the influence of the right mental set or purpose or demand (Vygotsky, 1962; Thorndike, 1974; Bruner, 1956; Inhelder et al., 1974). What distinguishes reading comprehension from many other problem-solving activities is the opportunity texts offer for contemplation and reconsideration. Students can learn to take advantage of this opportunity when the reading task is properly defined.

If left alone, the process of learning how to think about reading is shaped by the haphazard questioning techniques of everyday classroom instruction (Durkin, 1979). The outcome of such unsystematic exposure is that many students do not learn to use their texts in a functional manner. If by functional use of a text we mean the ability to examine it critically and to disentangle pertinent information from the manner in which it is presented, then in order to do so, students must develop a sense of composition of that text. That is, they must understand the role and practice of authorship (Meyer et al., 1980; Doctorow, Wittrock and Marks, 1978).

AUTHORSHIP VS. AUTHORITY

The concept of authorship is characterized by the sets of choices made at various points in the composition process. As illustrated in Figure 1, a writer brings a point of view and a sense of purpose to a topic. This leads the author to select not only the concepts, words, syntactic structures, and patterns of organization with which to develop the discussion, but to frame them within a coherent discourse. The need for logical relationships between ideas requires decisions at various points in the text about where transitions should be made as well as the type and amount of background information that is to be explicit or implied. Readers do understand "author" as the one who gave existence to the written statement. However, this inventor, composer, and writer of a treatise or book all too often is perceived or presented as an "authority," one whose opinion on a subject is *entitled* to be accepted because of presumed expertise on the particular topic. When viewed in this latter way, the author's text becomes a definitive statement. Comprehension becomes defined as mastery of that statement. The reader's role is one of trying to read the mind of the author and to match, as closely as possible, a "correct" interpretation of the text (Harris, 1962; Carnine and Silbert, 1979).

The one basic premise of the Directed Thinking about Reading (DTAR) approach to reading comprehension is that students must be taught to distinguish between authorship and authority. They must learn to view the text as a set of problems to be solved rather than as the final word on a subject. They must learn that they are entitled to criticize and evaluate a text for the extent to which it succeeds in communicating to them as individual readers. Teachers who take advantage of this increased awareness of the intimate relationship between composition and comprehension can help students improve their own writing, as well.

READING COMPREHENSION

Ever since Piaget's active rejection of behaviorist models of thinking (Piaget, 1950; Piaget and Inhelder, 1969), examination of reading comprehension has taken advantage of newer models of psycholinguistic theory (Goodman and Goodman, 1967; Goodman and Burke, 1980; Harste and Burke, 1978; and Smith, 1973) and cognitive development (Neisser, 1976; Doctorow et al., 1978; Carroll, 1981; Kentsch and Vipond, 1979; and Rumelhart, 1980). The resultant view of the

FIGURE 1. ILLUSTRATION OF THE COMPOSITION AND READING COMPREHENSION PROCESSES

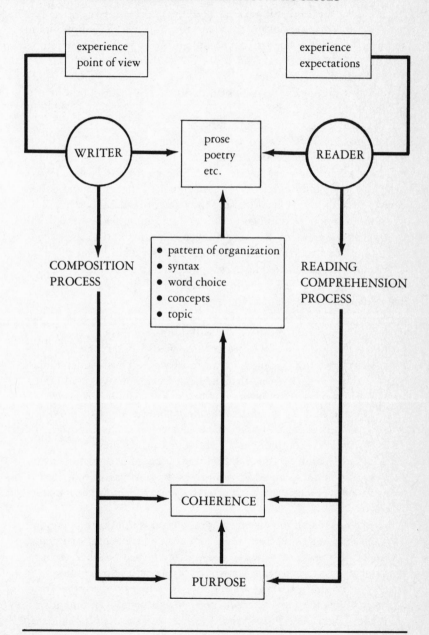

comprehension process is one of ever-increasing strategic complexity. The transaction between reader and text is clearly seen as guided by the reader's evaluation of information expressed and relationships explored. That this evaluation, in turn, is a function of the reader's background knowledge about the topic and recognition of the suppositions and structure that guide the development of the text has been amply demonstrated (Andre and Anderson, 1978–79; Pearson and Johnson, 1978; Rumelhart and Ortony, 1977; Spiro, 1975; and Taylor, 1982).

Attempts to simplify the task of thinking about reading by simplifying the text have led, in the past, to an interesting problem. Guided by superficial and inappropriate measures of text complexity (i.e., sentence length, and individual word features), attempts to lower readability have led to loss of referential details and to less coherent and, therefore, less comprehensible text (Taylor, 1982; Shimmerlik and Nolan, 1976). It is only by examining clarity of conceptual relationships and coherence of text selections in addressing the issue of readability that appropriate measures of text difficulty can and are being made through the use of the Degrees of Reading Power (Koslin, Koslin, and Zeno, 1979) and other variables related to text analysis. Thus, the technology of text analysis has allowed us to recognize and to create more "considerate" texts; those that contain sufficient explicitness and clarity of intersentential relationships (Beck et al., 1984).

No attempt at development of considerate texts will meet the needs of all students who read them. Nor will these attempts to reshape texts substitute for those already in use or those whose literary merit renders them worth reading if somewhat more obscure. Thus, students must learn to think in such a way that they can tackle, unravel, and understand any author's communication (Meyer et al., 1980; Lerner, 1982).

Attempts to simplify the task of thinking about reading by providing students with isolated skill practice are derived from an outdated and distorted view of comprehension and thinking (Skinner, 1957; and Scibior, 1984). Skill practice methodology is based upon the behaviorist view of reading as an additive process, in which skills practiced to the point of overlearning are expected to be transferred to new materials (Boning, 1977).

As recent research indicates, comprehension is not quantitative, nor is it merely a set of discrete skills, nor do comprehension strategies automatically transfer to new and unfamiliar materials. Rather, comprehension appears to involve selective reorganization of psycholinguistic and cognitive strategies that are highly dependent on the topic, structure, and style of the text selection and the expectations of the individual reader (Baker, 1979; Willows, 1974; Rumelhart, 1980; Spillich et al., 1979; and Spiro, 1975). What is necessary to improve comprehension of difficult text is a strategy that can exploit this diversity while providing the reader with the skill to apply it to new and even unknown materials.

DIRECTED THINKING ABOUT READING

The approach to teaching reading comprehension that is known as Directed Thinking about Reading (Stauffer, 1969) embodies many of the principles of effective teaching uncovered by Rosenshine (1983) and Brophy (Brophy and Good, 1974) in their extensive research on teacher behavior. The DTAR is a large group or whole class method. The intellectual sparks that a variety of individuals bring to a brainstorming session cannot be duplicated in guided silent reading. The presentation of new material is built firmly upon a review of previous learning and directed by the teacher. There is both guided and independent practice, each with its own corrective feedback, but the DTAR differs from traditional directed instruction in the role played by the students. In conventional directed reading lessons (D.R.L.), the reading objectives, the questions that must be answered, and the correct answers are all determined by the teacher and by the contents of the text. In a traditional D.R.L., students are encouraged to read for those details and relationships that the teacher believes are important. Answers are correct when they appear in the text and are incorrect when they do not (Harris, 1962; Carnine and Silbert, 1979; Omanson et al., 1984). In sharp contrast, the DTAR requires that those students about to read the text be the ones who determine the purposes for reading, the questions to be answered, and frequently, exactly what those answers should be.

Preparation for a traditional D.R.L. generally includes introduction of new or unfamiliar vocabulary prior to reading (Harris, 1969). Preparation for a DTAR involves review of important concepts that underlie the structure of the text and that guided the author's development. These concepts may not ever be explicitly stated but are represented in the text by means of examples or distinguishing characteristics (Smith, 1973; Pearson and Johnson, 1978).

The main purpose of the initial reading (and often the only reading) of the text in a D.R.L. is to gain that information and realize those relationships determined as appropriate or correct by the teacher (or suggested by a teacher's guide). In the DTAR, the readers first are required to speculate about the nature of information and/or relationships that might logically be contained in a selection on a given topic. Then they are asked to read and reread for verification of their conjectures. If hypotheses generated prior to the reading are, in fact, confirmed by the text, it merely means that both readers and writer share a common view of what constitutes important aspects of the topic. If, however, the readers discover discrepancies from their initial conjectures, it does not mean that they were wrong, ignorant, or stupid, but that they have priorities assigned to specific sets of information on the topic that differ from the writer's. Thus, students trained to read in a DTAR learn to think about texts in a very different way than those who have had only traditional instruction. In a DTAR the text is not viewed as an absolute set of details and relationships to be mastered as an end, in and of itself. Rather, it is viewed as the vehicle by which an author conveys selected aspects of a given subject. The author's choice of details and the manner in which they are presented are subject to critical evaluation by readers who may vary greatly in their reading competence. The clarity with which the information and ideas are communicated, the effectiveness of illustrations and examples, and the general coherence of the text all become the subject of discussion.

The outcome of this kind of systematic analysis is a more sensitive, active reader; one who engages in a transactive relationship with the text. More of the students trained to think about reading in this way display higher motivation and engage in more thoughtful response to reading than do those in a traditional directed reading lesson. In fact, so great is their involvement, students sometimes find it difficult to move on to a new selection if they have not had all their own questions answered.

Assumptions of a DTAR

There are several underlying assumptions which must be shared by all teachers engaged in any Directed Thinking about Reading activity.

Assumption 1

Text is worthwhile. The text selected for the DTAR lesson must be worth the time and energy that will be expended. It must be well written, contain important information, or represent a particular structure or pattern of organization that has transfer value. Although, in theory, it is possible to develop a DTAR lesson for any reading material, not all texts warrant this intensity of attention for a whole class lesson. It is pointless to develop a DTAR for a trivial or meaningless selection. If properly practiced, the DTAR approach will give students a means by which to identify and criticize less worthwhile texts on their own.

Assumption 2

Students can think. All students, even those with reading difficulties, can be taught to think critically about their texts. With systematic and appropriate direction, students can be guided to speculate about logical relationships and relevant details, make meaningful associations, weigh facts, and make inferences, judgments, and generalizations in virtually every area of study in which a text is used.

Assumption 3

Students have knowledge. All students know something about every selection they are asked to read. If the teacher has identified and carefully selected the concepts on which to focus the preliminary discussion, there should be a variety of tools for hooking student knowledge to the text. (A subordinate and prerequisite assumption is that teachers know their students well enough to make these connections.)

Assumption 4

Students use knowledge. Students can and must use their knowledge of concepts and relationships to improve their reading comprehension. They can generate hypotheses based upon their own experience. They can anticipate information and/or organizational features of the text. This active reading involves recognition of those text features that have been predicted. Rereading enables students to see that some of their predictions were not fulfilled because the author made other choices, which carried with them other sets of logical relationships and supporting details.

Assumption 5

Texts can be understood. Almost any reasonable text of an appropriate unit of length and readability can be read and understood by almost any student. With a well-organized DTAR, students need not read only those selections that appear to match their comprehension ability. The use of titles and picture clues, as well as other graphic features of text units, can serve to trigger useful associations. Discussion of conceptual relationships can help to anticipate context clues to new or difficult vocabulary. Anticipation of structure and organization of manageable text units can guide readers through a complex presentation. (The underlying assumption is that the teacher is thoroughly familiar with the text structure.)

Assumption 6

Rereading is necessary. No worthwhile text gives up all of its information in a single reading. Comprehension usually requires multiple reading of the text, each focused on a particular aspect of the presentation. Students can learn to refocus and reread and will be more willing to do so if they help to determine the purposes for rereading.

It should be clear from these assumptions that the two important factors that contribute most to an effective DTAR are teacher preparation (familiarity with the text, or willingness to apply the method to an unknown text) and selection of a worthwhile text, one that provides the reader with sufficient structure, challenge, and content. With these in order, the DTAR can be presented to any class from primary through secondary grades, whether they are compensatory education or gifted students, if the basic sequence of steps is followed carefully.

PLANNING THE DTAR

Step 1: Text Selection and Preview

1. *Find a text selection that is worth the study effort.* It should be well written and informative. Do not be concerned if the text is above the students' instructional level. With adequate preparation and direction, students will be able to read and understand it.

2. *Determine the appropriate objectives for the selection.* Identify the most important concepts. Note whether or not critical attributes and/or familiar examples are employed in the discussion and if, indeed, the concept actually is referred to by name. A checklist may prove helpful at this stage (see Figure 2). Develop a concept map that exploits the text information and structure. Check through the text for the presence of specific context clues to concept development, structure, and organization. Identify the suppositions made by the author and the need for background information.

3. *Survey the text for graphic cues.* Note such surface features as use of italics or boldface, marginal notes, sections headings, diagrams, introductory or summary statements, and even punctuation. Note the instances and frequency of novel or unusual uses of familiar words, unfamiliar words, and technical vocabulary or jargon. Note patterns of paragraph structure, including placement of

FIGURE 2. CHECKLIST FOR TEXT EVALUATION:
CONCEPT DEVELOPMENT

_____ 1. Definition is given in text when a new concept is introduced. Method
used:
— typographic cue
— text signal (e.g., "...which means...")
— marginal notes
— footnote or glossary reference
— other (please specify)

_____ 2. Examples are provided to illustrate concept.
— one example (+ discussion)
— several examples (+ discussion)

_____ 3. Contrasting ideas and objects are explained for comparison.

_____ 4. Related ideas and objects are presented and discussed for
comparison.

_____ 5. Attributes (characteristics) of the concept are clearly
described, aiding in discrimination of relevant and irrelevant
details.

_____ 6. Negative instances, exceptions and limitations are included
to clarify concept.

_____ 7. Applications of the concept are suggested by the text material.

_____ 8. Cause-effect relationship of concept to others is developed by
the text.

main ideas or topic sentences and supporting details. Note transitions or shifts in focus.

4. *Plan one or two introductory questions or statements.* These may relate to the content of the selection. For example, you may want to ask: "If you were writing about __, what would you include?" or "When you think of __, what comes to your mind?" These opening questions also may relate to the text structure. For example: "If you wanted to interest someone in the subject of __, how might you begin the discussion?" or "What kind of organization would be most effective for an article about __?"

Step 2: Directing Prereading Thinking and Discussion

1. *Encourage students to generate predictions about the content and/or structure of the material in response to the opening questions.* Use the chalkboard to classify and organize their predictions into categories that they can label or into a concept map that can be used for notetaking. *Avoid digression* from the main focus of the lesson. Emphasize only critical features of those concepts chosen for emphasis in that lesson. Illogical suggestions and speculations should be acknowledged with brief attention to why they are inappropriate. Those that are logical but irrelevant to the main purpose of the text should be acknowledged and can be duly noted in another section of the chalkboard. The main purpose of this portion of the lesson is to encourage students to speculate logically, based upon their experience with the topic and with the nature of text organization. The discussion should be relatively brief (8 to 10 minutes), focused, and to the point, and it should serve as the initial motivation for reading the selection.

2. *Build background information when it is apparent that students have insufficient information to handle the material.* Use this as an additional opportunity to motivate them to read the selection.

3. *Clarify purposes for reading.* As an outcome of the discussion, students will have raised a number of questions as well as speculated on content or organization of the text. These are, in fact, the purposes for which they will engage in the initial reading. Since there are likely to be several of these purposes, they may be divided up as a set of specific objectives for specific students (volunteers or draftees) within the group. Encourage students to select those questions or hypotheses that most interest them. Be

sure to have them clearly state their purposes before actually reading the text.

Step 3: Initial Reading and Thinking

1. *Students and teacher read to test predictions and answer questions raised in the prereading discussion.* Since this need not be a close reading, it is frequently helpful to team weaker students to help each other examine the text.

2. *Notetaking should be encouraged.* As they read, students should be encouraged to note unfamiliar words or other difficulties that impede comprehension. If the selection is fairly lengthy, some method is needed for noting the answers to questions or details that have been correctly predicted. Concept maps or other types of graphic organizers are excellent techniques for this purpose. *Note:* Close reading is inappropriate during this initial reading. Students should be skimming for those details that confirm or refute hypotheses, for examples to illustrate a point, for similarities and differences, for cause-and-effect relationships, for sequence of events, or for other structural features. Additional rereadings will be necessary to allow students to process the entire selection. (Don't worry about students missing anything important. They will gain a great deal more than you expect from the process of rereading.)

Step 4: Directed Discussion—First Reading

1. *Direct a discussion of the first reading.* This discussion should provide answers to at least some of the questions raised in the prereading phase of the lesson. Students must be required to support each answer by referring to the appropriate portion of the text. Encourage students to read aloud the supportive material. The other students are expected to indicate their agreement or disagreement by finding additional support or refutation in the text. At this time, the rereading can be directed toward finding additional examples, irrelevancies, similarities and differences, as well as observing relationships between new information and what was previously known.

2. *During this discussion phase, new conjectures, hypotheses, and confusions are going to be raised.* Closer rereading will be required to confirm or test these new conjectures. Once again, the set of new objectives for reading can be divided among the group or pursued by

those individuals who raised them in the first place. Alternatively, the entire class can investigate the text to find the answers to each new question or to test each new conjecture.

Step 5: Successive Rereading

1. This phase of the DTAR is the most flexible portion of the entire lesson. It owes its recursive nature to the fact that students can be encouraged to raise new questions and to peruse the text for as much detail as the teacher considers appropriate. Each conjecture or set of conjectures requires a closer subsequent rereading of all or a selected portion of the text, but for different purposes. Clearly, the text must contain material that lends itself to such continuous examination and a structure that reveals itself to the focused scrutiny of the readers.

2. *It is at this point in the lesson that the provision for individual differences in the group can be made most evident.* Advanced readers can be guided into thinking about more subtle text features such as the word choice, style, and structure the author used to communicate fine shades of meaning. Less able readers can be guided to observe the degree of explicitness of information. They can be encouraged to evaluate for themselves the effectiveness of the author's style and organization of detail. In both cases, readers must be encouraged to cite specific instances in the text that support their positions and to suggest specific alternatives to those features they have deemed ineffective. By so doing, they are being encouraged to develop increasing sensitivity to the stylistic choices involved in the composition process.

Step 6: Follow-Up Application

1. A wide variety of follow-up activities grow naturally out of a well-planned DTAR. They are limited only by the time and support resources available and by the focus of groups or individuals in the class. One set of activities can involve text revision and evaluation. Another set can involve additional readings and comparisons. In order to capitalize on and reinforce the thinking skills, which are so crucial to a DTAR, all follow-up activities must be derived from ideas, conjectures, or criticism evoked during the fifth step of the lesson. Thus, planning for a DTAR should include a mechanism for noting fruitful avenues for future work. This can range from simple mechanical starring or underlining key features

as they are discussed and listed on the chalkboard to a more elaborate follow-up lesson with specially prepared materials.

2. For less able readers who are being exposed to the initial stages of the DTAR, as much follow-up as possible should occur under the teacher's direct supervision. A gradual decrease in dependence of these students on teacher guidance makes it possible for them to become more efficient in self-directed reading and thinking, which is the ultimate goal of a DTAR.

SUMMARY

The main purpose of this Directed Thinking about Reading approach to teaching comprehension is to reshape the relationship between student, text, and teacher. Instead of presenting the text as a source of information against which the correctness of student responses is matched, the DTAR views it as the outcome of a series of choices made by the author, the purpose of which is to communicate information. The teacher's role is to help students to anticipate, recognize, and understand the writer's choices and the framework (i.e., organization, structure, point of view) within which they were made. In addition, the student is encouraged to evaluate the effectiveness with which the text succeeds as a communication. This approach forces the student into a more active and flexible role as a reader in the communication process. No longer can students taught through a DTAR conceive of the task of learning from a text as a one-time run-through to unravel the author's intent. Rather, they will have learned to redefine the task as a series of encounters with the text, each for a different purpose, each requiring a somewhat different rate and a somewhat different strategy. They will have learned to conceive of the text as a not necessarily perfect instrument of communication from a distant author who may or may not have great authority. They will have learned that they must share a certain point of view and set of expectations with that author in order to fully appreciate the meaning of any text aimed at a hypothetical audience. They will have learned that any text can be improved as a personal communication by judicious additions, deletions, or revisions that add explicitness or eliminate ambiguity.

The sense of audience, structure, and content that grow naturally out of systematic use of a DTAR ties reading of content-area text most closely to an appreciation of the writing process. It systematically encourages critical reading among students who may never encounter any other opportunities to develop this skill. They are continually made aware of the effect of and the need for clarity and organization in the expression of ideas, as they think more effectively about what they read.

About the Author

Susan Sardy is Associate Professor, Department of Education, at Yeshiva University.

References

Andre, M. and T. Anderson. "The Development and Evaluation of Self-Questioning Study Technique." *Reading Research Quarterly* 14 (1978–79): 606–623.

Baker, L. "Do I Understand or Do I Not Understand What Is the Question." Urbana: Illinois Center for the Study of Reading, Report #10, 1979.

Beck, J. et al. "Improving Comprehensibility of Stories: The Effects of Revisions That Improve Coherence." *Reading Research Quarterly* 19 (3) (1984):263–277.

Becker, W.C. and R. Gersten. "A Follow-up of Follow-through: The Later Effects of the Direct Instruction Model on Children in Fifth and Sixth Grades." *American Educational Research Journal* 196 (1982): 75–92.

Boning, R. *Specific Skill Levels.* New York: Barnell Loft, 1977.

Brophy, J. and T. Good. *Teacher-Student Relationships: Causes and Consequences.* New York: Holt, Rinehart, and Winston, 1974.

Bruner, J., J. Goodman, and G. Austin. *A Study of Thinking.* New York: Wiley, 1956.

Carnine, D. and S.J. Silbert. *Direct Instruction Reading.* Columbus, Ohio: Charles Merrill, 1979.

Carnine, D., E. Kameenei, and G. Coyle. "Utilization of Contextual Information in Determining the Meaning of Unfamiliar Words." *Reading Research Quarterly* 19 (2) (1984):188–204.

Carnine, D., E. Kameenei, and A. Maggs. "Components of Analytic Assistance: Statement Saying, Concept Training, and Strategy Training." *Journal of Educational Research* 75 (1982):374–377.

Carroll, J. "Ability and Task Difficulty on Cognitive Psychology." *Educational Researcher* 10 (1981):114.

Doctorow, M., M. Wittrock, and C. Marks. "Generative Processes in Reading Comprehension." *Journal of Educational Psychology* 70 (2) (1978):109–118.

Duffy, G. "Teacher Effectiveness Research: Implications for the Reading Profession." East Lansing: Michigan State University Institute for Research on Teaching, 1981.

Durkin, D. "What Classroom Observations Reveal about Reading Comprehension Instruction." *Reading Research Quarterly* 15 (1979): 481–533.

Frase, L. and B. Schwartz. "Effects of Question Production on Prose Recall." *Journal of Educational Psychology* 11 (1975):459–464.

Goodman, K. and C. Burke. *Reading Strategies: Focus on Comprehension.* New York: Holt, Rinehart, and Winston, 1980.

Goodman, K. and Y. Goodman. "Reading—A Psycholinguistic Guessing Game." *Journal of the Reading Specialist* (1967):126–135.

Harris, A.J. *Effective Teaching of Reading.* New York: McKay, 1969.

Harste, J. and C. Burke. "Toward a Sociopsycholinguistic Model of Reading Comprehension." *Viewpoints in Teaching and Learning* 45 (1978):19–34.

Harste, J. "Learning by Anomaly: A Response to Scibior." *Forum for Reading and Language Education* 1 (1984):27–31.

Inhelder, B., H. Sinclair, and M. Bonet. *Learning and the Development of Cognition.* Cambridge, Mass.: Harvard University Press, 1974.

Kintsch, W. and D. Vipond. "Reading Comprehension and Readability in Educational Practice and Psychological Theory." In Nelson (ed.), *Perspectives on Memory Research.* Hillsdale, N.J.: Erlbaum, 1979.

Koslin, B.L., S. Koslin, and S. Zeno. "Towards an Effectiveness Measure in Reading." In S.H. White (ed.), *Testing, Teaching, and Learning: Report of a Conference on Research on Testing.* Washington, D.C.: National Institute of Education, 1979.

Lerner, R.M. "Children and Adolescents as Producers of Their Own Development." *Developmental Review* 2 (1982):342–370.

Meyer, B., D. Brandt, and G. Bluth. "Use of Author's Textual Schema: Key for Ninth Graders' Comprehension." *Reading Research Quarterly* 16 (1980):72–103.

Neisser, U. *Cognition and Reality.* San Francisco: W.H. Freeman, 1976.

Omanson, R. et al. "The Effects of Reading Lessons on Comprehension: A Processing Description." *Cognition and Instruction* 1 (1984): 45–67.

Pearson, D. and D. Johnson. *Teaching Reading Comprehension.* New York: Holt, Rinehart, and Winston, 1978.

Piaget, J. *Psychology of Intelligence.* London: Routledge, 1950.

Piaget, J. and B. Inhelder. *The Psychology of the Child.* New York: Basic Books, 1969.

Rosenshine, B. "Teaching Functions of Instructional Programs." *Elementary School Journal* (March, 1983):336–351.

Ross, S. and F. DiVesta. "Oral Summary as a Review Strategy for

Enhancing Recall of Textual Material." *Journal of Educational Psychology* 68 (1976):689–695.

Rumelhart, D. "Schemata, the Building Blocks of Cognition." In Spiro, Bruce, and Brewer (eds.), *Theoretical Issues in Reading Comprehension.* Hillsdale, N.J.: Erlbaum, 1980.

Rumelhart, D. and A. Ortony. "The Representation of Knowledge in Memory." In Anderson, Spiro, and Montague (eds.), *Schooling and the Acquisition of Knowledge.* Hillsdale, N.J.: Erlbaum, 1977.

Schallert, D. and G. Kleiman. "Why the Teacher Is Easier to Understand Than the Textbook." Urbana: Illinois Center for the Study of Reading, Report #9, 1979.

Scibior, O. "Transactional Processes in Literacy Learning." *Forum in Reading and Language Education* 1 (1984):3–26.

Shimmerlik, S. and J. Nolan. "Reorganization and the Recall of Prose." *Journal of Educational Psychology* 68 (1976):779–786.

Skinner, B.F. *Verbal Behavior.* New York: Appleton, 1957.

Smith, F. *Psycholinguistics and Reading.* New York: Holt, Rinehart, and Winston, 1973.

Spillich, G. et al. "Text Processing of Domain Related Information for High and Low Domain Knowledge." *Journal of Verbal Learning and Verbal Behavior* 18 (1979):279–290.

Spiro, R. "Inferential Reconstruction in Memory for Connected Discourse." Urbana: Illinois Center for the Study of Reading, Report #2, 1975.

Stauffer, R. *Teaching Reading as a Thinking Process.* New York: Harper and Row, 1969.

Taba, Hilda. *Curriculum Development: Theory and Practice.* New York: Harcourt Brace Jovanovich, 1962.

Taylor, B. "Text Structure and Childrens' Comprehension and Memory for Expository Material." *Journal of Educational Psychology* 74 (1982):323–340.

Thorndike, R. "Reading as Reasoning." *Reading Research Quarterly* 9 (2) (1974):135–147.

Tierney, R., J. Readence, and L. Dishner. *Reading Strategies and Practices: A Guide for Improving Instruction.* Boston: Allyn and Bacon, 1980.

Vygotsky, L.S. *Thought and Language.* New York: Wiley, 1962.

Willows, D. "Reading Between the Lines: Selective Attention by Good and Poor Readers." *Child Development* 45 (1974):408–415.

Part V
Readability and the Future of the Textbook

Historically, the dominant focus in the instruction of students has been the text. Generations of students have wrestled mightily with varying degrees of success with the complexities of text content.

Well into the present century, the concept of instruction was one of fitting the student into the mold of the text. Some students did fit the mold and comprehended, but far more failed to achieve the required "comprehension fit." Fortunately, one of the concepts that received high priority in scientific studies of education beginning with the third decade of this century was that of the comprehensibility, or readability, of text. It has gradually become apparent that there was far too often a mismatch between student and text—a mismatch too formidable for many a student to overcome. As a result of years of investigation, teachers and publishers alike have begun to think more in terms of matching texts to students. Selecting the right text for the right student is the theme of the first article in this section.

As opportunities for schooling have mushroomed, particularly in the United States, to include the vast majority of children, the proliferation of texts has likewise reached unprecedented heights. Schools now face difficult problems in text selection, not only in terms of readability, but in terms of the quality of content, its instructional soundness, and the effectiveness of the teacher guidance and teaching aids offered. Those faced with making such decisions, especially about basal reading programs, are subject to intense selling pressures by publishers. Because at present there are neither uniform standards nor a common set of procedures for text selection, the future of the text may well rest upon improved regulation of text adoption standards and procedures.

It is a truism that for effective comprehension there must be reasonable correspondence between the reader's background of knowledge and experience and the difficulty of text material. How may we improve the way we match texts to readers? After a critical and scholarly discussion of the development and use of readability estimates, Klare makes a series of practical suggestions (when, where, why, how) for using readability estimates in conjunction with other information to determine the optimum match of text to reader.

Matching Reading Materials to Readers: The Role of Readability Estimates in Conjunction with Other Information about Comprehensibility

George Klare

MATCHING READING MATERIALS TO READERS

Most teachers and reading specialists readily accept two premises as essential to effective instruction in reading:

1. A primary goal of instruction is to increase the comprehension skills of readers.
2. Comprehension skills are most likely to increase when the difficulty levels of reading materials are matched appropriately to the capabilities of readers.

The centrality of comprehension needs little added emphasis. John Locke recognized this as early as 1697 in his discussion of understanding (see Garforth, 1966, p. 73). So also did the National Institute of Education in its recent Request for Proposal describing the need for a Center for the Study of Reading, now established at the University of Illinois (see Durkin, 1978–79, p. 433).

The importance of matching the difficulty of reading materials appropriately to reader capabilities also needs little further emphasis. Betts (1946, p. 442) credits McGuffey with having recognized this early in grading the difficulty of the basic reading materials in his readers published around 1840. Recent publications of reading specialists continue to stress this point. May (in Bond, Tinker, and Wasson, 1979, p. 75) states, "A learning task which is too easy for children will be boring, and one that is too hard will cause them to withdraw." Bond, Tinker, and Wasson (1979, p. 14) also point out, "If it were possible in day-to-day teaching to teach each pupil according to his capabilities there would be less need for remedial work."

The problem lies in achieving this ideal. Chall and Feldman (1966) found that the skill of assigning appropriate levels of material varied among teachers. Zintz (1970) found that appropriate matches were not common. This is clearly not an easy task for teachers. An obvious reason is the wide range of reading ability found in the typical classroom, a range that increases with grade level. This, plus related issues such as class size, make it difficult for teachers to judge an individual's reading ability and decide on appropriate reading material.

Testing Reading Comprehension

Early recognition of the need to supplement subjective judgments of individual reading abilities came in the form of standardized reading tests. Such tests existed around the time of World War I—the Gray Standardized Oral Reading Paragraph Tests (Gray, 1915) are one example—but the emphasis on "mental testing" during the war and soon after gave special impetus to this movement. Many tests were developed, but only two of the early tests especially relevant to later attempts at matching materials to readers need be mentioned here: the Stanford Achievement Test (reading), by Kelley, Ruch, and Terman (1922); and the Standard Test Lessons in Reading, by McCall and Crabbs (1925). Both measures provided scores in terms of grade levels, and both were popular enough with users to appear in a number of later editions. Such tests provided a way of meeting the reader-ability part of the match.

Estimation of Readability

An objective method of meeting the other part of the match, the reading difficulty of materials, was developing at about the same time in E. L. Thorndike's *The Teacher's Word Book* (1921). This book provided data on the frequency of occurrence of 10,000 printed words, including the most common in the language and thus words of great significance for the teaching of reading. Thorndike encouraged such use by providing guidelines for grades where particular words could be taught appropriately. His frequency count came to be widely used in teaching and research, appearing in two later, enlarged editions; in fact, only the relatively recent use of the computer provided those counts that have largely superseded it.

Early Readability Formulas

Evidence for the influence of Thorndike's count came quickly in the work of Lively and Pressey (1923). They developed what came to be regarded as the first of the "readability formulas," providing several indices of the difficulty of text largely in terms of the Thorndike frequency values of the words in 1,000-word samples.

Lively's and Pressey's criterion of validity consisted only of their judgments of the relative difficulty of 16 different pieces of reading material. Vogel and Washburne (1928) took the next step by providing a better criterion for their new formula. They used Lively's and Pressey's method to analyze 700 books that had been named by at least 25 out of almost 37,000 children as ones they had read during the school year and liked. And in conjunction with this, they had reading-grade scores for each child on the paragraph-meaning section of the Stanford Achievement Test. The median score for the children who read and liked a representative sample from the books could therefore be computed and used as a difficulty level in developing their new readability formula (Vogel and Washburne, 1928). This new "Winnetka" formula, a regression equation surprisingly modern in appearance, was also surprisingly predictive; even by today's standards it yielded estimates that correlated .845 with the reading test scores of the children who read and liked the criterion books.

With Vogel's and Washburne's work the circle was complete: the reading difficulty of materials could be matched objectively in terms of grade levels to the abilities of readers. This was not a perfect circle, but Vogel's and Washburne's method yielded better matches than subjective judgments, and it became widely used in one form or another as a way of getting readability estimates.

Large-Scale Estimation of the Difficulty of Reading Materials

The Lively-Pressey and Winnetka formulas, plus others developed soon after, formed the basis for large-scale estimations of the difficulty of reading material for children. The first book to appear was Washburne's and Vogel's *Winnetka Graded Book List* (1926), which presented their analysis of the 700 described above. Lively's and Pressey's method, as noted, was used in this analysis, and the Winnetka method was used in the enlarged edition, called *The Right Book for the Right Child.* Lewerenz used his own formula in providing vocabulary grade-placements of over 2,700 books (Lewerenz, 1937). Rue then used both the Winnetka and the Lewerenz grade estimates in compiling an analysis of 4,000 books for the intermediate grades (Rue, 1940).

Widespread Use of Readability Estimates

Around 1940 readability formulas began to change and become easier to use. Applying Thorndike's word-frequency values was time-consuming; this variable was abandoned, and the number of variables in formulas was reduced. Lorge's formula (1939) was a landmark not only for being easy to apply but also because it was the first developed with the McCall-Crabbs Standard Test Lessons in Reading as a criterion of difficulty. At that point, the problem of matching materials to readers was simplified. However, clouds of criticism have grown along with the growth of readability estimation.

CRITICISM OF READABILITY ESTIMATES AND THEIR USE

Critics of readability estimation have been around almost as long as readability formulas. Moore (1935), for example, predicted that readers would "recoil from reading" rewritten classics, and S.E. Fitzgerald (1953) felt that such "literature by slide rule" was unfortunate at best. But such comments were relatively rare until readability formulas began to be applied more widely to educational materials. Then the criticisms became more frequent and more specific. The major concerns about formula estimation are illustrated below through selected reports.

Formula Disagreements

As noted earlier, readability formulas are not perfect predictors of the difficulty of materials. Yet, as Chall points out (1979), formulas are quite predictive and compare well with the other educational and psychological tests. Furthermore, the intercorrelations of formula estimates, especially those from the best-known formulas, are often very high. Unfortunately, these same formulas do not always agree in the grade-level estimates they provide. Pauk, for example, found that the grade levels from the SMOG formula of McLaughlin (1969) differed widely from those of the Dale-Chall (1948) and Fry (1968) formulas. Such disagreements arise partly from the fact that definitions of *comprehension* and the levels used by developers of formulas vary so widely (Klare, 1984a). Most developers have used the grade level of readers who can answer 75 percent of the questions on a passage as their criterion of comprehension. This corresponds to the traditional "instructional" reading level (see Betts, 1946, p. 442). But some developers have used the more convenient statistical level of 50 percent, which unfortunately, is the traditional "frustration" level. And McLaughlin (1969) used what he called the more satisfactory 100 percent level, which, again unfortunately, differs from the traditional and more meaningful "independent" reading level of 90 percent. The use of these different levels of comprehension, each of which might be justified in itself, has contributed to the confusion in grade level estimates, especially since which level has been used is seldom clear and often forgotten.

Criterion Validity

One of the primary bases for evaluating a formula's predictive accuracy has always been correlation with a trustworthy criterion. Vogel and Washburne, as noted above, used as their criterion the values from a representative sampling of 700 books read and liked by children, in conjunction with their reading grade-level scores. Most developers, however, soon turned to the more convenient criterion provided by the McCall-Crabbs Standard Test Lessons in Reading. This would seem to be an almost ideal criterion for statistical purposes, with its many lessons varying in difficulty and content and its objective questions and detailed grade levels. Recently, however, use of this criterion has been seriously questioned—and by McCall himself. Stevens (1980) found him surprised to learn that the lessons had been used in formula development. He considered them only to be practice exercises, with their grade-level scores only rough equivalents for students to track their progress. This raises serious concern about the many formulas based directly or indirectly on the lessons, and particularly the grade levels they provide. A comparison (Klare, 1984b) of several formulas using the same variables but based on other criteria (as well as the lessons) actually shows relatively close grade-level agreement and thus reduces this concern; nevertheless, there is expressed need for improvement in this criterion as a basis for formula development. Harris and Jacobson (1974, 1975; Jacobson, Kirkland, and Selden, 1978), for example, argued that the norms of the lessons had become outdated and renormed certain of them for development purposes. Bormuth (1969) felt that a new and different kind of criterion would be superior and provided one, the most extensive one to date. He selected 330 passages of about 100 words each, ranging in difficulty from first-grade to college level and covering a wide range of subject matter. With cloze procedure as his measure of difficulty, he deleted every fifth word and used all five parallel versions of this deletion ratio. His subjects were 2,600 fourth- to twelfth-graders who took a total of 650 different passages. He checked the potential of 169 language variables against these data and developed 24 readability formulas of various types. Finally, he provided variations to predict the mean as well as the 35, 45, and 55 percent correct levels (corresponding roughly to frustration, instructional, and independent levels). The grade placement estimates yielded by these formulas clearly had the most extensive base of any before or since—and "extensive" is surely an understatement.

Grade Scaling

The notion of providing readability estimates in terms of grade levels appeared early and was embraced by most formula developers because these values could be compared so conveniently to school grades and reading test scores. Matching of reading materials to readers was thus a simple matter—too simple in the eyes of critics who argue that the scales do not compare perfectly with each other. Manzo (1979) specifically condemned the comparison of formula estimates with those derived from basal readers as a means of designating appropriateness for given grade levels, calling it "incestuous." He said this made readability research a construct without a point of reference. Problems with the grade scale subsequently led the Delegates Assembly of the International Reading Association to pass a resolution advocating that grade-equivalent scores be abandoned (Resolutions Passed by Delegates Assembly, 1981). Though specifically aimed at reading tests, this resolution also necessarily applies to readability estimates, raising still another question for formula users.

Sampling Variability

One of the problems with assigning a single value of any kind to indicate the degree of difficulty of a text is that it obscures what is often a high degree of variability. The traditional practice of analyzing 100-word samples rather than a complete text makes this an important consideration. And the growing encouragement for using only three such samples makes it an especially important concern. Coke and Rothkopf (1970), for example, found a range of Flesch Reading Ease values from approximately 35 to 120 (roughly from college level to below fourth-grade level, see Flesch, 1949) in a single book. They analyzed successive 100-word samples from a 20,000-word selection taken from a high school physics text and provided an interesting graph showing the probability of miscalculating the mean Reading Ease value of the text by five or more points as a function of sample size; the figures range from less than .01 for 60 samples up to almost .45 for five samples. G.G. Fitzgerald (1981) put the problem specifically in terms of grade levels. She defined a practical and statistically significant difference in sampling as more than one grade level of difference between sample and population means. Though the critical number of samples needed to avoid a difference of this size varied with the length of the book and other considerations, she characterized the entire set as "discouragingly large."

Degrees of Reading Power (DRP): Coordination of Reading Ability Scores and Readability Estimates

A recent article by Chall, herself the developer with Dale of the highly regarded Dale-Chall readability formula, is titled "Readability: In Search of Improvement" (1979). As noted above, traditional readability estimates do have a number of weaknesses that could be improved. The Degrees of Reading Power (DRP) program attempts to remedy many of these.

Briefly, the DRP program set about to improve the matching of reading difficulty to reader ability by coordinating readability estimates with reading test scores in terms of the same DRP units. The DRP reading test consists of passages about 325 words long from which words have been deleted and replaced with standard-length blanks. To that extent it is like a traditional cloze test; it differs, however, in that only seven selected words (rather than one-fifth of the words) have been deleted, and in that subjects are given five single-word options (rather than no added information) for arriving at the correct response to each blank. The DRP readability formula is based upon one developed by Bormuth in his readability study (1969). This formula, as noted earlier, was developed to predict cloze scores from a large number of passages varying in content and in level of difficulty.

No attempt will be made to provide details concerning the DRP reading test and readability formula; the *Users Manual* (1980) and the *Readability Report* (1982) already do that. Instead, attention will be focused on the ways in which the coordinated DRP program attempts to improve upon existing methods of matching reading materials to readers.

The criterion and grade-scale coordination problems mentioned above have been taken into account by using Bormuth's extensive criterion and by presenting both reading test scores and readability estimates in DRP units. In addition, many of the problems of formula disagreement and sampling variability have been sidestepped. The need to use readability estimates from different formulas has been minimized, since the *Readability Report* attempts to provide DRP estimates for as many published instructional materials as possible (currently about 3,500 books have been analyzed). The sampling of the materials is desirably large since the readability analyses are run by computer, which in turn makes possible estimates of variability as well as of average difficulty.

In addition to the above, the three traditional levels of comprehension—independent, instructional, and frustration—have been tabled for all DRP raw scores. Because of its importance, the instructional level has been provided with upper and lower bounds for still finer distinctions. Readers who have achieved a particular DRP test score can be matched through their scores to appropriate materials within the instructional range, or given materials for independent reading and steered away from materials likely to be frustrating.

The DRP program is able to provide detailed information of this sort partly because of the method of developing the test materials. The Rasch model makes it possible to calibrate a large group of passages from which parallel DRP tests can be built as needed. The modifications made to traditional cloze procedure yield further advantages. The traditional method deletes every fifth word, both function words (primarily articles, prepositions, and conjunctions) and content words (primarily nouns, verbs, adjectives, and adverbs). The contrasting DRP method deletes only seven selected and widely spaced content words from long, 325-word passages, with the following advantages.

1. Correct completion of a traditional cloze blank depends heavily upon the four or five words on each side of it, and in that sense provides a measure of comprehension at more nearly sentence level than the more desirable passage level. By spacing the blanks widely (i.e., with more than one sentence between them), DRP cloze comprehension is not predicated upon so narrow a base. Furthermore, by giving the reader five options, each one of which makes sense in its sentence but not its paragraph context, passage-level comprehension is further encouraged.

2. Correct completion of traditional cloze blanks, since they begin near the beginning of a passage and occur so frequently (i.e., every fifth word), are said to depend too heavily upon what readers already know and in particular upon their vocabulary. By using relatively long passages and placing the first blank some distance from the beginning, the DRP method starts readers who have a higher degree of background knowledge at less of an advantage over those with less background knowledge. Furthermore, by selecting words for deletion that are high in frequency, and by providing similarly common options from which to choose answers, the DRP method also gives readers who have a greater vocabulary less of an advantage.

3. Correct completion of traditional cloze blanks from which function words have been deleted is easier than completion of those from which content words have been deleted. In turn, typical readability variables are not as predictive for function as for content words (Bormuth, 1969). By deleting only content words (rather than both function and content words as in traditional cloze procedure), the DRP method yields a higher correlation between comprehension scores and readability estimates than would otherwise be possible.

The DRP program, in summary, appears to be a significant step forward in the development of ability testing and readability estimation, and the research reported to date supports this conclusion. As always, however, further reassurance on some questions would be desirable. Research attention to such points as the following, for example, would be welcome.

• Traditional cloze tests have been criticized as being primarily measures of redundancy rather than of comprehension (Kintsch and Vipond, 1979). To what extent is this true of DRP tests, considering their cloze heritage? How closely do DRP test scores correlate with other kinds of comprehension tests?

- Traditional cloze tests are said to avoid the problem (directed particularly at multiple-choice tests) of having easy questions over difficult text or difficult questions over easy text, since the text is the test. That is strictly correct, however, only if all five versions of an every-fifth deletion ratio are used, since the versions may differ so greatly in difficulty (Klare, 1982). To what extent does the DRP cloze method, where selected blanks are used, void this problem?
- Traditional cloze scores have been found easier to predict than other objective comprehension scores when using the same readability formulas (Miller, 1972). Would other well-regarded readability formulas do as well as the DRP formula on the DRP passages? How highly do estimates from the DRP formula correlate with those from these other formulas?
- Traditional prose research has been criticized because although it provides for generalizing to a subject population, it seldom provides adequately for generalizing to a language population (Coleman, 1964, and others). Since they are written specifically for DRP tests, to what extent are DRP passages representative of the population of instructional materials?
- Traditional among outside criteria for checking the validity of readability estimates have been judgments. To what extent would DRP estimates place materials at the same levels as pooled teacher judgments? (See Harrison, 1980, for such an evaluation.)

These questions aside, a much more disturbing issue has been raised: Should even the best of readability estimates be used? Has their overall effect been positive or negative?

The Use of Readability Estimates

Maxwell (1978) titled a recent study "Readability: Have We Gone Too Far?" The reason for her concern was the possibility that an "obsession" with readability might have been an important factor in the reported decline of 13- and 17-year-olds' inferential reading skills between 1970 and 1974 (*Reading in America,* 1976). Chall (1979; see also Chall, Conrad, and Harris, 1977) discovered evidence for this sort of speculation; she reported a study from her laboratory that found an association between the decline in textbook difficulty over a thirty-year period and the then-current decline in Scholastic Aptitude Test scores. She also described publishers as saying that teachers of the elementary grades were requesting science and social studies textbooks two years below the grade placement of their children.

Why should this be? Jorgenson (1977) uncovered an answer. He found a significant relationship between classroom adjustment ratings and differences in the matching of material difficulty to reader ability: behavior improved as the material became easier to read. In other words, less accurately matched material tended to be related to improved behavior, a finding that contradicts one of the basic premises of reading instruction and complicates the current social debate over low educational standards. If the difficulty level of reading materials is allowed to decline further, standards are likely to continue to fall and arouse further citizen concern. But if the difficulty of reading material is raised to more challenging levels—and Chall also reported that her study found a recent increase in the difficulty of primary texts to be associated with rising reading scores—behavior problems are likely to increase and further disrupt the instructional process.

What can be done to resolve this dilemma? There are no single or simple answers to so complex a problem, but certain suggestions might be helpful.

SUGGESTIONS FOR USING READABILITY ESTIMATES IN CONJUNCTION WITH OTHER INFORMATION ABOUT COMPREHENSIBILITY

Some critics have argued that the answer to the dilemma is to banish readability formulas and their estimates. Selzer (1981) says, "Readability is a four-letter word"; Battison and Goswami (1981, p. 10) say that formulas "have such a potential for mischief and misuse, we do not use them or recommend that others use them." But what would take their place in matching materials to readers? Specific studies may turn up various kinds of information related to the comprehensibility of text, but no metric is provided for their use. On the other hand, it is no longer enough to ask "Is readability real?" as Coupland (1978) does, and answer yes, or to say as Fry (1979) does, "In some respects, readability formulas have succeeded beyond their developers' wildest dreams." Though both may be true, there is now enough concern about readability estimation that Tibbett's (1973) query "How much should we expect readability formulas to do?" seems more appropriate. A review of the research literature suggests ways that other information, and particularly other kinds of information, about the comprehensibility of text can be used in conjunction with readability estimates to improve the matching of reading materials to readers. These suggestions are organized around five kinds of questions potential users might ask about applying formulas and the estimates they provide: when, where, why, what, and how?

When can readability formulas and their estimates be used? In 1976, the author looked carefully at the two chief reasons for applying reading formulas: the prediction and the production of readable writing (Klare, 1976). The two involve quite different processes. To predict comprehension scores, only "index" variables (such as sentence length) and a correlational approach to research are sufficient; to produce comprehensible text, "causal" variables (such as sentence complexity) and an experimental approach are needed. The former is consequently a much more straightforward process than the latter, and thus formulas can provide a good estimate for those levels of text in which the difficulty depends chiefly on "style" of writing as opposed to "content" of writing. This is most likely to be the case for primary-level materials and still reasonable enough for secondary-level materials; beyond beginning college-level materials it becomes less and less true. Users of formulas should be aware of two other cautions when evaluating a formula. First, the correlation coefficient can be a rubber yardstick, since the magnitude of the coefficient is sensitive to the range of talent in the materials being analyzed. Second, comprehension can be a rubbery criterion, since the desirable level varies with the reader's circumstances. But awareness of these limitations, as will be seen later, makes them less serious when using formulas for their intended purpose of predicting readable writing.

Using a readability formula when producing readable writing, on the other hand, is a far more questionable process; altering index variables, as Davison and Kantor (1982) have shown, does not necessarily produce a comparable change in comprehension. To put it another way, "writing to formula" is a bit like expecting to raise the effective temperature in a room by holding a match under the thermometer. If formulas are used, they should be kept strictly separate from the production process and only introduced afterward as a check on prediction.

To summarize when formulas and their estimates can be used, a good answer would be: for prediction, not production, of readable writing, and for material in which the level of difficulty depends primarily upon the style, not the content, of the writing.

Where can readability formulas and their estimates be used? One of the attractions of readability formulas is that they appear to be context-free, that is, to be applicable to all kinds of text. That characterization is not accurate, however. This is apparent from the realization that most may be applied—or rather misapplied—to passages in which the order of the words has been reversed; or to scrambled text (provided the punctuation remains); or to foreign-language text (provided the counts can be made). Users are unlikely to be misled into making such applications, but this does emphasize once again that typical formulas use only index variables, not causal variables. They only can be applied to considerate (i.e., meaningful continuous) prose, and then only under certain conditions.

As mentioned above, formulas are most appropriate for material in which style contributes more to difficulty than content, i.e., up to about beginning college level. They are also most appropriate for those levels of difficulty that correspond to the levels used in the criterion materials on which they were based, i.e., without extrapolation beyond those levels.

Formulas are therefore not appropriate for such material as plays or poetry, lists or tests, exercises or experiments, mathematics or music. Occasionally there has been research on special formulas for some of these special materials, but such formulas are generally not very predictive and must be used with caution.

To summarize where formulas and their estimates can be used, a good answer would be: with considerate prose, cautiously.

Why might formulas and their estimates be used? This question concerns the purpose of formulas in terms of matching materials to readers' circumstances. W. S. Gray, the pioneer in reading research, is said to have characterized the magnitude of the issue by describing reader motivation as ranging all the way from reading to learn to reading to forget. Readers, of course, are more willing to tolerate difficult material in the one setting than in the other.

A related but better breakdown for the purpose of reading instruction developed over the years. With the widespread use of reading tests, including informal ones, the three levels mentioned earlier—independent, instructional, and frustration—came to be accepted (Betts, 1946, p. 442). Relatively easy material is needed for readers to read successfully on their own; the traditional independent level, using objective comprehension tests, was considered to be that material on which they could answer 90 percent of the questions correctly. Bormuth (1967, 1968) and Rankin and Culhane (1969) found the comparable scores for traditional cloze tests to be from about 57 to 61 percent correct; for DRP cloze, the level has been adjusted again to a probability of .90. Relatively more difficult material can be used in an instructional setting; the traditional level was considered to be that on which 75 percent of the questions could be answered correctly. For traditional cloze tests, the figure was given as approximately 41 to 44 percent; for

DRP cloze, the probability figure once again is .75, with a range of about four DRP units provided on each side for refined assignment. Frustrating material traditionally was said to be that on which only 50 percent of the objective questions could be answered correctly; for DRP cloze a probability of .50 again has been set.

The important point is that one reader may be able to read a particular book independently, another may be able to read the same book with instructional help, and a third may be frustrated in trying to read it.

To summarize why formulas and their estimates might be used, a good answer would be: to help in deciding which materials might be used for which reader circumstances.

What other considerations affect formula estimates? Perhaps the most important consideration in using readability estimates appropriately is to use them in conjunction with other kinds of information about comprehensibility. And perhaps the most important kind of additional information concerns factors in readers that, for them as individuals, affect comprehensibility. Finally, perhaps the most important characteristic of these factors is that they may interact with the readability of the material in their effect upon comprehensibility. Some of the more critical factors are described briefly below through selected studies, with implications for how they affect the accuracy of readability estimates.

Ability

It may seem unnecessary to mention ability; its central role in determining whether or not something is comprehensible to an individual has long been acknowledged. However, the common practice of assigning reading material by readability grade level to all children in a particular class makes mention necessary. As studies have shown, the range of reading ability levels among the children increases with each passing year, so that ability becomes an increasingly important determiner of an individual's comprehension.

Sometimes an improvement in the readability of materials increases the comprehension for readers of different ability to much the same extent (see Klare, Mabry, and Gustafson, 1955). But sometimes an improvement affects such readers differently. Kincaid and Gamble (1977) found this in a study of standard and more readable versions of automobile insurance policies. They had three groups of readers: good, average, and poor. The good readers understood both the standard and the readable versions; the average readers understood the readable but not the standard; the poor readers understood neither version.

The implications for users of readability estimates include the following. First, select or recommend reading materials for individual readers whenever possible on the basis of a reliable test score rather than presence in a particular grade. Second, pay close attention to the less able readers when looking for more readable materials. Improved readability levels are more likely to help those struggling to understand than those already able to understand—and who may, in fact, profit from more challenging materials.

Interest

It may seem no more necessary to mention interest than ability; degree of interest has long been recognized as a prime determiner of an individual's comprehension. Yet the demonstrated effects of interest level upon comprehension are once again complex.

For example, Asher, Hymel, and Wigfield (1978) found that cloze comprehension scores on passages that fifth-graders rated as interesting were significantly higher than scores on passages rated as being of low interest. Walker (1976) also found that high-interest content had a positive effect on comprehension score; the effect, however, was clearer for average and below-average readers than for above-average readers, and for males more than females.

The implications of such studies include these. When interest in a topic is high, readability estimates tend to overestimate difficulty; when it is low, they tend to underestimate difficulty. More challenging material therefore can be assigned when interest in a topic is high then when it is low, and this appears to be particularly the case for males and for average or low-ability readers.

Knowledge

The amount of background knowledge, or "prior knowledge" as it is frequently called and as it is described by others in this volume, is another factor of acknowledged importance to comprehension. Yet the incorrect assumption that readability formulas are context-free makes emphasis on the role of knowledge desirable. Furthermore, the contribution of amount of knowledge to comprehension, and particularly to the accuracy of readability estimates as indicators of comprehensibility, is complex enough to call for special attention.

For example, Pearson, Hansen, and Gordon (1979) found that second-graders with greater background knowledge of spiders got significantly higher scores on a passage about spiders than those with lesser background knowledge. But were their higher scores due to greater comprehension of the information in the passage or simply to what they already knew? Perhaps the implications for teaching seem much the same either way, but that is not the case for Entin and Klare's study (1978). They found essentially no relationship between readability estimates and multiple-choice comprehension scores on the passages of a published reading test. Yet when prior knowledge was taken into account, the relationship became moderately positive. In a subsequent experimental study, Entin and Klare (1980; Entin and Klare, in press) found it difficult to separate the effect of prior knowledge from that of interest; it was not easy to find subjects (from a large pool available) who had both high prior knowledge and low interest in a particular topic, or vice versa. For the relative few who were located, knowledge (as measured) appeared to produce a greater effect than interest (as measured).

The implications of these results include the following. When amount of background knowledge is high, readability estimates tend to overestimate difficulty; when the amount is low, they tend to underestimate difficulty. Equally important, readability estimates become inappropriate as comprehension of material becomes increasingly complex due to content difficulty rather than style difficulty. As noted earlier, estimates are of greatest value at the primary and secondary levels.

Motivation

Since a reader's level of motivation may be a function of the intrinsic factors of interest or knowledge, it may seem unnecessary to list it separately. Because, however, it may also be extrinsic in origin (e.g., a function of incentives), and because it is related in a complex way to the accuracy of readability estimates, separate attention is needed.

Klare and Smart (1973), for example, found a high relationship (rank-order correlation of .87) between the readability estimates for correspondence courses and the probability that students would complete them. Yet Fass and Schumacher (1978) found that the significant influence of readability upon comprehension, apparent with a lower level of motivation, vanished when a higher level was induced (by offering five dollars to the five highest scorers).

The chief implication for instruction is similar to that with certain other factors: readability estimates may be overestimates of difficulty when the level of motivation is high, but be underestimates when it is low. In practice, those students whose motivational level is relatively low can especially be expected to profit from more readable material, provided their level is not so low that they abandon the reading material altogether. On the other hand, increasing the level of motivation among readers becomes especially important for challenging material.

Organization

The effect of organization upon the comprehension of text has been difficult to specify despite its apparent importance, chiefly because "organization" is itself so difficult to define and to manipulate experimentally. Recently, however, some inroads have been made in comparing different types of organization and their relative effectiveness. As might be expected, the experimental results are not simple when they are examined closely.

Meyer and Freedle (1978), for example, have described four types of organization for presenting information:

- adversative, with items contrasted
- covariant, with items presented as cause-effect relationships
- response, with items related as problems and solutions
- attributive, with items given a list-like pattern.

They found that listeners to passages organized with adversative and covariant structures remembered significantly more than listeners to passages organized with attributive and response structures. Irwin (1980) found, however, that some kinds of cause-effect organizations are significantly more comprehensible than others. Explicit cause-effect relationships fared better than implicit, and normal-order (cause first, effect second) better than reverse-order (effect first, cause second).

Marshall (1979) has provided one of the best brief summaries of the relationships between text structure and comprehensibility.

- Main ideas are remembered better than details, no matter where they occur in the text.
- Main ideas can be used to organize information best when they are explicitly stated and familiar.
- Repeated words and information are remembered better than non-repeated words and novel information.
- Information explicitly related to other information (particularly prior knowledge) is remembered better than unrelated ideas.
- The distance between a pronoun and its reference may affect comprehension of both the pronoun and its content.

The implication for instruction is that information not cohesively related is remembered less well than it may appear to be. Some materials for poorer readers, for example, use very short sentences with the intent of achieving greater readability. Such a structure, however, may require many connecting inferences on the part of readers and therefore actually be harder to understand than a structure having a more difficult readability estimate.

Preference

A reader is often able to state a preference for one piece of material over another, or one version of the same material over another. Sometimes the reader can give a reason for the preference, such as interest, ease of reading, etc. Other times, however, the reason may not be clear, yet the preference may be as likely to interact with readability to produce an effect upon comprehension—sometimes a surprising effect.

For example, Klare, Maby, and Gustafson (1955) found that even though two different contents were equated in terms of readability estimate, one was consistently judged easier and more pleasant to read than the other. Why this happened was not clear. Denbow (1973) found that although improved readability increased the comprehension of both a preferred and a nonpreferred content, the increase was greater for the nonpreferred content. The preferred content was comprehended better than the nonpreferred when both were at the less-readable level, and therefore presumably had less room for increased comprehension when both were made more readable.

The practical implication is that where a choice must be made, readability appears to be more critical for nonpreferred than for preferred material, at least when the comprehension level of the preferred material is already quite high. At the same time, more challenging material may be introduced when, for whatever reason, it is given a high preference by readers.

How else might the accuracy of difficulty estimates be improved? The reader factors described emphasize that readability estimates are not static levels above which readers necessarily will not comprehend and below which they will inevitably be bored. But these factors are not the only influences on the accuracy of such estimates; they were chosen only because research evidence exists for their effect upon comprehension, particularly in their conjunction with readability. What about such other factors as typography and format, illustrations and definitions, coherence and completeness, intriguing style and dramatic effectiveness? How can they be taken into account? What guidelines can be followed?

One approach is to look at the relevant literature; here bibliographics such as that of Macdonald-Ross and Smith (1977) on graphics in text can be helpful. For example, someone interested in the effect of typography might turn to it and find a reference to Watts' and Nisbet's *Legibility of Children's Books* (1974). The problem, however, is that the effects of this and many other such factors on comprehension have not been formulated as yet (if indeed they can be).

Therefore the better suggestion at this time is to ask the help of judges for such factors. But not just any judges; ask experts where possible, or get reliable consensus opinions (see Klare, 1982, p. 1521). This is important for readability also, even though formulas are available. The convenience of formulas and the usefulness of the benchmark estimates they provide for evaluation constitute reasons for retaining them, but also make it easy to forget that they can misinform as well as inform. Formula users, as noted earlier, are unlikely to consider scrambled text to be readable, even though it might appear so in terms of readability estimate alone. But the same users might miss the difficulty of text contrived only to get an acceptable readability estimate. Judges can help users to avoid such material and to make allowance for the many other unformulated factors that can affect comprehensibility.

Readability estimates are best thought of as screening devices or, in Monteith's (1976) terms, as probability estimates. If they are, users more likely will remember to use them only for tentative matching of materials to readers and be more willing to shift those materials around to the extent dictated by experience and by the factors described above. Once placed, materials can be made easier or more challenging as, for example, interest, knowledge, or motivation levels permit. That way readability estimates can play their appropriate role in helping to resolve today's educational standards dilemma.

About the Author

George Klare is Acting Dean of the College of Arts and Sciences at Ohio University.

References

Asher, S. R., S. Hymel, and A. Wigfield, "Influence of Topic Interest on Children's Reading Comprehension." *Journal of Reading Behavior* (1978) 10, 35–48.

Battison, R. and D. Goswami. "Clear Writing Today." *Journal of Business Communication* (1981) 4, 5–16.

Betts, E. A. *Foundations of Reading Instruction.* New York: American Book Company, 1946.

Bond, G. L., M. A. Tinker, and B. B. Wasson. *Reading Difficulties: Their Diagnosis and Correction,* Fourth Edition. New York: Prentice-Hall, 1979.

Bormuth, J. R. "Comparable Cloze and Multiple-Choice Comprehension Test Scores." *Journal of Reading* (1967) 10, 291–299.

Bormuth, J. R. "Cloze Test Readability: Criterion Scores." *Journal of Educational Measurement* (1968) 5, 189–196.

Bormuth, J. R. *Development of Readability Analyses.* Final Report, Project No. 7-0052, Contract No. OEC-3-7-070052-03266. Bureau of Research, Office of Education, March 1969.

Chall, J. S. "Readability: In Search of Improvement." *Publishers Weekly,* October 29, 1979, 40–41.

Chall, J. S., S. Conrad, and S. Harris. "An Analysis of Textbooks in Relation to Declining S.A.T. Scores." Princeton, N.J.: College Entrance Examination Board, 1977.

Chall, J. and S. Feldman. "First-Grade Reading: An Analysis of the Interactions of Professed Methods, Teacher Implementation, and Child Background." *Reading Teacher* (1966) 19, 569–575.

Coke, E. U. and E. Z. Rothkopf. "Note on a Simple Algorithm for a Computer-Produced Reading Ease Score." *Journal of Applied Psychology* (1970) 54, 208–210.

Coleman, E. B. "Generalizing to a Language Population." *Psychological Reports* (1964) 14, 219–226.

Coupland, N. "Is Readability Real?" *The Communication of Scientific and Technical Information* (1978) April, 15–17.

Dale, E. and J. S. Chall. "A Formula for Predicting Readability." *Educational Research Bulletin* (1948) 27, 11–20 and 37–54.

Davison, A. and Kantor, R. N. "On the Failure of Readability Formulas to Define Readable Text: A Case Study from Adaptations." *Reading Research Quarterly* (1982) 17, 187–209.

Denbow, C. J. "An Experimental Study of the Effects of a Repetition Factor on the Relationship Between Readability and Listen Ability." Unpublished doctoral dissertation, Ohio University, 1973.

Durkin, D. "What Classroom Observations Reveal about Reading Instruction." *Reading Research Quarterly* (1978–79) 14, 481–533.

Entin, E. B. and Klare, G. R. "Components of Answers to Multiple Choice Questions on a Published Reading Comprehension Test: An Application of the Hanna-Oaster Approach." *Reading Research Quarterly* (1980) 15, 228–236.

Entin, E. B. and G. R. Klare. "Relationships of Measures of Interest, Prior Knowledge, and Readability to Comprehension of Expository Passages." In B. Hutson (Ed.), *Advances in Reading/Language Research,* Vol. III. Greenwich, Conn.: JAI Press, in press.

Entin, E. B. and G. R. Klare. "Some Interrelationships of Readability, Cloze, and Multiple-Choice Scores on a Reading Comprehension Test." *Journal of Reading Behavior* (1978) 10, 417–436.

Fass, W. and G. M. Schumacher. "Effects of Motivation, Subject Activity, and Readability on the Retention of Prose Materials." *Journal of Educational Psychology* (1978) 70, 803–808.

Fitzgerald, G. G. "How Many Samples Give a Good Readability Estimate?—The Fry Graph." *Journal of Reading* (1981) 24, 404–410.

Fitzgerald, S. E. "Literature by Slide Rule." *The Saturday Review,* February 14, 1953, 15–16 and 53–54.

Flesch, R. F. *The Art of Readable Writing.* New York: Harper, 1949.

Fry, E. B. "A Readability Formula that Saves Time." *Journal of Reading* (1968) 11, 513–16 and 575–78.

Fry, E. B. "Fry's Readability Graph: Clarifications, Validity, and Extension to Level 17." *Journal of Reading* (1977) 21, 242–252.

Fry, E. B. "A Reappraisal of Formula Writing." *Publishers Weekly,* October 29, 1979, 41.

Garforth, F. W. (Ed.). *John Locke's "Of the Conduct of the Understanding."* New York: Teachers College Press, 1966.

Gray, W. S. *Gray Standardized Oral Reading Paragraph Tests.* Bloomington, Illinois: Public School Publishing Co., 1915.

Harris, A. J. and M. D. Jacobson. "Comparative Predictions of Tested Reading Comprehension of High School Seniors." Paper presented at the annual convention of the American Psychological Association, September 1, 1975.

Harris, A. J. and M. D. Jacobson. "Revised Harris-Jacobson Readability Formulas." Paper presented at the annual meeting of the College Reading Association, Bethesda, Maryland, October 31, 1974.

Harrison, C. *Readability in the Classroom.* Cambridge: Cambridge University Press, 1980.

Irwin, J. W. "The Effects of Explicitness and Clause Order on the Comprehension of Reversible Causal Relationships." *Reading Research Quarterly* (1980) 15, 477–488.

Jacobson, M. D., C. E. Kirkland, and R. W. Selden. "An Examination of the McCall-Crabbs Standard Test Lessons in Reading." *Journal of Reading* (1978) 22, 224–230.

Jorgenson, G. W. "Relationship of Classroom Behavior to the Match Between Material Difficulty and Student Ability." *Journal of Education Psychology* (1977) 69, 24–32.

Kelley, T. L., G. M. Ruch, and L. M. Terman. *Stanford Achievement Test (Reading).* Yonkers, N.Y.: World Book Co., 1922.

Kincaid J. P. and L. G. Gamble. "Ease of Comprehension of Standard and Readable Automobile Insurance Policies as a Function of Reading Ability." *Journal of Reading Behavior,* 1977, 9, 85–87.

Kintsch, W. and D. Vipond. "Reading Comprehension and Readability in Educational Practice and Psychological Theory." In L. G. Nilsson (Ed.), *Perspectives on Memory Research.* Hillsdale, N.J.: Erlbaum, 1979.

Klare, G. R. "Readability." In H. E. Mitzel (Ed.), *Encyclopedia of Educational Research,* Fifth Edition. New York: The Free Press, 1982, 1520–1531.

Klare, G. R. "Readability and Comprehension." In R. S. Easterby and H. Zwaga (Eds.), *Visual Presentation of Information.* London: Wiley, 1984a.

Klare, G. R. "Readability." In P. D. Pearson (Ed.), *Handbook of Reading Research.* New York: Longman, 1984b.

Klare, G. R., J. E. Mabry, and L. M. Gustafson. "The Relationship of Style Difficulty to Immediate Retention and to Acceptability of Technical Material." *Journal of Educational Psychology* (1955) 46, 287–295.

Klare, G. R. and K. Smart. "Analysis of the Readability Level of Selected USAFI Instructional Materials." *Journal of Educational Research* (1973) 67, 176.

Lewerenz, A. S. "Books Evaluated by Means of the Vocabulary Grade Placement Formula—Revised to March, 1937." Los Angeles: City School District, 1937.

Lively, B. A. and S. L. Pressey. "A Method for Measuring the 'Vocabulary Burden' of Textbooks." *Educational Administration and Supervision* (1923) 9, 389–398.

Lorges, I. "Predicting Reading Difficulty of Selection for Children." *Elementary English Review* (1939) 16, 229–233.

Macdonald-Ross, M. and E. Smith. "Graphics in Text: A Bibliography." IET Monograph No. 6. Institute of Educational Technology, The Open University, Milton Keynes, England, March 1977.

Manzo, A. "Readability: A Postscript." *Elementary English* (1970) 47, 962–965.

Marshall, N. "Readability and Comprehensibility." *Journal of Reading* (1979) 22, 542–544.

Maxwell, M. "Readability: Have We Gone Too Far?" *Journal of Reading* (1978) 21, 525–530.

McCall, W. A. and L. M. Crabbs. *Standard Test Lessons in Reading: Teacher's Manual for All Books.* New York: Bureau of Publications, Teachers College, Columbia University, 1925.

McLaughlin, G. H. "SMOG Grading—A New Readability Formula." *Journal of Reading* (1969) 12, 639–646.

Meyer, B. J. F. and R. Freedle. *The Effects of Different Discourse Types on Recall.* Princeton, New Jersey: Educational Testing Service, 1978.

Miller, L. R. "A Comparative Analysis of the Predictive Validities of Four Readability Measures." Unpublished doctoral dissertation, Ohio University, 1972.

Monteith, M. K. "Readability Formulas." *Journal of Reading* (1976) 19, 604–607.

Moore, A. C. "Recoiling from Reading: A Consideration of the Thorndike Library." *Library Journal* (1935) 60, 419–422.

Pauk, W. "A Practical Note on Readability Formulas." *Journal of Reading* (1969) 13, 207–210.

Pearson, P. D., J. Hansen, and C. Gordon. "The Effect of Background Knowledge on Young Children's Comprehension of Explicit and Implicit Information." *Journal of Reading Behavior* (1979) 11, 201–209.

Rankin, E. F. and J. W. Culhane. "Comparable Cloze and Multiple-Choice Comprehension Test Scores." *Journal of Reading* (1969) 13, 193–198.

Readability Report, Degrees of Reading Power, 1982–83. New York: The College Board, 1982.

Reading in America: A Perspective on Two Assessments. National Assessment of Educational Progress, Reading Report 06-R-01, 1974–75 Assessment. A Project of the Education Commission of the States, Funded by the National Center for Education Statistics, October 1976.

"Resolutions Passed by Delegates Assembly, April 1981." *Reading Research Quarterly* (1981) 16, unpaged (following page 613).

Rue, E. (Comp.). *Subject Index to Books for Intermediate Grades*. Chicago: American Library Association, 1940.

Selzer, J. "Readability Is a Four-Letter Word." *Journal of Business Communication* (1981) 4, 23–34.

Stevens, K. C. "Readability Formulae and McCall-Crabbs Standard Test Lessons in Reading." *The Reading Teacher* (1980) 33, 413–415.

Thorndike, E. L. *The Teacher's Word Book*. New York: Teachers College, Columbia University, 1921.

Tibbetts, S.-L. "How Much Should We Expect Readability Formulas to Do?" *Elementary English* (1973) 50, 75–76.

Users Manual, Degrees of Reading Power. New York: The College Board, 1980.

Vaughan, J. L. "Interpreting Readability Assessments." *Journal of Reading* (1976) 19, 635–639.

Vogel, M. and C. Washburne. "An Objective Method of Determining Grade Placement of Children's Material." *Elementary School Journal* (1928) 28, 373–381.

Walker, M. S. "The Effects of High- and Low-Interest Content on Instructional Levels in Informal Reading Inventories." Unpublished doctoral dissertation, Auburn University, 1976.

Washburne, C. and M. Vogel. *Winnetka Graded Book List*. Chicago: American Library Association, 1926.

Watts, L. and J. Nisbet. *Legibility of Children's Books*. National Federation of Educational Research, 1974.

Zintz, M. *The Reading Process*. Dubuque, Iowa: William C. Brown, 1970.

Text adoption procedures in the United States represent a kaleidoscope of standards, ways, and means. How may text selection, with special attention to adoption procedures, be improved? In a hard-hitting commentary on current adoption practices, Osborn and Stein conclude that there are a number of steps that can be taken to markedly improve adoption procedures, and they outline the nature and direction of some current efforts toward that end.

Textbook Adoptions: A Process for Change

Jean Osborn
Marcy Stein

Most of the textbooks, teacher's guides, workbooks, and other supplementary materials so prevalent in classrooms are parts of "series," "systems," or "programs" published by educational publishers. A visit to publishers' exhibit booths at the state and national conventions of any major reading, mathematics, science, or social studies professional organization reveals an enormous and often bewildering array of published programs. How do teachers decide which programs to use to help them teach their students? Ordinarily, this is done by a process called *adoption,* in which a variety of published programs are examined and evaluated by a committee of teachers and sometimes other people associated with schools.

A dictionary definition of *adoption* includes the phrase "to take up, use, and make one's own"; it is in this spirit that adoption committees select textbook programs. The programs that get through adoption committees and into schools and classrooms are those that teachers are expected to take up and make their own as they teach their students. But, how confidently should teachers take up and use the adopted textbook programs? And what do educational researchers have to say about the quality and effectiveness of published programs? Only during the past few years have researchers attempted to conduct systematic investigations and analyses of published textbook programs. These studies are of consequence to teachers and to adoption committees. Five different studies about five different aspects of textbook programs will be discussed here. Included are a comparison of basal readers and trade books, an analysis of content-area texts, an investigation of teacher's guides, a critique of workbooks, and a study of how the use of readability formulas affects a text's comprehensibility. These studies are examples of the available research on textbook programs.

RESEARCH ABOUT TEXTBOOK PROGRAMS

Basal Reader and Trade Book Stories

What are the characteristics of the books that students use as they learn to read? If basal readers are considered preparation for reading in the larger context, then how well do these readers prepare students to read "real life" texts—short stories, novels, expository articles, directions, and instructions—they will have to deal with once they have finished a basal reading program?

In a study comparing characteristics of basal reader stories with those of trade book stories, Bruce (1984) found a number of differences between the two groups of stories and concluded that publishers of basal programs should expand the range of story types they include in their student readers. Or alternatively, teachers should be made aware that children reading from basal readers are not exposed to many of the story types they will encounter in "real life" reading and should supplement the readers with trade books.

Content-Area Texts

Research about narratives has been carried out for a number of years; research about the characteristics of content-area texts is more recent. Anderson, Armbruster, and Kantor (1980) analyzed social studies and science texts on the basis of text structure, text coherence, text unity, and audience appropriateness. Their analyses revealed many examples of unclear text. These researchers speculate on how students are affected by unclear text. They point out that the effect of poor quality text on how much content-area knowledge students acquire in the early elementary grades may *not* be very great (primarily because many teachers do not use these textbooks as the primary learning source), but they suggest that poor quality texts may have a negative effect on how intermediate-grade students learn to learn and comprehend information from text.

Teacher's Guides

Although the textbooks students use have been analyzed rather extensively, there has been surprisingly little research about the texts teachers use. An exception is the research by Durkin (1984), who looked at the teacher's manuals associated with basal reading programs. In her analysis of comprehension instruction in the teacher's manuals of five basal reading programs, she categorized the suggestions to teachers in the manuals as *instruction, review, application,* and *practice.* She recorded the number of suggestions in each category and gave examples of their quality. For example, she found that when manuals specify comprehension instruction, the instructions are often vague and unclear. In addition, she found that the manuals "offer precise help (e.g., obvious answers to assessment questions) when it is least needed, but they are obscure or silent when specific help is likely to be required" (p. 31). Her observations about review are also disturbing. She remarks that "the frequency with which information or a skill is reviewed appears to have no connection with difficulty or importance for reading. Instead, the amount of review in all the series seemed more like the product of random behavior than of a pre-established plan" (p. 35). Her comments on application and practice are equally disturbing.

Workbooks

A number of classroom observation studies indicate that students spend a lot of time working in workbooks and other practice materials. Given the extensive use of workbook type materials, what are the characteristics of these materials? In an analysis of workbooks associated with basal reading programs, Osborn (1984) commented on many aspects of workbook tasks, including the relationship of workbook tasks to the rest of the program, vocabulary and concept level, instructional design, amount of practice, student response modes, number of task types, art, layout, quality of content, and clarity of instructions. Osborn found that workbook tasks in some programs had very little or nothing to do with the rest of the program; that instructions were often unclear, obscure, or unnecessarily lengthy; that the vocabulary of the workbooks sometimes was more complex than that of the rest of the program; and that the art and page layouts often were confusing. In addition, she found that although many tasks were trivial and had little to do with reading or writing, some of the most important tasks occurred only once or twice in an entire workbook. She found little "systematic and cumulative" review of what is taught in a program represented in the corresponding workbook. Although she also found examples of well-constructed tasks, she concluded that "workbooks are the forgotten children of basal programs," and urged publishers and teachers to attend to the problems inherent in these practice materials.

Readability Formulas

Research about another topic, readability formulas, is of particular concern to adoption committee members. The standard readability formulas are measures of sentence length and the complexity, unfamiliarity, or length of vocabulary. Everybody—teachers, adoption committee members, authors, and editors—assesses text with readability formulas. A group of linguists compared "original texts" (from magazines and books) with the same texts rewritten to conform to readability formulas (Davison, 1984). Davison comments that the rewritten texts "do their bit to lower the vocabulary scores and sentence length," but notes that the resulting simplifications are sometimes contradictory. For example, the practice of paraphrasing difficult vocabulary may considerably lengthen and add subordinate clauses to sentences. She also presents evidence that strongly suggests that making changes in text *solely* on the basis of readability formulas can have several harmful effects on comprehension. Changes of this type may seriously distort the logical relations between the parts of the text, disrupt the presentation of ideas, and make it difficult or impossible to convey the meaning of the original text. The original and rewritten texts below are taken from the Davison study (p. 124):

Original
I had kept my nerve pretty well till dawn, just as the faint light was coming, when we looked out and saw the water whirling against the bay window.

Adaptation
But we all kept our courage up. As the faint light of dawn was coming, we looked out. The water was whirling by.

In this example, the reader of the adapted version has to make more inferences and use more unstated background information than the reader of the original text. In conclusion, Davison finds that although steeped in tradition and simple to use, readability formulas generally have a harmful and negative effect on writing and revising written material for classroom use. She advises that *informed* subjective judgment is at this time the best replacement available for using readability formulas to both write and analyze student texts. However, when analyzing textbooks in the preceding article in this volume, Klare suggests that an appropriate use of readability formulas may be in conjunction with other factors affecting the comprehensibility of the text.

The implications of these analyses of textbook programs should lead adoption members to look at the programs they are considering very differently. While most of us share a belief in the efficacy of the printed word, these studies point to the use of a more critical eye for examining the words in the textbook programs that occupy such an important place in the classrooms of American schools.

THE USE OF TEXTBOOK PROGRAMS

Why are textbook programs so important? How much do they affect what happens in classrooms? Although most educators would agree that published programs are secondary in instructional importance to the classroom teacher, there is substantial evidence that teachers rely heavily on textbook programs. Textbook programs in reading, mathematics, social studies, and science often constitute the major part of the curriculum in these areas. A number of researchers have attempted to ascertain how much of what students and teachers do in school emanates from textbook programs. The popular estimates are that from 80 percent to 95 percent of what goes on in classrooms is derived from the many components of published instructional programs. One researcher (English, 1980) estimates that about 80 percent of the knowledge to which students are exposed comes from textbooks. A few researchers have tried to figure out how much time students spend with one component of published programs, the workbooks (and the worksheets run from the ditto masters) that accompany these programs. Fisher and his colleagues (1978) found that 70 percent of allocated instructional time was spent on workbook-type exercises. L. Anderson (1984) found that from 30 percent to 60 percent of the instructional time allocated for reading was spent on reading related workbook-type activities. In the classrooms they observed during reading periods, Mason and Osborn (1982) discovered that students spent more time working at their desks in their workbook activities than engaged in instructional activities with their teachers.

If it is acknowledged that the many components of textbook programs account for much of what happens in classrooms (despite the problems with the programs that researchers have documented, and surely that many of the teachers using textbook programs must have noted), then the question of teacher fidelity to the teacher's guides that accompany these programs needs to be raised. Do teachers follow the instructions in the manuals that are the guiding forces of most textbook programs? To answer this question, Durkin (1983) observed 16 elementary teachers from the first, third, and fifth grades as they taught reading on two successive days. She found a close match between how teachers conducted their reading lessons and what was prescribed in the basal manuals they were using. The major ways in which teachers departed from manual recommendations were in their lack of attention to the prereading activities recommended in the teacher's manuals, activities that have to do with the development of vocabulary and background knowledge. On the other hand, their adherence to all postreading recommendations (usually comprehension assessment questions and independent written work) was quite consistent, even for those activities described as supplemental.

Other observers of teachers (for example, Gerald Duffy, David Berliner, Jere Brophy, Carolyn Evertson, and Charles Fisher) have documented variations upon the theme of the relationship between published programs and the goals and decisions of teachers. We believe much of this research points up what is obvious; that is, teachers must consciously and consistently evaluate the textbook programs they use and modify these programs according to their own experiences and competencies—and according to the needs of their students. We contend, however, that most teachers are not trained to be textbook designers, and furthermore, we *know* that all teachers have a very limited number of work hours each week to accomplish an enormous number of instructional tasks for a large number of students. We suggest that efficient textbook programs and effective teacher decision making are especially critical to successfully teach students who are difficult to teach. It is for these children, especially, that teachers often ask for "expert" help. We suggest that it is not unreasonable for teachers to assume that the textbook programs selected by adoption committees are reflective of the best and most current "expert" knowledge in a subject area, and that the programs selected have been tried and shown capable of providing a basis for successful instruction for essentially all of the students for whom they are intended.

This discussion of textbook program adoptions has included some research about the quality of textbook programs and some estimates of how extensively and how exclusively these programs are used by teachers. By putting together the elements of this discussion, we arrive at a situation somewhat fraught with contradictions. Teachers count on textbook programs and follow them with varying degrees of fidelity.

Yet, researchers who have analyzed some of these textbook programs have delineated serious problems with them, and these problems are seemingly significant to the teachers and students using the programs. The question that emerges from this situation is, "Why do teachers use and adoption committees select textbook programs that, according to the researchers, are seriously flawed?" We attempt to answer this question as we discuss the environment and process of adoptions. We then describe a procedure that perhaps will be capable of removing some of the contradictions from the adoption-teacher-research triangle.

THE ADOPTION PROCESS AND THE IMPROVEMENT OF PROGRAMS

The remainder of this article is divided into three sections. The first section, *the adoption scene,* presents some background information about some of the factors (aside from the evaluation of textbooks) that influence how committees select textbook programs. The second section, *the textbook evaluation process,* examines the types of textbook evaluation procedures commonly employed by textbook adoption committees. The third section, *an alternative to current practice,* describes an alternative approach to evaluating textbook programs—one that will provide more accurate information about program content to program users and at the same time provide suggestions for program improvement to both users *and* developers of published programs.

Our major premise is that the textbook adoption process can be a means of improving the quality of textbook programs, as well as for selecting textbook programs. Anyone who has served on an adoption committee probably would claim that the primary goal of the group was to select, from an assortment of available programs, the best and most appropriate program (or programs). We would agree that program selection is the primary task of an adoption committee, but we also would like to suggest to the adoption committee the idea that textbook programs do not always offer the best, or even the most appropriate instruction. Therefore, a constructive adoption process should yield not only information about the content of programs, but also specific recommendations for the improvement of programs. We believe that textbook publishers will make significant changes in programs only when their consumers call for specific changes.

The Adoption Scene

The adoption of textbook programs can take place at many levels— at the school level, the district level, and the state level. In some states, called *adoption states,* a given number of textbook programs are selected by a committee (usually appointed by the governor and organized to represent the entire state) to be listed on a state list. To be eligible to buy textbook programs with state funds, local school districts must select programs from among those listed by the state adoption committee. In the other states, labeled by publishers as the *open territory* states, the selection of textbook programs is carried out by committees representing either an entire school district or just one school. The evaluation of textbook programs, whether at the state, district, or local levels, is conducted by committee, either appointed or voluntary. In an article in the *Reading Teacher,* one commentator summarizes some of the confusing realities of textbook adoption (Bowler, 1978):

> There are no uniform dates or forms, no common policies on bidding [by publishers], the length of the adoption cycle, sampling, extension of textbook contracts, price escalation clauses, number of school grades covered by adoption, adoption of audiovisual materials, or requirements that school materials be "learner-verified" before purchase (p. 518).

We will add to this list problems associated with how committee members are selected, what groups (and pressure groups) are represented, the number of issues adoption committees have to deal with, and how committees are organized to perform their important tasks.

The lack of uniformity among state and district adoption procedures need not be controversial. But some of the underlying problems characteristic of the adoption process are somewhat open to dispute. One problem lies in the nature of the producer and consumer relationship between the publishing industry and the adoption committees, and perhaps even more specifically, the relationship between the publishing industry and the committees in the adoption states of California, Texas, and Florida. Publishers expend great efforts to promote and advertise their programs in these big adoption states; they seem to respond more readily to the criticisms and demands of these adoption committees regarding, for example, the presence or absence of specific kinds of content, and the representation in student texts of conflict, politics, historical information, and minority groups. Another commentator on textbook adoption (English, 1980) concludes, "We like to think that there is no national curriculum in the United States. In practice, Texas, California, and Florida set our curriculum and most other school districts go along" (p. 277).

Though a fascinating topic, the intertwining of politics with pedagogy and with the sales practices of the publishing industry is not the major focus of this article. However, since the improvement of the quality of textbook programs is the focus, the role of the publishers of textbook programs must be acknowledged. Their role is a complex one —they produce programs that have an important educational function. On the other hand, they are in business and must develop products their customers will buy. Stiff competition among publishers probably contributes to their concern about being "different" and their caution about making changes. This caution affects the likelihood that findings from new lines of research will be translated readily into practice. When the research implies reasonable changes in practice, publishers are frequently reluctant to incorporate the changes until their customers begin to ask for them.

The Center for the Study of Reading has participated in two conferences for publishers of educational programs. During these conferences, researchers from the Center and other universities and research institutes reported on studies that have direct implications for the design of textbook programs. The responses from the executives and staff members who attended these meetings (essentially all of the major educational publishers) could be characterized as "cautious interest." While they generally acknowledged the relevance of the research to their programs, they pointed out that in the final analysis, their markets (that is, the states and school districts who adopt their textbook programs) would determine the changes that would be made in their programs. These responses highlight the need to reexamine the evaluation procedures used in the process of selecting materials and acknowledge the influence of the reports—and selections—of adoption committees on publishers.

The Textbook Evaluation Process

The primary function of most adoption committees is the evaluation of textbook programs. Typically a committee is responsible for organizing the evaluation procedures; for composing checklists, rating forms, and guidelines that reflect district objectives; as well as for engaging in the actual evaluation and selection process. The constraints put upon adoption committee members are numerous. For example, those serving on committees rarely receive remuneration or even release time from their daily responsibilities. Perhaps the biggest constraint is time. In a case study of the adoption process in the state of Indiana, Courtland and Farr and their colleagues (1983) reported that the textbook reviewers felt that not nearly enough time had been allowed for a thorough examination of materials.

An examination of the typical rating forms and checklists formulated and used by adoption committees reveals two outstanding problems: the level of objectivity seemingly inherent in the evaluation process, and the lack of representation of research-based criteria. Courtland and Farr report that the evaluation criteria employed by most reviewers in their adoption study were based on "personal interpretations" of the general criteria that were supplied to them. They write:

> When asked specifically to identify the factors that caused them to select as "best" one set of textbooks, the reviewers responded with a wide variety of general information and little specificity. The researchers' general impression was that the reviewers were often looking for reasons to exclude a set of texts rather than significant reasons to adopt one textbook series (p. 76).

An item analysis of basal reading evaluation forms and checklists gathered from 26 school systems in 14 states (Comas, 1983) revealed that rarely did there appear an item that required committee members to document or substantiate in a quantifiable form any of their conclusions about a program. We suggest that the subjectivity inherent in many adoption committee evaluations rests with an excessive reliance on checklists and rating forms. The very nature of these instruments precludes a certain amount of objectivity: for example, answering yes/no questions about sufficient review, or rating how well the teacher's guides are organized on a scale from 1 to 5, are measures that yield biased responses.

The lack of representation of research-based criteria on the items on rating forms and checklists is evident. There are usually more items about the physical features of textbooks than about more substantive topics, such as specific content, prose style in readers, pedagogy, and instructional design in teacher's guides.

We think that two types of research would help textbook program evaluators make more informed decisions: component research and program effectiveness research. Component research focuses on the *parts* of a given textbook program. For example, for a reading program, component research may address topics as narrow as sound-symbol correspondence or as broad as children's stories. Component research can focus on the characteristics of instructional design (irrespective of content) as well as on the specific content itself.

Program effectiveness research involves the testing of the effectiveness of an entire textbook program in a number of classrooms with a significant number of teachers and students. This type of research often is alluded to as "learner-verfication" information. Yet, although a certain amount of lip service is given to learner verification, we suspect relatively little careful learner verification takes place before a program is published, nor has much been expected by members of adoption committees.

Items that could tap component research and program effectiveness research are *not* a common feature of adoption committee evaluation forms. The Comas item analysis of evaluation forms found that only 34.6 percent of the districts sampled included research questions of any kind on their evaluation forms, as compared to 73.1 percent that included items about illustrations. Although practitioners and researchers are acutely aware of the length of time it takes to translate research into practice, it would seem that the adoption committee has a great deal of potential for facilitating this process.

An Alternative to Current Practice

The solution to some of the problems of the adoption process discussed in the previous section is a major goal of a project at the Center for the Study of Reading. Work there has begun on a set of pamphlets that adoption committees will be able to use to foster objective evaluation of reading programs. In addition, these pamphlets will incorporate the most appropriate and reliable findings from current component research.* Topics selected for the pamphlets represent aspects of reading that are of primary importance, are appropriate to a basal reading program, and are subject to quantifiable evaluation.

For each topic, a pamphlet will be developed that will provide the means for adoption committee members to examine that topic in the programs they are considering. The pamphlets will be written by different authors, but each pamphlet will follow a common framework and organization. The advantages of the pamphlet plan are considerable: People who are expert in various areas will be writing about what they know best; adoption committees will be able to pick and choose from among the pamphlets to evaluate programs for what they think is most important; different committee members can be assigned different topics. Committees may not like (or find useful) one pamphlet, but because of the separate authorship of each pamphlet, they can reject what they do not like and use what they do like. Another advantage of the pamphlet plan is that one group of pamphlets can be finished and be

---

*Component research will be emphasized in these pamphlets. Although a means of establishing standards for program effectiveness and learner verification practices may evolve as the pamphlets are developed, a good part of the responsibility for such practice must rest with publishers. A major problem for publishers is the expense of writing and field-testing new editions to meet the copyright standards that most adoption committees hold. Consequently, a frequent result of this problem is that programs are not adequately tried out in classrooms before they are published.

in use as more ideas for pamphlets emerge. The first set of pamphlets will focus on reading programs; a subsequent group will deal with social studies and science texts.

The pamphlet developed for each topic will include the research base or underlying assumptions on which the evaluation criteria are based, sampling procedures designed to allow for efficient application of the criteria, the criteria themselves, and an essay, entitled "An Insider's View," that will permit pamphlet authors to articulate ideas about how the topic ideally should be treated in instructional programs.

The topics of the first set of pamphlets are listed below:

1. **Introduction and Procedures** will include background information about the adoption process; the purpose and underlying assumptions guiding the set of pamphlets; a brief overview of each of the pamphlets; how to use the sampling and evaluation procedures of the pamphlets; an explanation of the section called "An Insider's View," and directions for pulling together information from each of the pamphlets in order to make selection decisions.

2. **Instructional Design** will contain procedures for evaluating the overall design of a program, including coordination across levels as well as coordination of the program's components (teacher's manual, student text, workbook); the design of lessons; the language used in instructional tasks; and the relationship of a program's scope and sequence chart to a program's stated objectives, to its actual content, and to a district's objectives.

3. **Readiness and Beginning Reading**

4. **Decoding Instruction** including phonics and structural analysis

5. **Vocabulary Knowledge and Concept Building**

6. **Comprehension Instruction**

7. **Organization of the Reading Lesson**

8. **Literary Appreciation**

9. **Study and Reference Skills**

10. **Reading and Writing**

11. **Student Textbooks**

12. **Workbooks and Supplemental Materials**

13. **Evaluation of Student Performance**

14. **Adaptations for Students with Special Needs**

In the introductory pamphlet, the point will be made that the pamphlets cover the topics that researchers at the Center for the Study of Reading think most crucial to reading instruction *and* most amenable to quantifiable analysis. The fact that some other topics are important but are not suitable for the kind of analysis proposed by the pamphlets will also be emphasized. Adoption committees may wish to evaluate these topics in ways they have used in the past.

The pamphlets on some topics (such as approaches to beginning reading) will cover alternative views; nevertheless, the evaluation of each alternative will include procedures for evaluating such things as internal consistency, consistency across components of the program, and sufficiency of practice. Pamphlet authors have been asked to consider the task of putting together a pamphlet as an exercise in answering two questions:

1. How would you help adoption committee members analyze a basal reading program so that they can find out some precise information about how your topic appears in that program?
2. How does this information relate to the research in your field— what implications does the research have for what should appear in a textbook program?

The answers to these questions must be translated into procedures that will be easy to use, that will produce precise and quantifiable information for adoption committee members, and that will make these evaluators aware of how well recent research about teaching and learning is reflected in the programs they are examining.

CONCLUSION

The major premise of this article has been that sound evaluation procedures are powerful tools, heretofore underemployed, for improving the quality of instructional programs in our schools. Given the importance of textbook programs, the tools that adoption committees use to assess the quality of these materials must be sharpened. We believe that evaluation procedures that yield specific information about the content of programs also have the capability of yielding recommendations for improving textbook programs.

About the Authors

Jean Osborn is Associate Director, Center for the Study of Reading, at the University of Illinois, Urbana-Champaign.

Marcy Stein is Visiting Professor, Center for the Study of Reading, at the University of Illinois, Urbana-Champaign.

References

Anderson, L. "The Environment of Instruction: The Function of Seatwork in a Commercially Developed Curriculum." In G. G. Duffy, L. R. Roehler, and J. Mason (Eds.), *Comprehension Instruction.* New York: Longman, Inc., 1984.

Anderson, T. H., B. B. Armbruster, and R. N. Kantor. *How Clearly Written Are Children's Textbooks? Or, of Bladderworts and Alfa* (Reading Ed. Rep. No. 16). Urbana: University of Illinois, Center for the Study of Reading, August 1980.

Bowler, M. "Textbook Publishers Try to Please All, But First They Woo the Heart of Texas." *The Reading Teacher* (1978), February, 514–518.

Bruce, B. "A New Point of View on Children's Stories." In R. C. Anderson, J. Osborn, and R. J. Tierney (Eds.), *Learning to Read in American Schools: Basal Readers and Content Texts.* Hillsdale, N.J.: Erlbaum, 1984.

Comas, J. *Item Analysis: Basal Reading Evaluation Forms.* Unpublished manuscript, Indiana University, School of Education, 1983.

Courtland, M. C., R. Farr, P. Harris, J. R. Tarr, and L. J. Treece. *A Case Study of the Indiana State Reading Textbook Adoption Process.* Unpublished manuscript, Indiana University, School of Education, 1983.

Davison, A. "Readability—Appraising Text Difficulty." In R. C. Anderson, J. Osborn, and R. J. Tierney (Eds.), *Learning to Read in American Schools: Basal Readers and Content Texts.* Hillsdale, N.J.: Erlbaum, 1984.

Durkin, D. *Is There a Match Between What Elementary Teachers Do and What Basal Reader Manuals Recommend?* (Reading Ed. Rep. No. 44). Urbana: University of Illinois, Center for the Study of Reading, October 1983.

Durkin, D. "Do Basal Manuals Teach Reading Comprehension?" In R. C. Anderson, J. Osborn, and R. J. Tierney (Eds.), *Learning to Read in American Schools: Basal Readers and Content Texts.* Hillsdale, N.J.: Erlbaum, 1984.

English, R. "The Politics of Textbook Adoption." *Phi Delta Kappan* (1980), December, 275–278.

Fisher, C., D. Berliner, N. Filby, R. Marliave, L. Cohen, M. Dishaw, and J. Moore. *Teaching and Learning in Elementary Schools: A Summary of the Beginning Teacher Evaluation Study.* San Francisco: Far West Laboratory for Educational Research and Development, 1978.

Mason, J. and J. Osborn. *When Do Children Begin "Reading to Learn?": A Survey of Classroom Reading Instruction Practices in Grades Two Through Five* (Tech. Rep. No. 261). Urbana: University of Illinois, Center for the Study of Reading, September 1982.

Osborn, J. "The Purposes, Uses, and Contents of Workbooks and Some Guidelines for Publishers." In R. C. Anderson, J. Osborn, and R. J. Tierney (Eds.), *Learning to Read in American Schools: Basal Readers and Content Texts.* Hillsdale, N.J.: Erlbaum, 1984.

Index